THE SMITTEN KITCHEN COOKBOOK

the
smitten kitchen
COOKBOOK

deb perelman

ALFRED A. KNOPF NEW YORK 2012

THIS IS A BORZOI BOOK
PUBLISHED BY ALFRED A. KNOPF

Knopf, Borzoi Books, and the colophon are registered trademarks of Random House, Inc.

Smitten Kitchen and SK Logo are registered trademarks of Deborah Perelman.
Used by permission.

Portions of this work were originally published on SmittenKitchen.com.

Library of Congress Cataloging-in-Publication Data

Perelman, Deb.
The smitten kitchen cookbook / Deb Perelman.—1st ed.
p. cm.
Summary: "The long-awaited cookbook from the food blogging phenom, Deb Perelman—
home cook, mom, photographer, and celebrated author of SmittenKitchen.com."
—Provided by publisher.
Includes index.
ISBN 978-0-307-59565-2 (hardcover)
1. Cooking. I. Title.
TX714.P443 2012
641.5—dc23   2012007711

Photograph on page xii by Elizabeth Bick
Jacket photographs by Deb Perelman
Jacket design by Carol Devine Carson

Manufactured in China
Published October 2012
Second Printing Before Publication, October 2012

FOR JACOB HENRY,

the best thing I ever baked

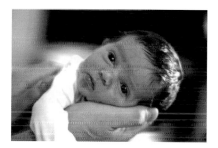

contents

introduction
ix

notes and tips
xiii

BREAKFAST
3

SALADS
53

SANDWICHES, TARTS, AND PIZZAS
81

THE MAIN DISH: VEGETARIAN
115

THE MAIN DISH: SEAFOOD,
POULTRY, AND MEAT
155

SWEETS
cookies
pies and tarts
cakes
puddings and candy
193

PARTY SNACKS AND DRINKS
283

measurements
305

build your own smitten kitchen
307

acknowledgments
313

index
314

introduction

*W*elcome. Welcome to my tiny kitchen. Wouldn't it be great if we could all fit in here? I'd make us mulled cider and gooey cinnamon squares. We could talk about pie. Jacob would probably bust out his guitar (actually, it's a ukulele, but don't tell him that) and sing "baa baa blakk shee!" because he's a total ham, and my husband would pour us some drinks. We'd have a great time.

Of course, unless you can squeeze yourself onto a fraction of a six-inch tile—grumbling, no doubt, that this was the worst party ever—this is probably not going to happen. I always wanted a kitchen big enough for a crowd, but instead, I chose to live in New York City, a place where the kitchens are barely usable but nobody complains because there's no reason to cook when there's a great restaurant on every corner. Besides, as my friend Jenn informed me shortly after I moved here in 2000, "ovens are for sweater storage."

And then, as if I'd missed the joke (I, um, often do), I decided to cook in my tiny kitchen anyway. I think I got my "if there's a will, there's a way" attitude from my mother. You could say there's no way to fit the ingredients you need in two cabinets or the enormous roast you'd like to prepare into a two-thirds-size oven; you could declare it impossible to prep any meal on a single two-by-three-foot counter, with only a few square feet to stand on . . . or you could clear the decks,

get to work, and an hour later maybe pull a killer pan of brownies out of the oven. I have a hunch that our great-grandmothers didn't refuse to cook because they couldn't fit their Vitamix on the counter. Well, perhaps other people's grandmothers. It should surprise absolutely nobody that I come from pesky stock.

Whenever I'm asked how I got here—presumably, to a place where you'd have my cookbook in front of you, not ~~my writing lair with~~ a bay ~~window overlooking the sea~~ my sofa with an explosion of wooden train tracks around me—I always wish I had a better kitchen story to share. "Just tell us your story!" people say, but I think that they're lying. I think that people want me to tell them a *good* story.

They want to hear that I'm a fifth-generation chili maker from Texas or that I only eat food that I hunt, forage, or find under the wheel of a car. That I went to cooking school and spent years on the line being yelled at by a French guy with his name over the door. Or maybe I was at a thrift store and found a collection of handwritten Hungarian recipe cards and made it my life's work to bring an old lady's cooking back to life. People want a story with drama and excitement. They don't want to hear that I've been a record store shift supervisor, a swirler of soft-serve frozen custard, an art therapist, and an IT reporter.

They don't want to hear that I just like to cook.

But I do, I really do.

That said, what drives my cooking is hardly so lofty. I never set out to build a website that would draw more than five million visitors a month. I never expected to have to quit my day job just to keep it up. I never looked into a crystal ball and saw my site flash across the television screen during a Google commercial, and when I read those last three sentences together, I still have to sit down until the spinning stops.

The reality of what drives me into the kitchen—despite living in a neighborhood where I can get the most tender meatballs or the most ethereally smooth hummus delivered in twenty minutes—is something far less bragworthy: I am picky as all hell.

And also, a little obsessive.

It's not enough for me to go to a restaurant and have a chicken dish that was mostly good but possibly in need of more acid. I have to go home and read about chicken for an hour. I have to figure out where I am most likely to find the best chicken that afternoon and then I have to buy that chicken and go home and weigh all the ingredients and make note of what size the potatoes were and exactly how far into the cooking time I turned them and the texture of the salt and the brand of the vermouth and tweak it and make

it again and again until the chicken is just as I had hoped it would be on that day I first ordered it.

And then I have to tell you about it. I cannot possibly spend all of this time fine-tuning what I think makes for the most incredible roast chicken there could be *and then let you make another recipe.* It would seriously bum me out.

These things—pickiness, ~~bullheadedness,~~ I mean, *obsessiveness*—can be terrible traits on their own but when I put them together, they seem to have grown into something so much better than their parts. And that, my friends, is because of you.

I may have known how to cook and known what I wanted my food to taste like when I registered the smittenkitchen.com domain name in the summer of 2006, but I didn't know a thing about the way people outside my head cooked until they started coming forward, through comments, and asking me questions.

"Did you mean table salt or kosher salt?"
"Would waxed paper work too?"
"Does this still work with store brand butter?"
"How on earth am I supposed to know if a dark chocolate cookie has become 'golden' at the edges?"
"What if I don't have and don't want to buy cream of tartar?"
"I hate sifting. Can I skip it?"
"Do I have to use the really expensive olive oil for this?"
"How is this brownie different from every other brownie on your site?"
"Have you completely lost your mind? I will not spend ten dollars on a box of salt!"

For six years, I have responded to every question I could possibly answer that has come up in the 150,000 comments on my site to date (I'll admit to ignoring ones about when I'll have another kid but only because *Mom, you are so busted*). More than any folding/whisking/butter-softening trick I've learned over the years, it's your comments, this question-and-answer game that we play, that have fine-tuned my cooking by forcing me to question everything.

Having answered your questions, I also came to realize that the vast majority of them boil down to one most pressing detail: "Will this recipe be really, truly worth it?"

I've noticed that nobody hates cooking as much as they hate the roulette of not knowing if their time, money, and efforts are going to be rewarded by a

recipe that exceeds expectations. And I'm no different; I don't really care if a meal is going to take more than thirty minutes to cook or if I'll have to chop three different vegetables. All I need to know is that a soup that may take a little longer and may be a little more involved will actually taste better than what I'm used to.

On the flip side, what I secretly hope when I read a cake recipe that asks me to use three different bowls is: Did this recipe's creator compare the results of this cake with one bowl, two bowls, and three bowls and find that the three-bowl method was *clearly* the winning cake? Or did they just ask me to use three bowls because that's the way it's always been done?

Wouldn't it be great if you knew the answer was "yes"?

This kitchen may be too tiny for me to throw the cooking party I've always dreamed of, but I've dragged you all in here with me and now I hope the recipes reflect it.

* * *

Here in the Smitten Kitchen, everybody agrees that cold fruit crisps make excellent breakfasts (Apricot Breakfast Crisp, p. 23) and that dropping everything to make the baked French toast embodiment of cinnamon toast (p. 7) is a perfectly respectable thing to do.

That you should be able to make pizza from scratch in under an hour (Rushed Pizza Dough, p. 104), and heavenly roast chicken too (Flat Roasted Chicken, p. 173). That vegetarian meals shouldn't be throwaways but as luxurious as the most classic French braise (Mushroom Bourguignon, p. 151). That the addition of fresh peas makes buttery Alfredo sauce totally okay to eat for dinner again (Sweet Peas and Shells Alfredo, p. 121). That it would be awesome if your new favorite lemon bar recipe required no zesting, juicing, and no more than a single bowl to assemble (Whole Lemon Bars, p. 217). And finally, that you simply cannot call a cake a S'More Cake unless you get to terrify your friends and family by whipping out a blowtorch to finish the "marshmallows" on top (S'More Layer Cake, p. 263).

Here, I hope we don't let tiny kitchens, tight budgets, long days, fussy ingredients, or people who tell you you're less of a cook if you need to look at a recipe keep us from making awesome food we're excited to eat and share.

Here, I hope that even if you weren't planning to cook tonight, at least one single thing in these pages looks so tempting that *not cooking* is no longer an option.

So, welcome. I hope you're hungry.

notes and tips

* Unless otherwise noted, any mention of sugar means white (granulated) sugar.

* Cornstarch is often sold as "corn flour" outside the U.S.

* Confectioners' sugar, or powdered sugar, is often sold as "icing sugar" outside the U.S.

* Whipping cream and heavy cream have slightly different fat levels (30 to 36 percent versus 36 to 40 percent) but for the purposes of the recipes in this book will work interchangeably. Outside the U.S. the equivalent is often sold as "double cream."

* You might notice that I call for table salt in most recipes, which might seem odd in an age where salt varieties can take up several grocery store shelves. I did this for consistency. Different types, and even brands, of salt have different weights and thus saltiness that they impart to a recipe—a tablespoon of table salt always weighs 18 grams but the same volume of sea salt could weigh a little less (14.5 grams, in the case of Morton's kosher salt) or a lot less (9 grams, in the case of Diamond kosher). The weight of sea salts is all over the map, as they all come in different-sized granules and flakes. This is good to keep in mind if you like to use the same measure of a type of salt different from what I have

specified; most salts will require a heavier hand to produce the same saltiness of table salt. I do call for kosher and sea salts in recipes where I feel the texture of the salt improves the final taste.

* In baking, I have a preference for baking powders without aluminum. Some bakers feel that aluminum contributes to a "metallic" or "tinny" taste in baked goods that use large volumes of baking powder, such as biscuits, scones, and muffins. I also find that baking powders with aluminum in them are more likely to discolor or give a blue-green tint to baked goods with fruit in them, such as the Whole-Wheat Raspberry Ricotta Scones (p. 15). Can't find an aluminum-free baking powder? Make your own: Mix ¼ teaspoon baking soda, ½ teaspoon cream of tartar, and ¼ teaspoon cornstarch to make 1 teaspoon baking powder.

* I love cooking with buttermilk but I know it is not available everywhere. If you don't have access to it (or don't wish to buy a large container for a recipe that calls for a small amount), you can make a substitute soured milk by mixing a scant cup of whole or low-fat milk with 1 tablespoon of lemon juice or white vinegar and letting it sit for 10 minutes. Thinning plain yogurt with a little milk works as well.

* You can make your own crème fraîche by mixing a scant cup of heavy cream with 1 tablespoon of buttermilk or yogurt in a covered container and leaving it out at room temperature for a day.

* You can make your own brown sugar by mixing 1 cup of granulated sugar with 1½ tablespoons molasses (for light brown sugar) or ¼ cup molasses (for dark brown sugar) and measuring what you need from this mixture.

* I mostly call for fresh herbs in this book. If you're substituting dry herbs for finely chopped fresh ones, use half the amount.

* Here's my favorite way to wash greens and other gritty vegetables: Fill a large bowl with very cold water. Add greens, a handful at a time, and pump them up and down gently a few times, so any sand and grit are deposited at the bottom of the bowl. Lift the greens out, being careful not to drag them through any dirt at the bottom of the bowl, and transfer to a colander, a spinner, or a bed of towels to drain.

* When using a recipe that calls for multiple egg yolks or whites, it's good to keep in mind that 1 large egg yields approximately 1 tablespoon of yolk plus 2 tablespoons of white.

* I use large eggs exclusively in the book, but should you have other sizes around, it's good to keep in mind that 5 large eggs, or 1 cup of eggs, are the equivalent of 4 jumbo, 4 to 5 extra-large, 5 to 6 medium, or 7 small eggs.

* When I measure flour or other dry ingredients from a bin to a cup, I use the "fluff, spoon, and sweep" method, which is to say that I fluff the flour before filling the cup with spoonfuls of it, then sweep the top of the cup to level it. This leads to cups of flour on the light side; they clock in at 125 grams or 4.4 ounces. (Read more about using weights on p. 305.)

* This is more of a philosophy than a technicality, but I tend to be a little stingy with my kitchen purchases. I'll pay up for good meat and produce from the farmer's market, but on most items, I'm using very basic grocery store ingredients—store brand butter, everyday eggs—and want you to feel that you can use whatever you have around and still have the same results. I don't assume that you have fancy imported olive oil or $30 aged balsamic in your pantry, and I won't suggest you use either unless I am convinced it adds something essential to the recipe.

THE SMITTEN KITCHEN COOKBOOK

breakfast

peach and sour cream pancakes

cinnamon toast french toast

gingerbread spice dutch baby

plum poppy seed muffins

whole-wheat raspberry ricotta scones

chocolate chip brioche pretzels

almond date breakfast bars

apricot breakfast crisp

big cluster maple granola

maple bacon biscuits

big breakfast latkes

greens, eggs, and hollandaise

baked ranchero eggs with blistered
jack cheese and lime crema

potato frittata with feta and scallions

new york breakfast casserole

fig, olive oil, and sea salt challah

cheddar swirl breakfast buns

peach and sour cream pancakes

*N*ow, I cringe remembering this story, but, seeing that I suspect it was my mother's proudest moment to date in my culinary development and that it related to pancakes, it seems only fitting that I tell you here about the day in my freshman year of college when my friends and I talked another friend, one with a car (cue clouds parting, angels singing), into taking us out to the IHOP in Arlington, Virginia, for a very exciting meal of Something, Anything That Wasn't on Our Meal Plan. Everything was going great until I realized—insert your best joke about dashed hopes that higher education might teach your narrator common sense—that the menu was mostly pancakes. And I didn't think their pancakes tasted very good. In fact, I always thought they tasted like the three very most scathing words in my mother's food vocabulary, and I said them there at the table that night: "from a *mix*."

My friends rightfully called me out. "You're such a pancake snob!" they said. The next day, I relayed that story to my mother, and I could sense her beaming even from hundreds of miles away. She still loves that story. In fact, if you ask her whether she ever knew that one day I was going to be someone who did a lot of cooking, she'll repeat the Pancake Story—right after she tells you about the time that I made brownies and forgot the flour—and say, "Maybe."

So, obviously, we must begin with pancakes. That are not from a mix. But not just any pancakes, upside-down cakes parading as pancakes. I made them on a whim one summer, and though I hadn't expected them to be terrible or anything, I hadn't anticipated the marriage of peaches and sour cream to be so weepingly delicious. The sugar in the peaches, it *caramelizes* in the butter and then melts into the pancake, and it left us with no other options but to spend all of the months of winter and spring lamenting how long it would be before I could make them again.

* * *

yield: eight 4-inch pancakes

1 large egg

1 cup (8 ounces or 230 grams) sour cream

¼ teaspoon vanilla extract

2 tablespoons (25 grams) sugar

¼ teaspoon table salt

¼ teaspoon ground cinnamon

Pinch of ground nutmeg

¾ cup (95 grams) all-purpose flour

1 teaspoon baking powder

½ teaspoon baking soda

Butter, for pan

1 peach, halved, pitted, and very thinly sliced (about ⅛-inch slices)

cooking note

On various occasions, I've replaced up to ½ cup of the flour with whole-wheat, white whole-wheat, or oat flour, and ¼ cup with rye flour; all make very delicious pancakes.

Preheat your oven to 250 degrees. Whisk the egg, sour cream, vanilla, and sugar together in the bottom of a large bowl. In a separate bowl, whisk together the salt, cinnamon, nutmeg, flour, baking powder, and baking soda. Fold dry ingredients into wet, mixing until just combined and still a little lumpy.

Heat your skillet or sauté pan to medium-low. A cast-iron skillet is my favorite to use for pancakes but if you don't have one, just use your heaviest skillet for best browning. Melt a pat of butter in the bottom of the pan, and ladle in ¼ cup batter at a time, leaving at least 2 inches between pancakes. Arrange two peach slices over the batter. Don't worry if they are bigger than the batter puddle, because the pancake will spread as it cooks. When the pancakes are dry around the edges and you can see bubbles forming on the top, after about 3 to 4 minutes, get your spatula all the way underneath the pancake-and-peach puddle, and flip it in one quick movement. If any peaches try to slide out from underneath, nudge them back where they belong.

Cook for another 5 minutes, until the pancakes are golden brown on the underside and the peach slices are nicely caramelized. If they're browning too quickly, lower your heat. Transfer the pancakes to a tray in your warm oven as they cook, which will ensure they fully set and keep them warm until you're ready to serve them.

cinnamon toast french toast

The only brunch I've ever hosted that left me downright regretful was the one on a New Year's Day when I decided I would make French toast. In my friends trickled, one at a time, but I could do little more than wave hello, because I was chained to the stove, dipping, flipping, frying, and then dipping and flipping and frying some more. This was no way to ring in the new year.

Shortly after that, I started baking French toast in a casserole dish, and I've never looked back. Not only do you not need to fry individual slices of custard-soaked bread, you don't really need to do anything the morning of a brunch besides preheat your oven and slide in the tray you prepared the previous night, before you went out to celebrate. Even better, you can make the french-toast casserole as thick and deep and decadent as you please—on the stove, it's hard to get the centers of thicker slices to set; in the oven, they always do.

I came late to cinnamon toast—buttery toast, thickly coated with cinnamon sugar and broiled until it becomes just caramelized enough that the heavens open up. I could blame my parents, I could blame my Yankee upbringing, I could blame the fact that I don't think I ever saw white bread in my parents' house growing up. Or I could just do my best to make up for lost time. This recipe does its best, and it feeds a crowd. I routinely question why I bother making anything else for breakfast.

*   *   *

make cinnamon toast Preheat your oven to 450 degrees. Whisk the cinnamon and sugar together in a small dish. Line two large baking sheets with foil. Place the bread slices on the baking sheets in one layer. Spread each slice of bread with 1 teaspoon of butter, then sprinkle each slice with 1 teaspoon of the cinnamon-sugar mixture. Toast the trays of bread in the oven until the bread is golden, and until the cinnamon sugar makes a caramelized crunch on top, about 7 to 10 minutes. Reduce the oven temperature to 375 degrees, and let the toast cool slightly.

yield: serves 8

1 tablespoon ground cinnamon

½ cup (100 grams) sugar

1-pound loaf (about 455 grams or 16 slices) white sandwich bread

8 tablespoons (115 grams or 1 stick) unsalted butter, softened

3 cups (710 ml) whole milk

6 large eggs

¼ teaspoon table salt

2 teaspoons pure vanilla extract

Maple syrup, yogurt, and/or berries (optional, to serve)

make casserole Generously butter a 9-by-13-inch baking dish. (You might have a little butter left over, but I wanted to build in some leeway in case, understandably, you weren't buttering your bread with precise teaspoon measurements.)

Cut two slices of the cinnamon toast in half horizontally and set aside.

Arrange the baking dish so that the longer side is horizontal to you on the counter. Place the bottom half of a divided slice of cinnamon toast in the upper left-hand corner, cut side facing left. Arrange your first full slice of cinnamon toast on top of it, so that the upper crust of the slice meets the left side of the pan. Arrange six more slices across the top of the pan, crusts in the same direction, overlapping each slightly. Finish with the top of a divided slice of toast.

Repeat across the bottom of the pan, with the toasts facing the opposite direction, starting and finishing with your second divided slice of toast.

Whisk the milk, eggs, salt, and vanilla in a medium bowl, and pour evenly over cinnamon toast in baking dish. Let sit for 15 minutes so that the custard absorbs a bit.

Before baking, if you've got any extra cinnamon sugar (you'll likely have a tablespoon or two), sprinkle it over the French toast. Bake for 30 minutes, until puffed and golden and until no liquid seeps out of the toasts when they are nudged about in the pan. Cut into squares and serve plain, with maple syrup, or with a dollop of plain yogurt and fresh berries.

do ahead You can prepare the dish up to the point where you add the custard, cover it with plastic, and rest it in the fridge overnight. Bake it directly from the fridge in the morning, just adding a few minutes to the baking time.

gingerbread spice dutch baby

*9*f you don't already have a Dutch-baby pancake in your breakfast repertoire, I simply cannot let you get any farther into this book without one. Closer to a thick crepe than a typical American pancake, it is, frankly, more interesting than both. The batter is practically austere in its brief ingredient list and in that it contains only a modicum of sugar, and it can be whirled up in a blender in a single minute before it is poured into a buttered frying pan and slipped into the oven. Faster than you can brew the coffee, slice some fruit, and set the table, you'll pull from the oven a rippling ocean of golden pancake—not puffed, but rumpled like a bedsheet. The edges are a little crisp. The center is something you'll daydream about later in the day. And the flavor, well, that's where I had fun. . . .

Traditionally, Dutch babies are a humble affair, dressed with lemon juice and dusted with powdered sugar. But this is one for a chilly morning, the kind that will fill your kitchen with a whiff of winter spice. Of course, this isn't the kind of gingerbread that would please your German great-grandmother; the intensity of the spices will not bring tears to your eyes. Everything here is a bit more gentle; it's breakfast, after all, and we all deserve to be gently eased into the morning after all that holiday nog and grog the night before.

*　　*　　*

Preheat your oven to 400 degrees. Run the eggs in a blender until they are pale in color. Add remaining ingredients except butter and confectioners' sugar, and process until smooth. Melt the butter over high heat in a 9-inch ovenproof skillet; swirl it up the sides, making sure the pan is nicely coated. Pour the batter into the prepared skillet, and bake for 15 to 20 minutes. Slide pancake onto a plate. Serve with powdered sugar, maple syrup, and/ or a drizzle of heavy cream.

yield: one 9-inch rumpled pancake, serving one to two

2 large eggs

1 tablespoon dark brown sugar

1 teaspoon unsulfured molasses

⅓ cup (40 grams) all-purpose flour

¼ teaspoon ground cinnamon

⅛ teaspoon ground ginger

Pinch of ground cloves

⅛ teaspoon ground or freshly grated nutmeg

⅛ teaspoon table salt

⅓ cup (80 ml) whole milk

2 tablespoons (30 grams) unsalted butter

Confectioners' sugar, maple syrup, or heavy cream, to serve

plum poppy seed muffins

She hasn't said so in so many words, but I have a hunch that my editor thinks I should explain why it took me no fewer than seven muffin recipes to stop fussing and find the perfect one to tell you about. Are muffin recipes that hard to come up with? No, not really. Do we perhaps just enjoy eating muffins so much that I looked for excuses to make more? Unfortunately, not that either. Am I really so terribly indecisive? Apparently, yes, but only in what I believed to be the quest for the greater muffin good. Okay, fine, and when I'm choosing earrings.

What finally led me here was, innocently enough, a basket of boring-looking lemon–poppy seed muffins at a bakery one morning; they got me wondering when poppy seeds would come untethered from lemon's grasp. Poppy seeds are delightful on their own—faintly nutty bordering on fruity—but they also play well with fruit that is richer in flavor and texture than lemon. Inspired, I went home and, a short while later, finally pulled a muffin out of the oven I'd change nothing about. Poppy seeds, plums, browned butter, brown sugar, and sour cream form a muffin that's rich with flavor, dense with fruit, and yet restrained enough to still feel like breakfast food. Seven rounds and six months in, I bet somewhere my editor is breathing a sigh of relief.

yield: 12 standard muffins

6 tablespoons (3 ounces or 85 grams) unsalted butter, melted and browned (see page 201) and cooled, plus butter for muffin cups

1 large egg, lightly beaten

¼ cup (50 grams) granulated sugar

¼ cup (50 grams) packed dark or light brown sugar

¾ cup (180 grams) sour cream or a rich, full-fat plain yogurt

½ cup (60 grams) whole-wheat flour

1 cup (125 grams) all-purpose flour

¾ teaspoon baking powder

¾ teaspoon baking soda

¼ teaspoon table salt

Pinch of ground cinnamon

Pinch of freshly grated nutmeg

2 tablespoons (20 grams) poppy seeds

2 cups pitted and diced plums, from about ¾ pound (340 grams) Italian prune plums (though any plum variety will do)

* * *

Preheat your oven to 375 degrees. Butter twelve muffin cups.

Whisk the egg with both sugars in the bottom of a large bowl. Stir in the melted butter, then the sour cream. In a separate bowl, mix together the flours, baking powder, baking soda, salt, cinnamon, nutmeg, and poppy seeds, and then stir them into the sour-cream mixture until it is just combined and still a bit lumpy. Fold in the plums.

Divide batter among prepared muffin cups. Bake for 15 to 18 minutes, until the tops are golden and a tester inserted into the center of a muffin comes out clean. Rest muffins in the pan on a cooling rack for 2 minutes, then remove them from the tin to cool them completely.

do ahead Generally, I think muffins are best on the first day, but these surprise me by being twice as moist, with even more developed flavors, on day two. They're just a little less crisp on top after being in an airtight container overnight.

cooking note

You don't create seven muffin recipes in a year without learning a few things. I found that you could dial back the sugar in most recipes quite a bit and not miss much (though, if you find that you do, a dusting of powdered sugar or a powdered-sugar–lemon-juice glaze works well here); that a little whole-wheat flour went a long way to keep muffins squarely in the breakfast department; that you can almost always replace sour cream with buttermilk or yogurt, but I like sour cream best. Thick batters—batters almost like cookie dough—keep fruit from sinking, and the best muffins have more fruit inside than seems, well, seemly. And, finally, in almost any muffin recipe, olive oil can replace butter, but people like you more when you use butter—and if you brown that butter first, you might have trouble getting them to leave.

whole-wheat raspberry ricotta scones

On my first Mother's Day, I decided I would host brunch for my husband's and my families. That morning, because I'm, well, me—someone who considers the constant monitoring of pantry staples exhausting, even though this always causes me trouble—I discovered that I was nearly out of the white flour I'd need for my scones. Also heavy cream. And, heck, even dried fruit.

So I cobbled together my remaining white flour with whole-wheat flour and ricotta and fresh raspberries. And here's the thing about scones and biscuits: If you try enough recipes, you realize that you're generally following some unspoken rules. Whole-wheat flour isn't a friend to biscuity things, because it makes them too dense; ricotta would just be weird; any fruit added must be dried. If you added fresh fruit, such as berries, the dough might be too sticky, and in the oven maybe the berries would melt into pockets of jam, and maybe they'd look a little wild, with buckled indents from the cooked fruit and craggy shapes . . . and . . . Wait, what? Why is this a bad thing again?

This is what I realized when I pulled them from the oven: Everything I thought would go wrong had gone really, really right. Raspberries plus ricotta plus whole-wheat flour equaled everything I wanted out of a breakfast baked good, tucked neatly into a portable shape

*   *   *

yield: nine 2-inch (5 cm) square scones

1 cup (120 grams) whole-wheat flour

1 cup (125 grams) all-purpose flour

1 tablespoon (15 grams) baking powder, preferably aluminum-free

¼ cup (50 grams) sugar

½ teaspoon table salt

6 tablespoons (3 ounces or 85 grams) unsalted butter, chilled

1 cup (4¾ ounces or 135 grams) fresh raspberries

¾ cup (190 grams) whole-milk ricotta

⅓ cup (80 ml) heavy cream

Preheat your oven to 425 degrees. Line a large baking sheet with parchment paper.

In the bottom of a large, widish bowl, whisk flours, baking powder, sugar, and salt together.

with a pastry blender Add the butter (no need to chop it first if your blender is sturdy), and use the blender to cut the butter into the flour mixture until the biggest pieces are the size of small peas. Toss in the raspberries, and use the blender again to break them into half- and quarter-berry-sized chunks.

without a pastry blender Cut the butter into small pieces with a knife, and work the butter into the flour mixture with your fingertips until the mixture resembles coarse meal. Roughly chop the raspberries on a cutting board, and stir them into the butter-flour mixture.

both methods Using a flexible spatula, add the ricotta and heavy cream to the butter mixture and stir them in to form a dough. Then use your hands to knead the dough gently into an even mass, right in the bottom of the bowl. Don't fret if the raspberries get muddled and smudge up the dough. This is a pretty thing.

With as few movements as possible, transfer the dough to a well-floured counter or surface, flour the top of the dough, and pat it into a 7-inch square about 1 inch high. With a large knife, divide the dough into nine even squares. Transfer the scones to the prepared baking sheet with a spatula. Bake the scones for about 15 minutes, until they are lightly golden at the edges. Cool them in the pan for a minute, then transfer them to a cooling rack. It's best to cool them about halfway before eating, so they can set a bit more. I know, way to be a big meanie, right?

cooking note The trickiest thing about these scones is the dampness of the dough. Yet that same trickiness yields something that seems impossibly moist for a scone and, especially, for a whole-wheat one. Remember to keep your counter and your hands well floured and you won't have any trouble getting the scones from bowl to counter to oven to belly—which, after all, is the whole point.

do ahead

Scones are always best the day they are baked. However, if you wish to get a lead on them, you can make and divide the dough, arrange the unbaked scones on your parchment-lined baking sheet, freeze them until firm, and transfer them to a freezer bag. If you're prepping just 1 day in advance, cover the tray with plastic wrap and bake them the day you need them. If you're preparing them more than 1 day in advance, once they are frozen transfer them to a freezer bag or container. Bring them back to a parchment-lined sheet when you're ready to bake them. No need to defrost the frozen, unbaked scones—just add 2 to 3 minutes to your baking time.

chocolate chip brioche pretzels

When it comes to ludicrously delicious, butter-laden French breakfast treats, enthusiasts generally fall into one of two categories: croissant-eaters and brioche-eaters. Me, I'm on Team Brioche; I'd choose a buttery, lightly sweet, stretchy, and deceivingly plain knob of bread over all thousand layers of a great croissant any day. It might be my inability in my mid-thirties to eat like a grown-up that has made this choice for me, evidenced by the telltale flakes I find still clinging to my coat and sweater hours after the croissant is a distant memory. Or it might be the fact that, if you're going to pick your breakfast indulgences based on the ease of making them at home, the brioche will win.

It is, after all, a fairly simple bread dough, enriched with milk, eggs, and butter, and even simpler after I got to it. Though I don't doubt that the flour-lidded starter, and butter that has been bashed into soft submission on a counter and then added in delicate dabs at the end, make a phenomenal proper brioche, I am not a morning person, and thus, this became lazy brioche. I've found out that you can squash the standard procedure into one rise and not miss out on as much as you'd think. And since I'd already long abandoned proper brioche etiquette, I went ahead and roped it into a stretchy, rich pretzel, brushed it shiny and a bit salty, and then studded it with coarse sugar. It was my husband who suggested adding chocolate chips—well, technically, that's his suggestion for improving every baked good, but on this I think it was especially inspired. Eat these warm from the oven and I promise there won't be a telltale crumb left behind.

*   *   *

make brioche Whisk the milk and yeast together in a small dish until the yeast has dissolved. In the bowl of an electric mixer with the paddle attachment, stir together flour, sugar, and salt. Add the eggs and the yeast mixture, and mix at a low speed until the dough comes together in a shaggy pile. Raise the speed to medium, and beat for 10 minutes; the long

dough

⅓ cup (80 ml) whole milk

1 teaspoon instant yeast

2¼ cups (280 grams) all-purpose flour

2 tablespoons (25 grams) granulated sugar

½ teaspoon table salt

2 large eggs, at room temperature, lightly beaten

8 tablespoons (115 grams or 1 stick) unsalted butter, at room temperature

1 cup (6 ounces or 170 grams) well-chopped chocolate (for the best chocolate flavor) or miniature chocolate chips

¼ teaspoon freshly grated orange zest (optional, but lovely if you're into that chocolate-orange thing)

glaze

1 large egg

½ teaspoon table salt

1 teaspoon water

Coarse or pearl sugar, for finishing

mixing time creates the soft, stretchy strands brioche is known for. Add the butter, a third at a time, mixing the dough between additions. Now switch to the dough hook, and knead at low speed until a silky-smooth dough forms, another 5 minutes. Add the chocolate and zest, if using, and run the machine until it is mixed into the dough.

Transfer to a lightly oiled bowl, cover with plastic wrap, and allow to rise in a warm spot for 2 hours, until almost doubled. Alternatively, you can rest the dough in the fridge overnight (or up to 24 hours), bring back to room temperature, and let the rise complete before continuing to the next step.

Meanwhile, line two baking sheets with parchment paper and set aside. Preheat your oven to 350 degrees.

form pretzels Gently deflate the dough, and divide it into eight pieces, about 3¼ ounces (93 grams) each. Working with one piece at a time, roll each piece into an 18-inch-long rope about ½ inch thick. Curiously, I find these ropes easier to roll and stretch on an unfloured or very lightly oiled surface, but if you find yours sticking too much, lightly flour your counter before continuing.

To form the pretzel, draw the ends of a rope together to form a circle. About 2 inches from both ends, twist the rope ends together to close the circle—a full twist, so that the rope end that started on the right side finishes there. Fold the twist down into the circle, adhering the loose ends of the rope at five and seven o'clock on the base. Repeat to make eight pretzel twists. Transfer them to prepared baking sheets, brush them with glaze, and let them rest for about 15 minutes, during which they'll puff slightly again.

to finish Brush pretzels with glaze one more time, sprinkle with pearl or coarse sugar, then bake for 12 minutes, or until puffed and lightly bronzed. Cool slightly on a rack before serving, if you can bear it.

cooking note Unfortunately, I find this to be the rare bread dough that's radically easier to make with a stand mixer. Nevertheless, should you feel up for the challenge, you can vigorously "knead" the dough in a large bowl with a wooden spoon for a good 10 minutes before adding the butter. Yes, this takes longer than your average bread dough, but that long kneading time is what yields the long, stretchy strands essential to great brioche.

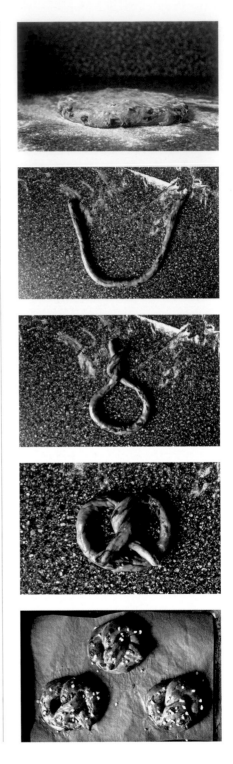

almond date breakfast bars

I can't say enough good things about having a stockpile of breakfast bars in your freezer—they make an accompanying cup of yogurt you grabbed on the way to work less depressing, they're the perfect toddler snack, they're a fantastic gift to bring a new mama, and could you imagine sending dinner party guests home with a little wholesome homemade breakfast for the next morning? Yeah, me neither. But I sure wouldn't mind going somewhere where the host was so clever.

Now, if you're thinking that *yeah right, I'm going to* make *breakfast bars*, you know, right after you etch glass canisters with an intricate leaf pattern, you'd be exactly in the same boat as I was six years ago—at the time, it seemed inconceivable, when they're actually a cinch. Nevertheless, breakfast bars are *exactly* the kind of thing that can be sketchy and/or, at least, overly sweet when purchased in a wrapper (no doubt, boasting all of the ways it will change your life for the better). My early attempts to make them at home weren't much better. Most were delicious, but almost all were loaded with butter and other desserty ingredients and one—my favorite, actually—had corn syrup and was sweeter than your average birthday cake. Oops.

So I got to tinkering. And this is the result: something that totally fits my own breakfast bill—not too sweet, full of wholesome ingredients, etc.—and yet still tastes like a treat, which is a relief. After all, it's breakfast, not an apology for an extra helping of dinner the night before.

* * *

yield: sixteen 2-inch square bars

1 cup (150 grams) chopped dried pitted dates

1¼ cups (110 grams) quick rolled oats

3 tablespoons (22 grams) barley or whole-wheat flour

⅓ cup (35 grams) wheat germ

½ cup (55 grams) thinly sliced almonds

½ teaspoon table salt

¼ teaspoon ground cinnamon

¼ cup (65 grams) almond butter

¼ cup (60 ml) olive oil

¼ cup (85 grams) honey

¼ teaspoon freshly grated orange zest

¼ teaspoon almond extract

Preheat your oven to 350 degrees. Line an 8-by-8-by-2-inch pan in one direction with parchment paper, allowing the paper to go up the opposing sides. Do the same in the opposite direction. This parchment "sling" makes it easy to remove the bars from the pan in one piece.

Stir together the dates, oats, flour, wheat germ, almonds, salt, and cinnamon in the bottom of a large bowl. In a separate bowl, whisk together the almond butter, olive oil, honey, orange zest, and almond extract until smooth. Pour the wet ingredients over the dry mixture, and stir them together until the dry ingredients are evenly coated. Spread the batter in the prepared pan, pressing the mixture firmly into the bottom, edges, and corners to ensure they are molded to the shape of the pan. I like to use a piece of plastic wrap to protect my hands as I do so.

Bake the bars for 20 to 25 minutes, until they're brown around the edges—don't be afraid to get a little color on the tops too. They'll still seem soft and almost underbaked when you press into the center of the pan, but do not worry—they'll set once completely cool.

Cool the bars in their pan placed on a cooling rack or in the fridge. (Alternatively, after about 20 minutes you can use your parchment "sling" to lift and remove the bars, and place them in their paper on the rack to cool the rest of the way. This can speed the process up.)

Once they're cool, use a serrated knife to cut the bars into squares. If bars seem crumbly, chill them further in the fridge for 30 minutes, which will fully set the "glue," then cut them cold.

cooking notes

This recipe can easily be doubled, to fit in a 9-by-13-inch baking pan and make thirty-two bars.

My recipe owes some credit to King Arthur Flour's Chewy Granola Bars, which use different ingredients and levels but helped me find the fat/grain/seed balance that makes these wonderful.

do ahead

To store, wrap the bars individually in plastic, or stack them in an airtight container—even if they seem firm to begin with, they'll soften overnight in a container. They also freeze well.

apricot breakfast crisp

*I*f you're only eating baked fruit crisps for dessert, you're totally missing out. Or maybe you've already figured out how amazing they are when eaten cold, the next day, straight from the fridge? You have, I can tell.

A few years ago, I started making breakfast crisps—that is, fruit crisps intended for the breakfast meal, baked hot only to be served cold. Cold desserts are kind of my favorite anyway, so it didn't feel like a compromise. This revelation came at about the same time that I realized that great apricots, unlike most stone fruits, don't even require a knife to take them apart; you can split them at their seams with your fingertips, and tear them in half again to make perfect chunks. The simplicity of this procedure is ideal for something I promise you'll want to make a new breakfast habit. I adapted this recipe for the morning hours by using a lot less sugar, a good volume of oats, and some almonds. When I'm feeling especially goody-goody, I replace half the butter with olive oil, and half the white flour with whole wheat. If I have it around, I really like making this with a natural sugar, such as a coarse turbinado (often sold as Sugar in the Raw); natural sugar is a nice fit for the subdued breakfast meal, and I'm convinced it gives the topping more crunch.

But mostly, the weeks I make this are my favorite weeks, and they lead me to question why I'd ever buy premixed yogurts, with overly processed and sweetened flavors, when I could be having this instead. Baked at the top of the week, and scooped out little by little each morning (or packed in a container to go to the office), it quickly becomes the highlight of the morning.

* * *

prepare fruit Preheat your oven to 400 degrees. Pull apart the apricots at their seam, remove the pits, and tear them one more time, into quarters. Place the fruit in a small baking dish (a 1-quart gratin dish is perfect). Stir in the sugar, flour, and a pinch of nutmeg.

yield: 2 to 3 cups of fruit crisp

fruit

1 pound (455 grams) apricots

2 tablespoons (25 grams) sugar (granulated or natural turbinado)

1 tablespoon all-purpose flour

Pinch of freshly grated nutmeg

topping

4 tablespoons (55 grams or ½ stick) butter

⅓ cup (65 grams) sugar (granulated or natural turbinado)

½ cup (40 grams) rolled oats

½ cup (65 grams) all-purpose flour (or a mixture of whole-wheat and all-purpose flour)

Good pinch of salt

2 tablespoons sliced or chopped almonds

Yogurt of your choice, to serve

apricot breakfast crisp (continued)

make topping Melt the butter in a small saucepan, and stir in first the sugar, then the oats, then the flour, and finally the salt and almonds, until large clumps form. Sprinkle the mixture over the fruit. Bake for about 30 minutes. Eat warm or chilled, with a scoop of your favorite yogurt.

cooking note Are apricots unavailable? This crisp also works with other stone fruits (a mixture of peaches and plums is fantastic), and, in the fall, apples and pears. If using apples or pears, you should cut your fruit into smaller chunks and bake it for closer to 40 to 45 minutes, covering the top with foil if it browns too quickly.

big cluster maple granola

The gap between store-bought and homemade granola is so vast, there's no bridging it; there's only accepting that, once you learn how to make it at home, you cannot go back to buying it, and if you make this once, you will make it again.

Because nobody warned me of this before I made granola the first time, I've made a lot of it in the last ten years. And although no batch went to waste, I was a bit unhappy with each. Most homemade-granola recipes contain many things that perplex me: a large amount of sugar when a little will do; an epic amount of fat—often melted butter, which seems awfully guilt-inducing for first-thing-in-the-morning fare; and directions that suggest that you stir and stir, which inhibits the clumping we unabashedly adore in store-bought granolas. Over the years, I've dialed back the sugar further and further, and still found the granola perfectly sweet. I've replaced butter with olive oil, which bakes up wonderfully, and scaled back the volume so that you don't end up with an oily mass that never clumps. And for the biggest clusters? An egg white. Nothing "glues" quite like protein.

But the real inspiration behind this recipe is my friend Anna, who brought me a jar of wheat-germ-studded walnut-and-dried-cherry granola weeks after my son was born. It was perfection; I don't think granola flavor gets any better than that. Anna and I met nearly a decade ago, when we both hated our jobs and daydreamed about quitting them to ice cupcakes all day. Seven years later, she's a pastry chef and I get to hang out with you all day, fiddling around with oats until I find my granola nirvana. With Anna's flavors and the big-cluster tricks I've picked up over the years, I don't think I'll get any closer than this.

*　　*　　*

yield: about 7 cups granola

3 cups (240 grams) old-fashioned rolled oats

1 cup (50 grams) unsweetened shredded or flaked coconut

1 cup (100 grams) walnuts, coarsely chopped

¼ cup (25 grams) toasted wheat germ

2 tablespoons (30 ml) olive oil

½ teaspoon coarse salt

½ cup (120 ml; or increase to ⅔ cup if a sweeter granola is preferred) maple syrup

¼ teaspoon ground cinnamon

1 large egg white

1½ cups (215 grams) dried cherries or another dried fruit, diced if large pieces

Preheat your oven to 300 degrees. Combine all ingredients but the egg white and dried fruit in a large bowl, tossing to coat evenly. Whisk the egg white in a small bowl until frothy. Stir into the granola mixture, distributing it throughout. Spread it in a single layer on a parchment-lined baking sheet. Bake for 45 to 55 minutes. About halfway through the baking time, use a large spatula to turn over sections of the granola carefully, breaking them up as little as possible. Rotate the pan if granola is baking unevenly. When it is evenly browned and feels dry to the touch, transfer the pan from the oven to the cooling rack. Cool completely. Once it's completely cool, break up granola into whatever size clusters delight you. Sprinkle in dried fruit.

The granola keeps at room temperature in an airtight container for 2 weeks. It keeps even longer in the freezer, if you're the stockpiling type.

maple bacon biscuits

I would like to tell you that all of my recipe ideas come from warm, glowing places—a favorite restaurant that I now live far from, a great-aunt who makes something better than anyone else, a daydream—but it's just not the case. A whole big lot of the time, recipes come from disappointment, from something I'd ordered out somewhere, imagining it would taste one way, when really it tasted another way. (And not a good way.) Usually, my husband is sitting across from me, enjoying his meal without complaint, and I'll say, "Try this!"

It's hardly the most honorable of inspirations—being convinced that everyone else is doing it wrong, that I alone can do things well. It probably makes me outright wrong a lot of the time. But it did produce a fine biscuit when my husband pointed out—astutely, as always—that perhaps I might stop kvetching across the coffee shop table and go home and make us some better biscuits. The results of my complaints are sweet but salty, buttery and bacony and as light as can be. You should probably serve them alongside eggs, but they have a tendency not to last long enough for you to scramble some.

*　　*　　*

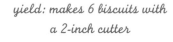

yield: makes 6 biscuits with a 2-inch cutter

3 slices (about 3 ounces or 85 grams) bacon

¼ cup (60 ml) maple syrup

1½ cups (190 grams) all-purpose flour

2 teaspoons baking powder

½ teaspoon baking soda

½ teaspoon table salt

Approximately 4 tablespoons (55 grams or ½ stick) unsalted butter, chilled, chopped into small chunks

¼ cup (60 ml) buttermilk

Fry the bacon until it is crisp. Remove the bacon from the pan and drain it on a few stacked paper towels. Pour the bacon fat into a glass measuring cup so that you can see how much you have. (I usually end up with 2 tablespoons; note if you have more or less, so that you can adjust the butter quantity, as noted below.) Place your measuring cup in the freezer, and freeze until fat is solid.

Chop the bacon into small bits, and place it in a small dish. Pour the maple syrup over the bacon and stir; then set the mixture aside.

Remove the solidified bacon fat from the freezer. Preheat your oven to 425 degrees. Line a baking sheet with parchment paper. Mix the flour, baking powder, baking soda, and salt in large bowl. Using a pastry blender or your fingertips, rub the chilled bacon fat and 4 tablespoons butter (the amount needed for 2 tablespoons bacon fat; adjust up or down if you ended up with less or more bacon fat) into the dry ingredients until mixture resembles coarse meal. Add the bacon–maple-syrup mixture and the buttermilk, and blend together with a rubber spatula until it is evenly moistened. Knead just a couple times (as little as needed) to form the scraps into a dough. Pat out to 1-inch thickness on a well-floured surface, and cut into biscuits with a 2-inch cutter. Arrange the biscuits on the baking sheet, and bake for 12 to 14 minutes, until they are puffed and golden. Serve warm.

do ahead

Biscuits are best the first day they are baked, but they can be prepared in advance. I like to make double and triple batches, freeze them on a tray until they're firm (and won't stick together), and then keep them in a bag in the freezer until I'm ready to bake them. When the need for biscuits arises, you can bake them directly from the freezer and just add a couple minutes to your baking time.

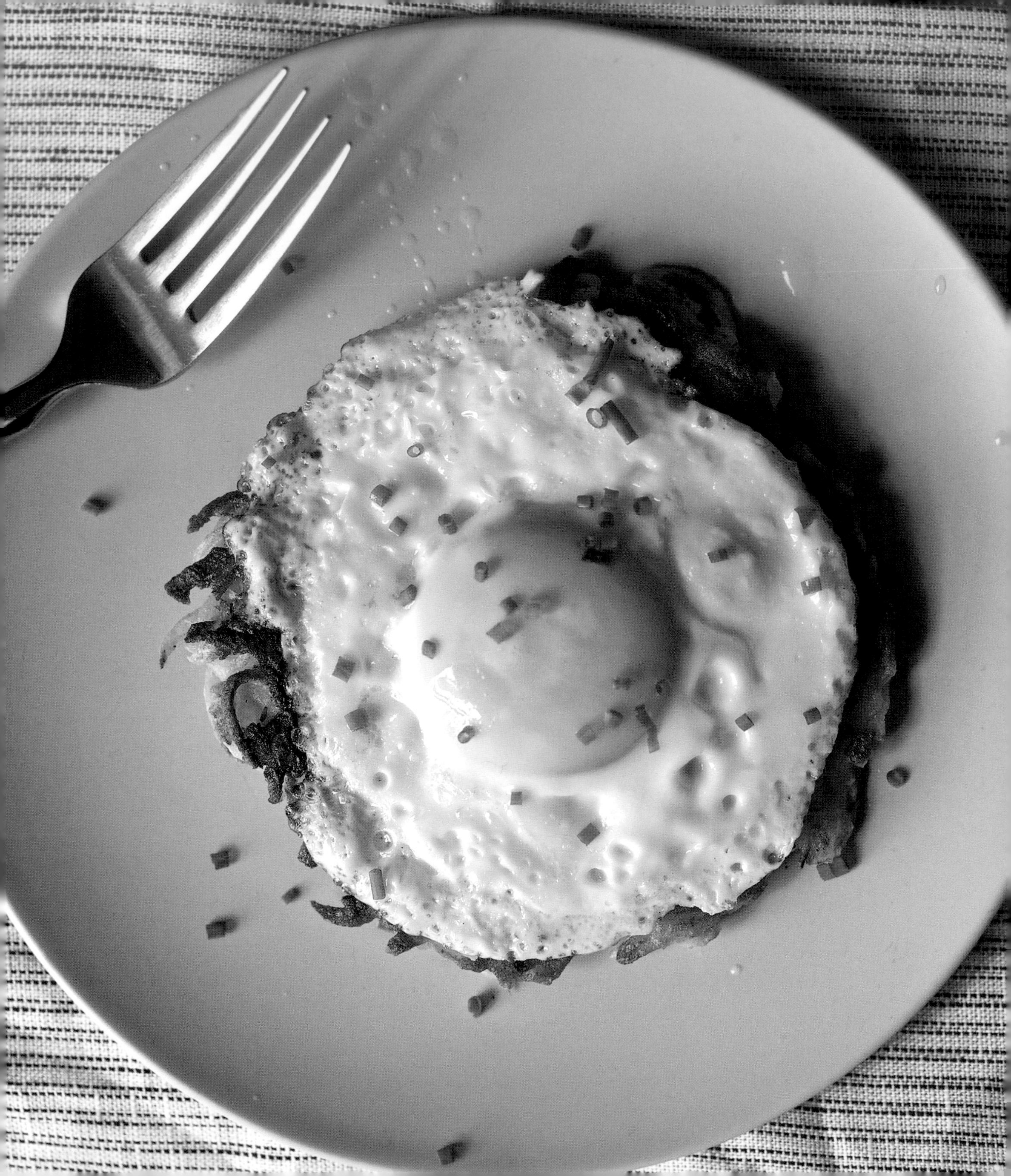

big breakfast latkes

Just about everyone who makes breakfast has a version of breakfast potatoes, be they hash browns or home fries or skillet-smashed potatoes. And just about all cooks make them their very own way—the way they think potatoes should be—and though they may tolerate other breakfast-potato formats, they secretly always think that their personal method, the one they learned from their mama/that diner on Main Street/their friend the chef is the best.

Personally, I just want to eat latkes all year round, and I maintain that if you're limiting your latke consumption to the eight nights of Hanukkah, you are missing out. The latke, at its base, is the ideal breakfast potato—humble russets and everyday onions, shredded, mixed with the slimmest amounts of egg and flour, and fried until brown and crisp on both sides. Latkes hold together better than hash browns, which allows you to make them bigger. And the bigger they are, the more ideal base they become for the other perfect breakfast, a fried egg.

*   *   *

Preheat your oven to 250 degrees. Line a baking sheet with foil, and keep in oven until needed.

In a food processor or on a box grater, coarsely shred the potato and onion. For longer, moplike strands, I prefer to lay the potato sideways in the chute of the food processor. Transfer the shredded mixture to a square of cheese-cloth or lint-free dishtowel, and gather the ends to wring out as much water as possible. Let it stand for 2 minutes, then squeeze it out again.

In a large bowl, whisk the flour, baking powder, salt, pepper, and egg together. Stir in the potato-onion mixture until all the pieces are evenly coated.

In a small, heavy skillet (cast-iron, if you have one), heat 2 tablespoons of vegetable oil until it shimmers. Drop one-quarter of the potato mixture into the skillet, and flatten with the back of a spoon to a 5-inch round. Cook the latke over moderate heat until the edges are golden, about 4 to

yield: four large (5-inch) latkes

1 large baking potato (1 pound or 455 grams), peeled

1 small onion (¼ pound or 115 grams), peeled

¼ cup (30 grams) all-purpose flour

1 teaspoon baking powder

¾ teaspoon table salt

¼ teaspoon freshly ground black pepper

1 large egg, lightly beaten

Vegetable or olive oil, for frying

Fried eggs, to serve (optional)

cooking note

For neat edges and a thinner rostilike appearance, you can press each pancake into a 6-inch skillet and proceed to cook according to directions. For lacy, craggy-edged latkes, form the pancakes in a larger pan.

5 minutes; flip, and cook until golden on the bottom, about 3 to 4 minutes more.

Transfer latke to the prepared baking sheet in the oven. Repeat process with remaining latke batter in three batches, creating a total of four large latkes, being sure to add more oil as needed and letting it fully reheat between pancakes. Keep latkes warm in oven until needed.

Serve latkes warm in four wedges with eggs or whole with a fried egg atop each.

do ahead Latkes are a do-aheader's dream. You can also keep the latkes warm in the oven, on low heat, for an hour or more, if you're waiting for stragglers to arrive. If already cooked, they keep well in the fridge for a day or two, or in the freezer, well wrapped, for up to 2 weeks. Reheat the latkes in a single layer on a cookie sheet in a 300-degree oven until they're crisp again. Bonus: If you undercooked them a bit, or didn't get them as brown as you'd hoped, you can compensate for this in the oven.

greens, eggs, and hollandaise

For a very long time, almost every time I went out to brunch at a place I didn't recognize, I'd order eggs Florentine—a split English muffin topped with sautéed spinach, a poached egg, and hollandaise sauce. I was convinced that it was a safe choice, that it was such a standard dish that nobody could really mess it up, right?

So—you know where this is going. Sometimes, the spinach was creamed. Often, the egg had been poached until it was hard-boiled. And one time, I saw an empty bucket of something called hollandaise out by the trash, and let's just say it didn't contain many recognizable ingredients.

Obviously, it was time to take this party home. At home, your eggs are never overcooked, and even if they are, at least you didn't pay $14 plus tax and tip for the honor. At home, your vegetable options are not limited to spinach, likely frozen. At home, your hollandaise never comes in a bucket. If you're like me, you might be assuming that the hollandaise is the dealbreaker. Who can make hollandaise at home? Well, you. It turns out that hollandaise, which was once the bane of the cooking student's sauce series, can be whirled up in a blender in less than 5 minutes, and it tastes like buttery, buttery perfection.

*   *   *

prepare your greens Wash your greens, but no need to dry them—just place them in a large pot over high heat. Cook with just the water clinging to the leaves, stirring occasionally, until they are wilted. If you use mixed greens, first add those that cook more slowly—about 2 minutes for baby spinach, 3 to 4 minutes for grown-up spinach, 6 minutes for chard, and a bit longer for heavier greens.

Press or squeeze out the excess liquid any number of ways, either by wringing it out in cheesecloth (my favorite method), putting the greens in a mesh strainer and pressing the moisture out with a spatula or large spoon, or letting them cool long enough so you can grab small handfuls and squeeze them to remove as much water as possible.

yield: serves 4 generously (2-egg portions) or 8 modestly (1-egg portions), with 1 cup hollandaise

greens and eggs

1¼ pounds (570 grams) mixed greens (chard and spinach make a nice mix, or any greens you prefer), heavy stems removed, leaves cut into ¼-inch ribbons

2 tablespoons (30 grams) butter, plus more for the egg cups

½ small onion, or 2 medium shallots, finely chopped

1 garlic clove, minced

Salt

Freshly ground black pepper

Pinch of ground or freshly grated nutmeg

2 tablespoons (30 ml) half-and-half or heavy cream

8 large eggs

hollandaise

10 tablespoons (140 grams or 1¼ sticks) unsalted butter

2 large egg yolks

1 to 2 tablespoons freshly squeezed lemon juice

Salt

Dash of hot sauce (optional)

4 English muffins, split and sliced into 1-inch "fingers," for serving

meanwhile, make the hollandaise sauce Cut the butter into small bits. Melt it gently in a small saucepan or a small bowl in the microwave until three-quarters melted. Remove the butter from heat, and stir until the remaining pieces dissolve; this ensures that your melted butter doesn't get too hot and lose moisture.

In a blender, combine the yolks, 1 tablespoon lemon juice, a pinch of salt, and a dash of hot sauce, if you're using it. Blend at high speed until the sauce is pale yellow and smooth, for about 30 seconds. Open the pour spout on the lid, run the motor of the blender, and drizzle in the butter a few drops at a time, then a spoonful at a time, and finally in a long, thin stream, until all of it is added. The sauce should have thickened quickly. Taste for seasoning. If necessary, you can thin the sauce with water or additional lemon juice. Add more salt if needed. Transfer hollandaise to a serving dish, which you can keep warm by setting it in a larger dish of warm water, to keep it loose and warm while you prepare the eggs.

assemble egg cups Preheat your oven to 375 degrees. Wipe a large skillet dry, then melt the butter in it, over moderate heat. Cook the onion and garlic in butter over moderately low heat until they are softened, about 6 minutes. Stir in greens, and season to taste with salt, freshly ground black pepper, and nutmeg. Raise the heat, and drizzle cream over the greens; cook them with the cream for 2 to 3 minutes.

Butter four (for larger portions) or eight (for smaller portions) ramekins and arrange them on a baking sheet. Distribute the greens evenly among rame-kins. Break two eggs each into four ramekins, or one each into eight rame-kins. Bake single-egg ramekins for 10 to 15 minutes, or until egg whites are set and yolks are not. The double-egg ramekins will take 15 to 18 minutes.

Arrange English-muffin "fingers" in a single layer on a baking sheet, and toast them in the oven while the eggs bake.

to serve Generously dollop each egg dish with hollandaise sauce. Serve immediately, with English-muffin toast soldiers.

do ahead
Wilted and wrung-out greens can be kept in the fridge for 2 days in a covered container.

baked ranchero eggs with blistered jack cheese and lime crema

I am fairly certain that nothing could possibly go wrong when eggs and tomatoes intersect. Just about every culture has its own format of the two: In North Africa and the Middle East, there's *shakshuka*, eggs cooked in a spicy tomato sauce; in Turkey, a similar dish is *menemen*; in Italy, there's the awesomely named *uova in purgatorio* (eggs in purgatory), involving a garlic-and-basil marinara sauce. But the one that I cannot ignore on any brunch menu at any time is *huevos rancheros*, which my husband jokes I am contractually obligated to order as part of my studies at Huevos Rancheros University. What can I say? I take my spicy egg-tomato mashups seriously.

To be picky, the "rancheros" sauce in huevos rancheros—a salsa-like tomato sauce—is usually dolloped on eggs that are served on tortillas, rather than in the sauce. But we're so into this dish in my apartment—and I'm so keen on breakfast preparations that will allow you to feed a whole brunch crowd without actually standing over the stove and frying eggs and tortillas individually—that I switched it up. And added a lid of broiled Monterey Jack cheese. And a lime *crema*. And tortilla strips that crisp in the oven while you cook the sauce and eggs.

I know you're probably thinking, "A *dozen* eggs? You want me to cook a dish that could feed the better part of a dozen people? Who do you think we are, Jon & Kate Plus 8?" But I have found that when you make food, good food, at home, even in excess, it never goes to waste.

*   *   *

make ranchero sauce   Preheat your oven to 450 degrees. First, taste your jalapeño for heat. I find that they can range from mild-as-a-green-pepper to why-didn't-you-warn-me! and look the same, so I like to see what kind of jalapeño I ended up with before using the whole thing. Adjust the amount accordingly, halving or quartering the pepper, if needed, and toss into a blender. Add the tomatoes, onion, garlic, and several pinches of salt

yield: serves 6 generously (2-egg portions) or 12 modestly (1-egg ortions)

ranchero sauce

1 jalapeño

3 cups (from a 28-ounce or 795-gram can) whole tomatoes, fire-roasted if you can find them

1 medium white onion, roughly chopped

1 large garlic clove, crushed and peeled

Salt and freshly ground black pepper to taste

1¾ cups cooked black beans (or from a 15-ounce or 425-gram can), drained (optional)

crisp tortilla strips

2 tablespoons (30 ml) olive oil

4 small (6-inch) corn tortillas

Salt, to taste

12 large eggs

1¼ cups (4 ounces or 115 grams) coarsely shredded jack cheese

baked ranchero eggs with blistered jack cheese and lime crema (continued)

and pepper, and blend until smooth. Pour into a 12-inch ovenproof skillet, add black beans (if using them), and bring to a simmer. Cook for 10 minutes, or until it has reduced slightly.

make tortilla strips Meanwhile, brush a baking sheet with 1 tablespoon of the olive oil. Cut the tortillas into ½-inch-wide strips, and arrange them on the oiled tray. Brush the tops of the tortilla strips with the remaining tablespoon of oil, and sprinkle with salt. Bake for 3 to 6 minutes, or until they are brown and crisp, turning over once if needed. Remove strips from oven, then preheat broiler.

make crema In a separate bowl, stir together the lime juice, *crema,* and a pinch of salt.

cook eggs Once the sauce has thickened slightly, remove the pan from heat, and break the eggs across the surface of the sauce, distributing them as evenly as possible. Return to heat, cover the pan, and simmer eggs gently in sauce for about 10 to 12 minutes, until the whites are nearly but not completely opaque. (You'll finish them up in a minute.) Sprinkle the surface of the tomato-egg mixture with cheese, and broil until the cheese is bubbly and a bit blistered—just a few minutes.

to serve Garnish with dollops of lime *crema,* broken-up pieces of tortilla strips, and cilantro. Serve immediately.

garnishes

2 tablespoons freshly squeezed lime juice (from about 1 lime)

1 cup crema mexicana or sour cream (240 grams)

¼ cup chopped fresh cilantro

cooking note

Of course, you could always scale this down. It works well halved in a 9-inch skillet, or even quartered and baked in a 1-quart gratin dish. I am so obsessed with my cast-iron skillet that I used it the day I took the photo on page 36 but it is not recommended for tomato-based dishes as their acid wears away at the pan's seasoning.

do ahead

This is not the best dish for planning ahead, because reheated eggs are always overcooked eggs. However, you can prepare the sauce in advance and reheat it when you need it, and then prepare all of your garnishes and crispy things, so that only the eggs are saved for the last minute.

potato frittata with feta and scallions

When I first moved to New York City, my friends and I gathered for brunch every Sunday at Stingy Lulu's, an Art Deco–styled diner in the East Village that was famed for drag-queen servers but, more recently (oh, my liver aches just to remember this), an all-you-can-drink brunch for a respectably low price. We ate at 1 p.m. each week, sometimes 1:30, never sooner. Breakfast before 1:30 p.m. was for old people, obviously.

I ordered the same thing every single week—a frittata with feta, scallions, potatoes, and bacon, except I was still a vegetarian back then and had them hold the bacon. The addictiveness of this frittata, which I have seen nowhere since and thus have been forced to re-create in my own kitchen, should not be underestimated. It is an all-in-one breakfast dish, and, baked in a large frying pan, it easily serves a small crowd. I've replaced their red potatoes (surely, their leftover home fries) with discs of roasted-until-crisped buttery Yukon Golds. The scallions are wonderful, the bacon is great (especially if you can find the thicker-cut stuff), but the real magic is the feta. Feta, eggs, and potatoes go wonderfully together, I learned over a weekly series of watered-down mimosas; the sharp saltiness stands out in a way that cheeses chosen for their ability to melt into omelets do not.

*   *   *

yield: serves 6 to 8

3 tablespoons (45 ml) olive or vegetable oil

1¾ pounds (795 grams) Yukon Gold potatoes

½ teaspoon table salt, plus more for roasting potatoes

Freshly ground black pepper

¼ pound (115 grams) bacon, thick-cut if you can get it, cut crosswise into ¼-inch matchsticks

½ bunch (about 3 to 4) scallions, trimmed and thinly sliced

⅔ cup (3 ounces or 85 grams) crumbled feta

6 large eggs

2 tablespoons (30 ml) milk or cream

cook potatoes Preheat your oven to 400 degrees. Coat a roasting pan or baking tray generously with oil, about 1 to 2 tablespoons. Peel potatoes, and cut them into ¼-to ½ inch slices, and then halve them lengthwise into half-circle shapes. Pile them in the prepared pan, and generously season them with salt and freshly ground black pepper. Don't worry if they don't fall into one layer—the combination of some steamy/softer and some crisp-edged potatoes will work great in this dish. Roast 30 minutes, or until potatoes are mostly cooked (they'll finish cooking with the eggs), tossing once halfway through. Let cool slightly.

potato frittata with feta and scallions (continued)

Alternatively, you can place all of the potato slices in a saucepan and cover them with an inch of cold water. Bring to a simmer and cook slices for 5 to 7 minutes, or until tender but not falling apart. Drain, and let them cool slightly. You won't have the crisp edge on the potato, but you will save a lot of time.

cook bacon and prepare pan Cook bacon in well-seasoned 9-inch cast-iron frying pan until crisp. Scoop out with slotted spoon and drain on paper towels. Add additional tablespoon oil to the bacon drippings in the pan, and reheat it over medium heat. Swirl the oil and drippings around in the pan and up the sides, being sure to coat it fully.

assemble and bake frittata Arrange roasted potatoes in your skillet. If there are pieces with browned undersides, I like to flip the toasty sides up, mostly because they will look bronzed and pretty. Scatter bacon, then scallions and feta over potatoes. Whisk eggs with milk, ½ teaspoon salt, and several grinds of black pepper in a medium bowl, and pour over potatoes. Cover skillet with foil, and bake for 20 minutes. Remove foil, and bake for another 10 to 15 minutes, or until puffed at edges and set in center.

to serve Serve right from the skillet, in 6 to 8 wedges.

new york breakfast casserole

I'm not sure how it is where you live, but in New York City there are few more popular breakfasts than (1) an egg and cheese on a roll or (2) cream cheese and lox on a bagel. You can get either made to order frighteningly cheap anywhere—the deli, the bodega, some bars, the average corner store, where you can stock up on beer, lottery tickets, or cat litter along with breakfast. The randomness of these transactions is one of my favorite things about New York.

Does New York need an all-purpose breakfast vehicle like the one below? Arguably, no. But I came up with it one day as an attempt at a Yankee spin on the kinds of breakfast casseroles I've had in the South—usually with Tater Tots, lots of cheese, and bacon or ham; and, yes, they are insanely delicious—and got back to that corner-store breakfast (minus the pack of cigarettes and bottle of vitaminwater). I found it to be better balanced than your average egg sandwich—which always feels too heavy on the bread for me—and was delighted to discover that, in the oven, bits of cream cheese puff and bronze like tiny marshmallows. Plus, as I always prefer, it serves a crowd, and can be assembled in advance, even the night before it is needed.

*   *   *

prepare casserole Spread a third of the bagel cubes in a 9 by 13 inch pan (or other 4-quart baking dish, if necessary). Dot the bagels with a third of the cream-cheese bits, and mix in the red onion and cherry tomatoes. Repeat in two more alternating layers. Whisk eggs with milk, salt, and freshly ground black pepper. Pour the egg mixture over bagel-and-cheese mixture, and feel free to turn any seedy sides of the bagel croutons faceup, in order to pretty up the dish. Cover tightly with plastic wrap, and refrigerate overnight.

to cook The next morning—I mean, whenever you are forced from bed—remove casserole from the fridge and preheat your oven to

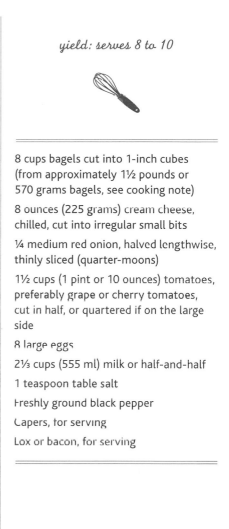

yield: serves 8 to 10

8 cups bagels cut into 1-inch cubes (from approximately 1½ pounds or 570 grams bagels, see cooking note)

8 ounces (225 grams) cream cheese, chilled, cut into irregular small bits

¼ medium red onion, halved lengthwise, thinly sliced (quarter-moons)

1½ cups (1 pint or 10 ounces) tomatoes, preferably grape or cherry tomatoes, cut in half, or quartered if on the large side

8 large eggs

2⅓ cups (555 ml) milk or half-and-half

1 teaspoon table salt

Freshly ground black pepper

Capers, for serving

Lox or bacon, for serving

350 degrees. Bake on a tray, uncovered, in the middle of the oven until it has puffed, turned golden brown, and cooked through (a knife inserted into the center of the casserole and rotated slightly shouldn't release any liquid), for 1 to 1¼ hours. Let it rest 10 minutes before serving.

to serve Serve in big scoops with a sprinkle of capers and a side of lox. Or bacon.

cooking note

Bagel sizes tend to be very inconsistent, making it difficult to estimate the number you will need. You might need up to a dozen freezer-aisle bagels or merely four or five large ones from a bagel shop. Do your best to eyeball what you'll need and if you overestimate, well, nobody ever complained about a freezer full of bagels.

fig, olive oil, and sea salt challah

*T*he terrain of updating old, beloved recipes is fraught with land mines. People don't travel by planes, trains, and automobiles, and sit in three-hour traffic jams on Thanksgiving afternoon because they're secretly hoping their mother decided to make not their family's favorite stuffing this year, but a new one she clipped from a gourmet food magazine. And my people haven't been sitting down to Friday night and High Holiday dinners with a braided loaf of egg bread for thousands of years with the nagging suspicion in the back of their minds that it really could use an update—perhaps with some imported sea salt?

Because of this, I always *try* to tread carefully when making old-school dishes, yet usually fail because my curiosity gets the better of me. This time, I wasn't sorry at all. I took my favorite recipe for challah and replaced the vegetable oil with olive oil, the sugar with honey, the raisins I might use in a sweeter loaf with a fig paste cooked with orange zest, and then I finished it with sea salt and proceeded to watch a table full of carb-eschewing people fall upon it like a pride of hungry lions. This challah gets requested by name.

Leftovers, should they survive the dinner table, make some fine French toast, especially when drizzled with warm honey and served with a dollop of fresh ricotta.

*   *   *

to make dough with a stand mixer Whisk the yeast and 1 teaspoon honey into ⅔ cup warm water, and let it stand for a few minutes, until foamy. In a large mixer bowl, combine the yeast mixture with remaining honey, ⅓ cup olive oil, and eggs. Add the salt and flour, and mix until dough begins to hold together. Switch to a dough hook, and run at low speed for 5 to 8 minutes. Transfer the dough to an olive-oil-coated bowl (or rest the dough briefly on the counter and oil your mixer bowl to use for rising, so that you use fewer dishes), cover with plastic wrap, and set aside for 1 hour, or until almost doubled in size.

yield: 1 large loaf

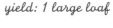

bread

2¼ teaspoons (1 packet—¼ ounce or 7 grams) active dry yeast

¼ cup (85 grams) plus 1 teaspoon honey

⅓ cup (80 ml) olive oil, plus more for the bowl

2 large eggs

2 teaspoons flaky sea salt, such as Maldon, or 1½ teaspoons table salt

4 cups (500 grams) all-purpose flour

fig filling

1 cup (5½ ounces or 155 grams) stemmed and roughly chopped dried figs

⅛ teaspoon freshly grated orange zest, or more as needed

½ cup (120 ml) water

¼ cup (60 ml) orange juice

⅛ teaspoon sea salt

Few grinds of black pepper

egg wash

1 large egg

Coarse or flaky sea salt, for sprinkling

to make dough by hand Proof the yeast as directed above. Mix the wet ingredients with a whisk, then add the salt and flour. Mix everything together with a wooden spoon until the dough starts to come together. Turn the mixture out onto a floured counter, and knead for 5 to 10 minutes, until a smooth and elastic dough is formed. Let rise as directed above.

meanwhile, make fig paste In a small saucepan, combine the figs, zest, water, juice, salt, and a few grinds of black pepper. Bring to a simmer over medium heat, and cook, stirring occasionally, until the figs are soft and tender, about 10 minutes. Season with salt and pepper to taste. Remove from heat, and let cool to lukewarm. Process fig mixture in a food processor until it resembles a fine paste, scraping down the sides of the bowl as necessary. Set aside to cool.

insert figs After your dough has risen, turn it out onto a floured counter and divide it in half. Roll the first half of the dough into a wide and totally imperfect rectangle (really, the shape doesn't matter). Spread half the fig filling evenly over the dough, stopping short of the edge. Roll the dough into a long, tight log, trapping the filling within. Then, gently stretch the log as wide as feels comfortable (I take mine to my max counter width, about three feet) and divide it in half. Repeat with remaining dough and fig filling, creating four ropes.

weave your challah Arrange two ropes in each direction, perpendicular to each other, like a tight tic-tac-toe board. Weave them so that one

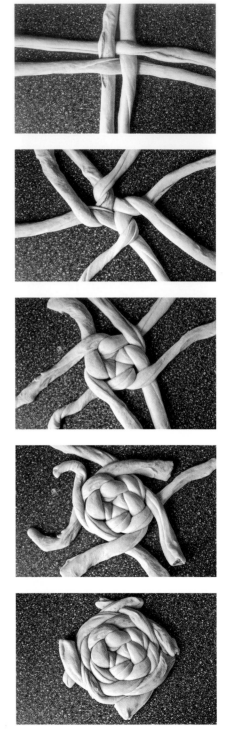

side is over, and the other is under, where they meet. So now you've got an eight-legged woven-headed octopus. Take the four legs that come from *underneath* the center, and move them over the leg to their right—i.e., jumping it. Take the legs that were on the right and, again, jump each over the leg before, this time to the left. If you have extra length in your ropes, you can repeat these left-right jumps until you run out of rope. Tuck the corners or odd bumps under the dough with the sides of your hands to form a round.

Transfer the dough to a parchment-covered heavy baking sheet or, if you'll be using a bread stone, a baker's peel. Beat egg until smooth, and brush over challah. Let challah rise for another hour, but 45 minutes into this rise, preheat your oven to 375 degrees.

bake your loaf Before baking, brush loaf one more time with egg wash and sprinkle with coarse salt if you're using it. Bake in middle of oven for 35 to 40 minutes. It should be beautifully bronzed; if yours starts getting too dark too quickly, cover it with foil for the remainder of the baking time. The very best way to check for doneness is with an instant-read thermometer—the center of the loaf should be 195 degrees.

Cool loaf on a rack before serving. Or, well, good luck with that.

cheddar swirl breakfast buns

What kind of cookbook photographer sneaks a bun from the pan before taking a photo? One who had already waited twenty excruciating minutes in a kitchen so fragrant with everything delicious in this world—cheese, butter, and freshly baked bread, of course—for these to come out of the oven that, by the time they emerged, she'd had enough. And, no, she's not sorry. It was totally worth it.

These are dangerous, dangerous buns, as the photo on page 51 will attest. Think of this as cinnamon buns for people who find them too achingly sweet first thing in the morning. I know you're thinking, "Who doesn't like eggs? Or cinnamon buns? Do these people have pulses?" I'm going to tell you two things: (1) I wondered the same when I realized I had a friend in such a camp. (2) Since I've made these, I only question my own sanity for eating anything else for breakfast.

The secret ingredient, however, isn't the cheddar, or the dill, or the dough, rich with milk and butter. It is the humblest of things, ½ cup of grated onion, which—baked against the cheese within the swirly walls of the bread—becomes so sweet and subtle it raises this breakfast treat to an entirely new level.

*   *   *

make the dough Combine the flour, salt, pepper, and sugar in the bottom of a large bowl. In a separate bowl, whisk the yeast into the milk until it dissolves, then pour the yeast-milk mixture and the melted butter into the flour, and mix them together with the paddle of an electric mixer, or with a wooden spoon, until a shaggy ball can be formed.

If you are using a mixer, switch to the dough hook, and knead at a low speed for about 6 minutes, or until a smooth and slightly sticky ball is formed. If you are making these by hand, turn the dough out onto a lightly floured counter and knead it for about 8 minutes, until smooth.

Place the dough in a lightly oiled bowl, and cover with plastic wrap. Let it

dough

3 cups (13¼ ounces or 375 grams) all-purpose flour

1 teaspoon table salt

Few grinds of black pepper

1 tablespoon sugar

2¼ teaspoons (1 packet— ¼ ounce or 7 grams) instant yeast

1 cup (235 ml) milk

4 tablespoons (55 grams or ½ stick) butter, melted, cooled to lukewarm, plus 1 tablespoon for brushing

filling

½ cup (½ medium) grated white onion

1½ cups (6 ounces or 170 grams) grated sharp cheddar cheese

2 teaspoons minced fresh dill

¼ teaspoon table salt

Few grinds of black pepper

rest until it doubles, about 2 hours. Alternatively, you can chill the dough in the fridge overnight, or up to 3 days, then bring it back to room temperature and pick up where you left off when you're ready.

form buns Scoop the dough out of the bowl onto a well-floured counter, and roll into a 12-by-16-inch rectangle. Mix filling ingredients, and spread thinly over the rectangle, leaving a ½-inch border at the short ends. Roll tightly from one short end to the other, into a 12-inch log. With a sharp serrated knife, carefully cut the log into twelve 1-inch rolls.

Using parchment paper, line the bottom of two small pans (either 9-inch round or 8-inch square) or one 9-by-13-inch baking pan, and arrange six rolls in each of two smaller pans or twelve rolls in the larger one, with an even amount of space between them. Brush the tops with additional melted butter, cover the pan(s) with plastic wrap, and let rise at room temperature until doubled again, about 2 hours. When they're almost doubled, preheat your oven to 350 degrees.

bake buns Once the rolls have fully doubled, bake for 20 to 25 minutes, until the tops are golden brown and the cheese bubbles from their centers. Serve immediately.

cooking note

If you're not into cheddar, you can substitute the same volume of Swiss, provolone, or even mozzarella. Parsley can be substituted for dill. Olive oil can be substituted for butter. Breakfast can be swapped for dinner, a meal where these would be equally welcome in a bread basket. Feeling clever? Make them into miniature buns and serve them at a cocktail party. But, please, invite me.

salads

vinegar slaw with cucumbers and dill

zucchini ribbons with almond pesto

fingerlings vinaigrette with sieved eggs
and pickled celery

iceberg stack with blue cheese and radishes

tomato scallion shortcakes with
whipped goat cheese

kale salad with cherries and pecans

sugar snap salad with miso dressing

broccoli slaw

cranberry bean salad with
walnuts and feta

roasted baby roots with
sherry-shallot vinaigrette

honey and harissa farro salad

vinegar slaw with cucumbers and dill

*I*f, thus far, you've only known slaw to be limp and mayo-sogged, and you've understandably avoided it, well, consider this the anti-slaw, or everything that the white stuff isn't: bright, crunchy, and lightly pickled instead of slick with dressing. It's also a little bit habit-forming. I made it before a Fourth of July rooftop barbecue on a broiling summer day—the kind of weather mayo jars warn you about—and by the next morning no fewer than two friends had texted me for the recipe. (Of course, because my fat little Eastern European fingers were never designed with texting in mind, I wrote back something like "1 media head green carnage" and they all yelled at me to join the modern age. I digress.)

Nevertheless, there's no reason to limit this salad to the summer's burger and hot dog toppings. We eat it with pork chops and beside pressed sandwiches, and I regularly have it for lunch in January when I'm trying to offset holiday excess. That said, it's equally delicious with *additional* fried excesses, from everything Milanese and schnitzel to fried chicken. The ingredients list is short and its fridge life is long, or as long as it takes for other family members to get hooked on it.

* * *

Toss the cabbage, cucumber, and dill together in a large bowl. Don't be freaked out by how big the salad looks; it settles as it marinates. Whisk the vinegar, salt, and sugar together in a small bowl until the salt and sugar dissolve. Stir in the water. Pour the liquid over the salad, and let it marinate, tossing the cabbage occasionally. After 1 hour, it should be a bit wilted and crunchy; at 2 hours, the flavor is even better.

yield: serves 12

1 medium head green cabbage (about 2 pounds or 900 grams), cored and thinly sliced or shredded

1 large seedless or English cucumber (about 1 pound or 455 grams), sliced in round discs as thinly as possible (you can double this if you cannot get enough of cucumber)

2 tablespoons chopped fresh dill

½ cup (120 ml) white wine vinegar

2 tablespoons kosher salt

4 teaspoons sugar

½ cup (120 ml) cold water

cooking note

I use Diamond brand kosher salt. If you're using another brand, use less as it will be more densely salty.

do ahead

The salad keeps, covered, in the fridge for a week.

zucchini ribbons with almond pesto

Can we promise to never talk about the weather? For example, New York in July is hot. So very hot. Also humid. And unpleasant. And have I mentioned this heat? It's unbearable. But tomorrow the weather will change, and you'll have spent fifteen minutes talking about something that you don't even remember. In my mind, this is infinitely worse than spending an evening discussing the finer points of different vegetable-roasting temperatures. (You are welcome to pity my husband right now. I understand.)

But if I were going to discuss the weather—which I won't, I promise—on those days in July when the zillion inhabitants of this tiny island are squeezed into structures coated with heat-soaking concrete from floor to sky, while vehicles weave through the grid in a way that makes living in New York City challenging, I would suggest an antidote in the form of a cold, refreshing salad. One that required no heated cooking and, even better, helped us with summer's real torment—zucchini population control. Two pounds at a time, this salad hopes to do its part.

* * *

prepare the pesto Grind the almonds, Parmesan, garlic, and red pepper flakes in a food processor until they are finely chopped. Add the lemon juice, salt, and olive oil and pulse the machine a few times, until combined. Pour the dressing in the bottom of a large salad bowl, and let it roll up and around the sides.

prepare the zucchini Using a vegetable peeler (a Y-peeler or mandoline works great if you have one here, but any old peeler will do) and working from the top to bottom of each zucchini, slice the zucchini into ribbons (about 1/16-inch thick). Place the ribbons in dressing-coated bowl.

assemble the salad Toss the ribbons gently—frankly, your hands are best for this as they won't break up the ribbons while tossing them—attempting to coat the zucchini as evenly as possible with the dressing. Serve at room

yield: serves 4

½ cup (142 grams) almonds, toasted and cooled

¼ cup (20 grams or ¾ ounce) grated Parmesan cheese

1 small garlic clove, peeled and crushed

Pinch of red pepper flakes

2 tablespoons (30 ml) lemon juice

¼ teaspoon table salt

⅓ cup (80 ml) olive oil

2 pounds (about 900 grams) medium zucchini, trimmed (about 4 medium, thin, and longer if you can find them)

temperature. This can sit out for a while (the longer it does, the more relaxed the ribbons will be) but I like to eat it right away, when the ribbons still make tall loops and twists in the bowl.

cooking notes

If you can find thinner, longer zucchini, all the better. I've found that the prettiest ribbons happen when the length of your peeler blade exceeds the width of your zucchini, because it keeps the green-skinned edges intact. Of course, nature doesn't always adjust itself to your food-styling needs. If you can only find short and squat zucchini, fear not; the salad will be just as delicious.

Too hot to even consider toasting almonds? Use them raw, and this will still be delicious.

fingerlings vinaigrette with sieved eggs and pickled celery

*T*his salad started as a love letter to one of my favorite cold French dishes, leeks vinaigrette, where leeks are braised until fork-tender and served at room temperature with a sharp Dijon vinaigrette. Sometimes there's a sieved hard-boiled egg on top, and those times are my favorite, because it's incredible the way a mesh strainer can turn a firm but perhaps rubbery hard-boiled egg into a pile of fluff that clings tenderly to other ingredients.

Of course, while my head, as it often is, might have been gallivanting in Paris in the springtime, my fridge had some leftover fingerling potatoes and not a whole lot else in it that day. And so I decided a lunchtime potato salad was in order, an elegant one that could be plated, not scooped. Halved lengthwise and spread in one layer, the cut sides of fingerlings are an excellent platter for anything you wish to heap upon them, in this case, a coarse Dijon and shallot dressing, eggs, herbs, and, well, pickled celery.

I know, I know "Pickled celery?" You see, you cannot marry into a Russian family without quickly developing affection for all things pickled, and the essential way that vinegar soaked ingredients can perk up an ordinary dish. Pickled celery is also a grand thing to keep around; if you've been slipping minced pickles or celery into your egg salads, pickled celery is both at once. If you like celery in your tuna, you'll like this better. And when you want to make an audience surer than they ever were before that you've gone off the deep end by further blaspheming an already blasphemed classic French dish, pickled celery and you should quickly make an acquaintance.

*   *   *

pickle your celery In a small bowl, whisk together the vinegar, water, salt, and sugar. Add the celery, and set the mixture aside for about an hour in the fridge. If you don't have an hour, 30 minutes will still pickle them to deliciousness, but they will only get better with age.

yield: serves 2 to 4

pickled celery

¼ cup (60 ml) white wine vinegar

¼ cup (60 ml) water

1 tablespoon kosher salt

1½ teaspoons sugar

2 stalks celery, thinly sliced on an angle

vinaigrette

2 tablespoons (30 ml) olive oil

2 teaspoons whole-grain mustard

1 teaspoon Dijon mustard

2 teaspoons white wine vinegar

1 small shallot, minced

1 pound (905 grams) fingerling potatoes, boiled until fork-tender and fully cooled

2 large eggs, hard-boiled (see page 85), peeled, cut into 4 quarters

Crumbled bacon, minced fresh herbs, few tufts of frisée or arugula leaves (optional)

fingerlings vinaigrette with sieved eggs and pickled celery (continued)

make the dressing Whisk the vinaigrette ingredients together until smooth. Adjust seasoning to taste. Set aside.

assemble the salad Halve the fingerlings lengthwise, and arrange them, cut sides up, on a platter. Drizzle the vinaigrette generously over the potatoes. Press each chunk of egg through a mesh sieve over the potatoes and vinaigrette, yolk first (this makes it neater), so that all of the fingerlings are coated with tufts of egg. Garnish with pickled-celery slices, and enjoy immediately.

do ahead
Potatoes can be boiled and kept in fridge for up to 3 days, or until needed. Pickled celery will keep in fridge for up to a week.

iceberg stack with blue cheese and radishes

*I*f you've ever wondered why iceberg wedges are still on the menu at most restaurants, wondered who still orders them, look no farther than your humble host.

It's me. I order iceberg wedges, everywhere. At bars, at steakhouses, and at that random restaurant around the corner, the one that makes great burgers and knows that we iceberg junkies might have thinning ranks but we're a loyal bunch. If there's one on the menu, you can guarantee not only that I will order it, but that it will be the highlight of my meal. Between forkfuls, I will lament iceberg's low place on the lettuce totem pole, how silly it is that elite food people revile it, considering it unfit in a world of mesclun mixes and baby field greens that are so delicate, so fresh, that a little grit still clings to them. I like a salad that has both taste and structure.

You can't eat as many iceberg wedges as I have without forming an opinion or two about them, and what some places get right, most get very wrong. The first is bottled dressing. Do you know how easy it is to make blue-cheese dressing? Seriously, just skip ahead to the recipe for a second; did you see that? And it tastes the way blue-cheese dressing was always meant to taste but so rarely actually does. My next gripe is with the wedge itself. Pretty, yes, but not the ideal geometry for dressing incorporation. One day, I had an iceberg salad that consisted of a large horizontal disc, allowing the dressing to seep between all the leaves, and I've made it this way ever since. Do you miss the *Ta-da!* display of a vertical salad? Stack it. My final gripe with most iceberg salads is that their creators seem to think that packaged croutons are an acceptable form of crunch—yuck, I say, and so I dice celery and radishes on top instead.

The result is a teetering, overloaded, craggy, drippy tower of everything I don't ever want to grow too old, smart, or refined to eat. Also, I have found that if you serve this salad where a normal host would offer something leafy, green, and quiet to chew, you'll find, among relieved faces, that I'm not alone in my preference.

yield: serves 4 to 5

dressing

½ cup (120 ml) well-shaken buttermilk

½ cup (105 grams) mayonnaise

1 tablespoon freshly squeezed lemon juice

½ teaspoon Worcestershire sauce

1 small garlic clove, minced

¼ teaspoon table salt

⅛ teaspoon freshly ground black pepper

for the stack

4 ounces (115 grams) pancetta in ¼-inch dice, or bacon in slices

1 stalk celery, cut into ¼-inch dice (about ⅓ cup)

⅓ cup radishes in ¼-inch dice

1-pound head (455 grams) iceberg lettuce, trimmed and cored, sliced into 1-inch-thick rounds (you'll get about 6)

½ cup (2 ounces or 55 grams) firm blue cheese, crumbled

¼ cup finely chopped fresh chives

*   *   *

In a medium bowl, whisk together dressing ingredients until smooth. Adjust seasonings to taste.

Brown the pancetta or bacon in a frying pan until it is crisp. Drain it on paper towels, and let it cool. If you are using slices of bacon, once they have cooled, either chop or crumble them into small bits.

Toss the celery and radishes together in a small dish.

Place your largest slice of iceberg carefully on a platter. Drizzle with a few tablespoons of dressing, then sprinkle with a little of the radish-celery mixture, a little bacon, a little blue cheese, then chives. Place the next largest slice of iceberg on top (or angled onto it, if it is not sturdy enough to hold the weight), and repeat, adding dressing, radishes and celery, bacon, blue cheese, and chives; then repeat with remaining slices, stacking and staggering them decoratively. If any ingredients remain, sprinkle them over the top.

Serve and enjoy, unapologetically.

cooking notes Don't eat bacon? Try this: Cut a shallot into thin slivers, submerge them in ½ inch of hot oil in a small saucepan, fry them until crisp, drain them well, and immediately salt them; now give a little smirk in the direction of all those who believe there's nothing better than bacon. If they only knew!

The dressing will yield 1 cup, about twice what you need for one iceberg stack, but I feel it would be reprehensible for me to divide the recipe, because you'll immediately want to use the dressing again and shouldn't have to make it twice. For a traditional, awesome blue-cheese dressing without this salad recipe, you'd then either stir in ½ cup crumbled blue cheese (for a very chunky version) or blend it in so that just some chunks remain (for a more typical texture).

tomato scallion shortcakes with whipped goat cheese

I like to go easy on tomatoes. I know that they get along famously with herbs, with fistfuls of garlic, with hearty onions and creamed soups. I know you can pair them with cumin, with ginger, with lime, and with horseradish and vodka (and my husband very much wishes you would). I know that tomatoes make an excellent backbone. But when tomatoes are as good as they get in August, it seems rude to do anything but give them a chance in the spotlight, so I find myself making a lot of lightly dressed salads—just olive oil, red wine vinegar, a pinch of sugar to bring out their natural sweetness, salt, and freshly ground black pepper, all delivered with a light hand.

The problem, if there could be one, is the puddle. You know, that fresh-tomato-and-diluted-dressing runoff that puddles in the plate? That cannot be lifted with a fork? I can't bear to rinse it down the sink, and, short of tipping the plate into my mouth—well, that's not something we need to admit to, do we?—I started looking for something to sop it up before it had a chance to escape. Sometimes it was a piece of thick garlic-rubbed toast, but one of the best times it was something as tender as the tomatoes themselves—a biscuit, at a friend's barbecue one summer.

From there, I went home and decided that shortcakes had been vested in the sweet for long enough. Tomatoes are every bit as much of a fruit as strawberries, and they make a fine, fine pairing with a biscuit, accented with mild green onions. Of course, a shortcake without a whipped topping is no fun at all, and so I whipped some goat cheese. The result was one of the most delicious embodiments of fresh tomatoes I've had to date.

*   *   *

make biscuits Preheat your oven to 425 degrees. Line a baking sheet with parchment paper. Whisk the flour, baking powder, and salt together in a large, wide bowl. Using your fingertips or a pastry blender, cut the butter into the dry ingredients until the mixture resembles coarse meal.

yield: 6 to 8 shortcakes

scallion biscuits

2 cups plus 2 tablespoons (265 grams) all-purpose flour, plus more for dusting

2 tablespoons (30 grams) baking powder

¾ teaspoon table salt

5 tablespoons (70 grams) unsalted butter, chilled, cut into ¼-inch pieces

1 scallion, thinly sliced

1 cup (235 ml) whole milk

tomato salad

1 tablespoon olive oil

1½ tablespoons red wine vinegar

⅛ teaspoon salt

Pinch of sugar

Freshly ground black pepper

½ pound (approximately 1⅓ cups or 225 grams) cherry or grape tomatoes (mixed colors, if you can find them)

toppings

3 tablespoons (45 ml) heavy or whipping cream

4 ounces (115 grams) goat cheese, softened

Greens from 2 scallions, thinly sliced

Stir in the scallion. Add the whole milk, and stir until evenly moistened. Pat out to ¾-to-1-inch thickness, and cut into six to eight 3-inch rounds, re-forming scraps as needed. Arrange the biscuits on the parchment-lined sheet, spacing 2 inches apart. Bake until they are golden brown on top, for about 15 minutes. Rotate the pan to ensure even baking.

make tomato salad In the bottom of a bowl, whisk the olive oil, red wine vinegar, salt, sugar, and freshly ground black pepper. Quarter the cherry tomatoes lengthwise, and add them to bowl with the dressing, tossing together gently.

make whipped goat cheese In a separate bowl, use an electric mixer (or whisk by hand, if you like the workout) to whip the cream until peaks form. Add the goat cheese, and beat until the cheese topping is light and fluffy.

assemble shortcakes Split each warm biscuit in half, and generously spoon each half with the tomato salad and its dressing. Dollop with whipped goat cheese, and sprinkle with scallion-green slivers. Eat at once.

kale salad with cherries and pecans

I have spent a good part of the last few years believing that the world would be a better place if we could all stop pretending that kale tastes good. Every barn-tabled, locavore-bent, small scrappy restaurant with Brooklyn beers on the menu and pictures of old guys on the wall—that would be, every restaurant we have a weakness for—seems determined to convince diners that kale is (a) delicious and (b) worth adding to everything. It's been a tough couple of years to order salad. In kale's defense, it is full of many good things—iron, vitamin A, C, beta carotene. It's a hardy plant, and it grows well into the fall. In my defense, it can be tough and bitter and I don't eat things just because they're good for me. I eat things because I like them.

Here is how I made peace with it: I sent it back to 1993. Do you remember 1993? I vaguely remember it as the year when the food universe was trying to get us to trade our iron grip on romaine and iceberg lettuces for mixes of baby field greens sold as mesclun. Except mesclun mixes tasted like greens, and this freaked people out until some brave soul figured out that there was a salad trifecta—dried fruit, goat cheese, and a honey-Dijon dressing—that made anything else in a salad palatable. I applied the same theory to kale, and it worked—we not only ate this salad, we had seconds. Seconds! Of raw kale! Who are we?

*   *   *

Preheat your oven to 350 degrees, and spread the pecans on a tray. Toast them for 5 to 10 minutes, tossing them once or twice to make sure they toast evenly. Remove them from the oven, and set them aside to cool.

Wash your kale and let it dry on spread-out kitchen or paper towels. Then, with a knife, remove the rib from each stalk, leaving long strips of kale leaves. Stack the leaves in small batches, roll them tightly the long way, and cut the roll crosswise into thin ribbons. Add the kale ribbons to a large salad bowl.

yield: serves 4

salad

½ cup (70 grams) pecans

8 ounces (225 grams) Black Kale, also known as Cavolo Nero or Lacinato, Dinosaur, or Tuscan Kale

4 ounces (115 grams or about 4 medium-large) radishes

½ cup (70 grams) dried cherries

2 ounces (55 grams) soft goat cheese, chilled

dressing

3 tablespoons (45 ml) olive oil

1½ tablespoons (23 ml) white wine vinegar

1 tablespoon smooth Dijon mustard

1½ teaspoons honey

Salt and freshly ground black pepper to taste

kale salad with cherries and pecans (continued)

Thinly slice the radishes, and add them to the bowl. Coarsely chop the pecans and cherries, and add them as well. Crumble the goat cheese over the top. Whisk dressing ingredients together in a small dish, and pour the dressing over the salad. Toss the salad until it is evenly coated with dressing. This salad is great to eat right away, but even better after 20 minutes of tenderizing in the dressing.

sugar snap salad with miso dressing

My friend Dan used to make fun of the salad-dressing commercials that would come on while we watched *Buffy* back in the day—you know, back when you had to suffer things like commercials. "Yuck! Vegetables are icky! Gotta drown them!" he'd say sarcastically as the thick ribbons of creamy dressing rained down over the bowls of greens and tomatoes. But he's right, in a way. Fresh vegetables—especially the ones you wait all year to see at the stands, and when you do, they're brighter and snappier and more peppy and sweet than you'd remembered, and you'd already remembered them fondly—are a fine thing. Why slick them into sameness?

So that's the earnest side of this story. That would be, like, the speech I'd give my kid if he woke up one day and only wanted salad oozing with creamy stuff (which, realistically, is going to happen, if only out of rebellion). The other side is what happens when you taste sesame-miso dressing—you know, the stuff they put over your salad at sushi restaurants, usually with ground carrots inside. Sesame-miso is a game changer, a substance so delicious, so nutty and salty and toasty and sweet at once, that you start ordering salads just to get to it, kind of like how you order cupcakes just for the frosting. (You know you do.)

Realistically, this salad could contain anything, and as long as it was doused in sesame-miso manna, it would be hard to hate. But I especially love it in the early parts of the summer, when sugar snaps show up at the markets and are begging to be left crunchy. I back it up with ribbons of almost weightless Napa cabbage, mild green onions, and radishes, and then I don't apologize for dousing it in dressing. Not this dressing, not this salad. I save the apologies for when I've polished off the salad before my husband got to try any.

*   *   *

blanch sugar snaps Bring a large pot of salted water to a boil, and prepare a small ice-water bath. Boil the sugar snaps for about 2 minutes, or until just barely cooked but still crisp. Scoop them out with a large slotted

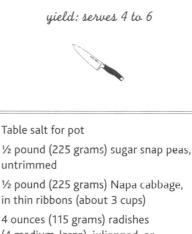

yield: serves 4 to 6

Table salt for pot

½ pound (225 grams) sugar snap peas, untrimmed

½ pound (225 grams) Napa cabbage, in thin ribbons (about 3 cups)

4 ounces (115 grams) radishes (4 medium-large), julienned, or quartered and thinly sliced

3 large scallions (about ½ bundle), white and green parts, thinly sliced on bias

3 tablespoons (⅞ ounce or 24 grams) sesame seeds, well toasted (300-degree oven for 5 to 8 minutes)

sesame-miso dressing

1 tablespoon minced fresh ginger

1 large garlic clove, minced

2 tablespoons (1¼ ounce or 36 grams) mild yellow or white miso, plus up to 1 more tablespoon (⅝ ounce or 18 grams) to taste

2 tablespoons (⅝ ounce or 16 grams) sesame seed paste or tahini

1 tablespoon honey

¼ cup (60 ml) rice vinegar

2 tablespoons (30 ml) toasted sesame oil

2 tablespoons (30 ml) vegetable or olive oil

spoon, and drop them in the ice-water bath. Once they're cool, drain and pat dry. Trim ends and cut sugar snaps on bias into thin slices. Toss in large bowl with cabbage, radishes, scallions, and 1 tablespoon sesame seeds.

make the dressing Whirl all ingredients, using the smaller amount of miso, in a blender until smooth. Taste and adjust ingredients—use the extra tablespoon miso if desired. Don't fret if it is a tad salty, and try to resist the urge to compensate with extra honey. The sugar snaps have a mellow sweetness to them that balances well with a saltier-than-normal dressing.

assemble the salad Toss salad with half of dressing, and taste. Use more if you desire, which I bet you do. If not, be delighted that you will have extra for your next salad. Sprinkle with remaining sesame seeds. Dig in.

cooking note

If you can't get sugar snaps, this is also lovely with snow peas, green beans, and even thinly sliced cucumber. If you're not into radishes, grated carrot is a wonderful replacement.

broccoli slaw

My husband's cousin makes a fantastic broccoli salad. I can never remember exactly what's in it, but I have a vague recollection of uncooked broccoli, creamy dressing, and dried cranberries. I pretty much eat the whole thing whenever she brings it over for a holiday meal. On a table piled with crepes and caviar, potato pastries, mushroom salads, pickles, olives, garlicky roasted red peppers, smoked fish, black bread—and did I mention the caviar?—you can imagine why the broccoli doesn't get the love it deserves. But I never ignore it. In fact, now that I think about it, she probably makes it just for me. I married well.

When I tried to re-create it a couple years ago, I cut the broccoli into matchsticks and thin slices. I made a ranch-ish dressing with buttermilk and apple-cider vinegar. I toasted almonds. I chopped dried cranberries. I soaked onions in the dressing. And then I stood in the kitchen and ate nearly the entire bowl, the entire 2 pounds of broccoli salad. Sure, I was five months pregnant at the time. Apparently, pregnant women need their iron. I made fun of my broccoli habit on my website. And then, more than two years later, I decided to include the salad in this book, and when I went to retest it, the same thing happened. I inhaled it. I couldn't have been less pregnant at the time (though the result of the first pregnancy was sitting on the floor chomping adorably on a raw floret), which led me to the conclusion that this salad might just be good.

*   *   *

Trim the broccoli, and chop it into large chunks; then cut each chunk into thin slices. I usually cut the stems into thin slices, then stack the slices and cut them in the other direction, into thin matchsticks; if you have a mandoline with a julienne blade, this will also do the job. Then I cut the florets vertically into thin slices, slicing from the stem up to the floret top. This helps them stay together, but keeps them lying nicely against each other in the salad.

yield: about 8 cups slaw, serving several people or 2 pregnant ones

2 heads broccoli (¾ to 1 pound, or 340 to 455 grams each)

½ cup (45 grams) thinly sliced almonds, toasted

⅓ cup (40 grams) dried cranberries, coarsely chopped

½ cup (120 ml) buttermilk, well shaken

½ cup (105 grams) mayonnaise

2 tablespoons (30 ml) cider vinegar

1 teaspoon granulated sugar

½ teaspoon table salt

½ small red onion, finely chopped

Lots of freshly ground black pepper

Toss the sliced broccoli with the almonds and cranberries. In a small bowl, whisk the buttermilk, mayo, vinegar, sugar, and table salt until smooth. Stir in the onion. You can let the onion marinate in the dressing for 10 minutes, to mellow it. Pour the dressing over the broccoli mixture, and add a generous amount of black pepper. Stir the salad until the broccoli is evenly coated with the dressing. Serve immediately, or keep covered in the fridge for 2 to 3 days; really, though, it's never lasted that long around here.

cranberry bean salad with walnuts and feta

The first time I saw fresh cranberry beans, I demanded to know where they'd been my whole life, because they are jaw-droppingly gorgeous—the pods are a bright pinkish magenta with white speckles, and the beans inside are the reverse, white with pink-magenta speckles. I want to wear them; surely there's a market for cranberry-bean dresses and scarves, yes? Unfortunately, their beauty was short-lived. I was crushed to discover that when you cook them both the hot pink and the speckles completely disappear, leaving a muddy lavender color behind, which is just not the same.

Fortunately, the aesthetics aren't the only reason they were exciting to me. As a self-described bean obsessive, I find surprisingly few that I can easily buy fresh and de-pod myself in the summertime, and this is one of them. Even if you have a beloved brand of dry beans that never lets you down, there's little comparison in the depth of flavor you can get from fresh ones—and the 20-minute cooking time, versus multiple hours, cannot be beat.

So here is my favorite formula for bean salad. What, everyone doesn't have one? This is one of the things I like to keep around as often as possible; a small bowl of it with some toasted pita wedges makes an excellent lunch, and it keeps for the better part of a week. You can easily substitute a standard can of whatever beans you've got around, or the same volume of cooked ones. The red onions and walnuts are a nod to a Georgian kidney-bean salad that my mother-in-law makes called "lobio," though if you want to go further in that direction you'll want to use some garlic and cilantro. The celery is for extra crunch, and the feta—well, the feta was the kind of thing that happened one day when this salad landed on a plate with a salad with feta in it and I realized they were better together.

*   *   *

yield: serves 4

1¾ cups cranberry beans (from a 15.5-ounce can, or a heaped pound—455 grams—of fresh beans in pods)

¼ teaspoon table salt, plus more for the pot

1 tablespoon red wine vinegar

2 tablespoons (30 ml) olive oil

Freshly ground black pepper

1 stalk celery, finely diced

¼ small red onion, finely diced

¼ cup (28 grams) chopped walnuts, toasted (350 degrees for 10 minutes) and cooled

⅓ cup (roughly 2 ounces or 55 grams) crumbled feta

1 to 2 tablespoons chopped flat-leaf parsley (optional)

Shell the fresh beans, if you're using them. In a small saucepan of boiling salted water, cook the beans over moderate heat, stirring occasionally, until just tender, about 20 to 25 minutes. In a sieve, drain the beans and rinse them under cold running water to stop them from cooking further. Set aside.

Whisk together the vinegar, olive oil, table salt, and black pepper in a medium bowl. Add the beans, celery, red onion, walnuts, feta, and parsley, if using, to the bowl, and toss to combine. Adjust seasoning to taste, adding more vinegar, salt, pepper, or onion as you prefer. Serve immediately, or pack away in the fridge for future lunches.

roasted baby roots with sherry-shallot vinaigrette

There's a point in the New York City winter when the sky seems endlessly gray, the streets are piles of grimy islands of half-melted sleet, and the greenmarkets are a sea of brown and beige vegetables, and the only way I can save myself from the late-winter doldrums is to (a) take a vacation someplace warm and sandy where the colors are always bright against the horizon or (b) embrace beets. Seeing as I sadly lack the ability to fly off to St. Thomas at a moment's notice, beets it is.

But beets and I have never gotten along. Something about the intensity of the color (and the way it bled into everything), the texture, the vaguely fruity flavor when softly roasted threw me, and I knew my reaction was an immature one (I mean, they didn't really taste terrible), I knew it was unreasonable (if they didn't taste terrible, why didn't I eat them?). I couldn't quite hurdle it. I could not rise above it for the sake of rationality. I am hardly a model eater.

But I can handle almost anything in small, crackly doses, and so the day I found teeny-tiny beets, gateway beets, lingering among the big beastly beets at a market was the day when I began, tepidly, to embrace them. Halved and roasted until blistery and sweet, studded with coarse salt, and tossed with faintly crunchy quinoa, this preparation had texture. It had depth of flavor, against an intense, almost syrupy vinaigrette. And it had color, a veritable half–color wheel of pretties to gaze at in months that are notably bereft of reds, oranges, and golds. The beets won. Well, they won this round. Still, it's a start.

*   *   *

Preheat your oven to 400 degrees.

cook quinoa Bring the quinoa and 1 cup salted water to a boil. Cook for 10 to 15 minutes, until quinoa has absorbed water. You're looking for about 1½ cups cooked quinoa. Set aside.

roast roots While grain cooks, prepare vegetables. Peel shallots and separate cloves, if there are two inside. Place in a medium square of alumi-

yield: serves 4

½ cup (65 grams) uncooked plain quinoa, rinsed

Coarse salt

3 small shallots

Olive oil

1½ pounds (680 grams) mixed root vegetables (I used radishes, turnips, and mixed beets), tiny if you can find them, scrubbed, trimmed of all but a bit of stem, and halved lengthwise

Juice of ½ lemon

Freshly ground black pepper

dressing

2 tablespoons (30 ml) sherry vinegar

1 tablespoon balsamic vinegar, plus more for finishing

2 big pinches of coarse salt

3 tablespoons (45 ml) olive oil

Freshly ground black pepper

to serve (optional)

Dabs of soft goat cheese

Dollops of thick yogurt

num foil, coat with a few droplets of olive oil, and wrap in foil, creating a packet. Place on rack in oven.

Coat a baking sheet or roasting pan lightly with olive oil. Arrange the root vegetables in one layer, and drizzle lightly with additional olive oil. Squeeze lemon juice over the vegetables. Sprinkle generously with salt and freshly ground black pepper.

Add roasting pan to oven. Roast vegetables for 20 minutes, then flip them and roast for another 10, or until tender and a bit crackly. (Larger ones might take longer to cook through.)

make vinaigrette Remove vegetables from oven, and set aside. Remove shallot packet with tongs. Carefully remove the shallots from foil packet, and toss into the blender. Blend with sherry and balsamic vinegars and 2 pinches of coarse salt and some pepper. Drizzle in olive oil. Sample vinaigrette, and adjust seasoning to taste.

assemble and serve Spoon three-quarters of quinoa onto a platter. Arrange roasted roots over quinoa, and sprinkle with remaining quinoa. Drizzle the entire dish with shallot-sherry vinaigrette. For a little extra, you can finish it with additional droplets of your balsamic. Serve with goat cheese or yogurt, if using.

cooking note

The proportion of this salad is a bigger ratio of vegetables to a smaller ratio of grain—I wanted the roots to be the focus. If you like more grains with your salad, as grain salads more commonly contain, double the suggested amount.

honey and harissa farro salad

One of the best salads I've ever made isn't this. I'm sorry. I didn't mean to start out by sorely disappointing you, but I do hate to bury the lede. The near-best was a beloved carrot salad recipe sent to me by a reader halfway across the world; it sounded so delicious, I immediately dropped what I was doing to march to the fridge. In that salad, carrots are peeled, grated, and tossed with feta, mint, and a lemon-harissa dressing, and then your family inhales the whole thing quickly. Or at least mine did.

But a grated carrot salad is . . . you know, generally only half of a meal. No matter how much of it we were able to eat in a sitting (and please, don't ask), we were always a bit hungry a couple hours later. In time, I used it to inspire a heartier, meal-like salad, bulked with grains. Carrots share the spotlight with parsnips, at first due to poor planning and later because we liked it better with them included. The dressing gets a touch of honey as well. But I kept the mint, feta, and harissa intact. They lace the hearty farro and root vegetables with something punchy and bright, while leaving us sated enough that we don't come prowling for scraps a few hours later. Unless those scraps are cake, in which case, all bets are off.

*   *   *

cook farro Bring the farro, water or broth, and a few pinches of salt (if using water or unsalted broth) to a boil. Once it's boiling, reduce the heat to a simmer and cook the farro until tender, for about 15 to 20 minutes. If any extra water or broth remains, drain it. Set the farro aside until the vegetables are ready.

prepare vegetables Preheat your oven to 400 degrees. Coat two large baking sheets with one tablespoon olive oil each. Peel carrots and parsnips, and cut them into 2-inch lengths. If they're skinny, quarter them length-wise to make batons. If they're thicker, cut them into matchsticks about ¼ to ½ inch thick. Spread the vegetables on prepared baking sheets, and sprinkle them with salt. Roast for 20 minutes, then toss them about in their pan, before roasting them for a further 10 minutes.

yield: serves 4 to 6

farro
1 cup (215 grams) uncooked farro

4 cups (950 ml) water or broth

vegetables
2 tablespoons (30 ml) olive oil

½ pound (225 grams, about 4 medium) carrots

1 pound (455 grams, about 2 large) parsnips

Salt

dressing
5 tablespoons (75 ml) olive oil

½ teaspoon harissa, or to taste

1 teaspoon honey

2 tablespoons (30 ml) freshly squeezed lemon juice, plus more to taste

Pinch of ground cumin

Salt

¼ cup chopped fresh mint leaves, or half parsley and half mint

¾ cup (4 ounces or 113 grams) crumbled feta

assemble salad   Whisk the dressing ingredients together, seasoning to taste with pinches of salt. Use more harissa if you'd like more heat; I suggest a restrained amount, because the heat of harissas can vary widely. In a large bowl, combine farro and roasted vegetables. Stir in most of the mint and feta, leaving a spoonful of each for garnish. Stir in dressing, to taste. Serve, garnished with the reserved feta and mint.

do ahead   This salad keeps in an airtight container for 3 to 4 days in the fridge.

cooking note   The baton shape of the carrots and parsnips actually conflicts with one of my salad pet peeves—large and small pieces together that don't fit logically on a fork. But somehow it works here. Nevertheless, there's no reason not to cut your vegetables into more traditional chunks or slices, or any way you see fit.

sandwiches, tarts, and pizzas

avocado tartine with cucumber
and sesame seeds

chicken and egg salad toasts with
lemon aioli and fennel

emmentaler on rye with sweet
and sour red onions

ratatouille sub

broccoli rabe panini with mozzarella

wild mushroom tart

butternut squash and caramelized
onion galette

pizza dough

rushed pizza dough

leisurely pizza dough

everyday margarita pizza

shaved asparagus pizza

eggplant and three cheese calzone

avocado tartine with cucumber and sesame seeds

*B*ack when I was a vegetarian, when it was time to go out with friends I always insisted that our restaurant choices not be limited by my dietary rules. This may sound as if I was playing the part of a martyr—"Don't worry about me, I'll just eat the lettuce that comes under the fried chicken!"—the thing was, I held in my head a detailed map of all the great dishes nobody notices on a menu unless they're looking, and I could eat anywhere. At steakhouses, I'd eagerly anticipate the garlic-buttery broiled mushroom caps, flawless asparagus spears, and just about anything they could do with potatoes. At French bistros, I'd eat leafy green salads and just about anything that promised to contain goat cheese, leeks, or haricots verts. And at sushi restaurants, I ordered avocado-cucumber rolls, and believe to this day that anyone who does not is missing out.

That's the inspiration behind my own fussy hack on avocado toast. Classic avocado toast is hardly a recipe—you simply toast bread, smash up some avocado on it with a fork, and sprinkle with salt, pepper, and a few drops of olive oil. But this is the way I make it when I miss that sushi roll. Inspired by the gorgeous, rhythmic sushi-bar preparation, I lay out delicate avocado slices—but, seriously, no reason not to just mash it up if you're (I hope) a tad less obsessive than me. What comes after that is a cucumber caviar of sorts, though I promise, it's hardly fancy, just a finely chopped cucumber dressed with rice vinegar and nutty toasted sesame oil with lots of black and white sesame seeds on top. It's crunchy, creamy, nutty, and one of my favorite midafternoon snacks.

*   *   *

Split your bread into top and bottom halves, and toast the halves. Arrange slices of, or mash, half your avocado on each toasted baguette half. Stir together the cucumber, vinegar, sesame oil, and salt. Dollop half the cucumber salad on top of each bread half. Sprinkle with mixture of seeds, if using. Adjust seasonings to taste—I often find that I want a few more drops of rice vinegar, or another pinch of salt. Eat immediately.

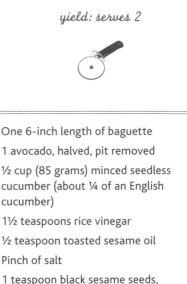

yield: serves 2

One 6-inch length of baguette

1 avocado, halved, pit removed

½ cup (85 grams) minced seedless cucumber (about ¼ of an English cucumber)

1½ teaspoons rice vinegar

½ teaspoon toasted sesame oil

Pinch of salt

1 teaspoon black sesame seeds, toasted (optional)

1 teaspoon white sesame seeds, toasted (optional)

chicken and egg salad toasts
with lemon aioli and fennel

Prior to reading Laurie Colwin's *Home Cooking*, I found chicken salad anything but glamorous. I mean, really, what is there to love about cold leftover chicken dressed with a scoop from a jar of mayonnaise? It's about stretching scraps, filling two slices of bread in time for lunch—it's about function, not gastronomy.

But in Colwin's voice, chicken salad becomes something elegant—for children's lunches, and their tea parties; for ladies in hats wearing strings of pearls; for grown-up dinner parties. She encourages things like cooking your chicken gently at a low temperature for a very long time, and even letting the chicken cool in its broth overnight for extra moisture. She insists that you use fresh herbs, and that you make your own mayo. I realize that same people would scoff at putting this much effort into chicken salad, but only because they haven't tried the results yet.

So it was with Colwin's gentle encouragement that I decided to up my chicken-salad game and create something I'd order in a fancy restaurant but also enjoy eating at home. But I don't want you to blame her for the weird stuff I put in there—for the fennel, the hard boiled eggs, etc. No, that's purely my strange tendencies, not hers, but it works. Dolloped on toasted whole-grain bread and garnished with extra herbs, it makes a lunch that feels civilized, like something from a time of fine dishes, pressed linen napkins, and lunch eaten slowly and deliberately.

*   *   *

cook your eggs Place whole eggs in a small pot of cold water, and bring to a boil. Once the water is boiling, reduce to a simmer and cook for 10 minutes exactly. Drain the eggs, and rinse them in cool water. Let them cool completely in the fridge until needed.

yield: 6 to 8 toasts

2 large eggs

Table salt

1 pound (455 grams) boneless, skinless chicken breasts or thighs; or 2¼ cups leftover chicken, skinned, deboned, and cubed

½ cup finely chopped fennel bulb

1 to 2 tablespoons chopped fennel fronds (greens), plus more for garnish

1 tablespoon chopped fresh chives, plus more for garnish

Freshly ground black pepper

Slices of whole-grain bread, toasted

lemon aioli

1 small garlic clove

½ teaspoon table salt

1 large egg yolk

½ teaspoon Dijon mustard

Few gratings of fresh lemon zest

½ cup (120 ml) olive oil

1 tablespoon white wine vinegar

Lemon juice to taste

if starting with uncooked chicken Bring a medium pot of salted water to a boil. Reduce to a very low simmer. Gently add chicken cutlets, and cook slowly until 155 degrees in the middle—if you trust the source of your chicken—or 160 degrees if you don't wish to get yelled at by food police, about 10 minutes total. If you have the time, place the chicken in a bowl, cover with the cooking broth, and store in the fridge overnight. The next day, scrape off any thickened stock and chop the chicken. It will be more tender after resting like this. If you don't have the time, simply cool the chicken and cut it into small cubes.

make the aioli First, on a cutting board, mince the garlic clove, and mash it with the salt to a paste with side of your knife.

to continue by hand Add the garlic paste, egg yolk, Dijon mustard, and zest to a medium bowl. Begin whisking in the olive oil drop by drop, as slowly as you can bear. (I find having a second person dripping it in makes it easier. I do not recommend using your toddler as this second person.) Continue in this manner until the mixture begins to thicken. Once the mayo has emulsified, you can add the rest of the oil in a slow, steady stream, whisking all the time. Arm getting tired? Try to murmur, "Jiggle-free upper arms . . . sleeveless sundresses . . . ," to yourself. I find it helps morale. Add the vinegar and a squeeze of lemon juice, and whisk until combined. Taste, and adjust lemon and seasonings to your liking.

to continue with a blender Add the garlic paste, egg yolk, Dijon mustard, and zest to your blender. Run the machine, and begin adding the oil drop by drop, as slowly as you can bear. Continue in this manner until the mixture begins to thicken. Once the mayo has emulsified, you can add the rest of the oil in a slow, steady stream, running the machine all the time. Add the vinegar and a squeeze of lemon juice, and blend until combined. Taste, and adjust lemon and seasonings to your liking.

assemble the salad You should have ¾ to 1 cup aioli. Add half of it to a large bowl, and combine with the chopped chicken, fennel, fennel fronds, and chives. Add additional aioli in small increments until you have your desired amount of dressing. Season with salt and freshly ground black pepper to taste. Dollop generously on toasts, and garnish with extra greens. Eat and enjoy.

do ahead

Chicken salad keeps in the fridge for 3 to 4 days.

emmentaler on rye with sweet and sour red onions

Oh, stop giving me that look. I know my tastes in grilled cheese are weird. My husband says so all the time. He says that normal people embrace, not fight, those good old jellied, individually wrapped orange squares of American "singles." Normal people enjoy an occasional slice of white bread, or at least a soft whole wheat, in their cheese sandwiches. Normal people leave it at that: Grilled cheese was never broken, so why try to fix it?

I've found that if you call it a "panini," people let you put whatever you want between your slices of bread. Vegetables and sweet things and nontraditional cheeses are allowed to melt and muddle together in peace. If it helps, you can pretend this is a panini. But I hope you trust that there is great deliciousness within: Those onions are cooked slow and low until sweet and tart and resonating with immense flavor. Swiss cheeses have a vaguely bitter nuttiness that goes dreamily with this, and rye, well, I know you probably don't like the caraway seeds; it seems nobody does. So, if you can't find seedless rye, and you can't find the best substitute, which is a seedless pumpernickel, you can use plain old white or whole-wheat bread. But I think you're missing out.

P.S. This is amazing with a side of vinegar slaw (see page 54).

*   *   *

cook onions Heat the olive oil and 1 tablespoon butter in a large skillet over medium-high heat. Add the onion, and sauté for 5 minutes. Add the brown sugar and salt, lower the heat to medium-low, and cook another 10 minutes, stirring occasionally. Add the vinegar, and scrape any stuck onion bits from the bottom of pan with a spoon. Simmer for 1 to 2 minutes, until the onion mixture thickens, and season to taste with black pepper. Cool to lukewarm, or store in an airtight container in the refrigerator until needed, up to 5 days. You should have just shy of ½ cup of cooked onions.

yield: 2 sandwiches

onions

1 tablespoon olive oil

1 tablespoon unsalted butter

1 large red onion, halved and thinly sliced (about 2 cups)

2 teaspoons brown sugar, light or dark

¼ teaspoon table salt, plus more to taste

1 tablespoon balsamic vinegar

Freshly ground black pepper

sandwiches

Four ½-inch-thick slices rye bread

2 tablespoons (30 grams) butter, salted or unsalted, softened

¾ cup (about 3 ounces or 85 grams) grated Emmentaler or another Swiss cheese *assemble the sandwiches* Generously butter one side of each slice of bread; these will be the outsides of your sandwiches. Arrange one slice, buttered side down, on a plate. Spread thickly with jammy onions (about 2 tablespoons per sandwich; you'll have extra). Sprinkle with half the grated cheese. Arrange a second slice of bread on top of the cheese, buttered side facing up. Repeat with the remaining slices to make a second sandwich.

cook sandwiches Heat a heavy 12-inch skillet over medium-low heat. Once it's hot, arrange your sandwiches in the pan, and cook them until crisp and deep golden brown, about 5 minutes per side. If you are making a larger batch and want to keep them warm and melty, arrange them in a single layer on a baking sheet in a 200-degree oven. When ready to eat, slice the sandwiches in half. Don't expect leftovers.

cooking note
I probably don't have to tell you how fantastic this sandwich is with a thin slice of speck, prosciutto, or even duck prosciutto.

ratatouille sub

With all due respect to avocado and hummus, vegetarian sandwiches can be awfully . . . flimsy. Just because someone is a short-term or lifelong meat ascetic doesn't mean that they are therefore all sprouts and earnestness. I can assure you, my vegetarian friends are none of these things.

With this in mind, I attempted to create a sandwich as rib-sticking, belly-warming, and mammoth as a meatball sub but, you know, minus the meatballs. Except instead of simply replacing them with the typical alternatives—gobs of cheese, perhaps some lentil patties—I instead turned to my favorite hearty vegetarian stew, ratatouille. I don't make ratatouille in the traditional way (that would be with each vegetable cooked in its own pot in a multihour process, no doubt creating something so heroic, you wouldn't dare squeeze it onto a bun) but in the manner of Pixar's *Ratatouille*. Yes, *like the movie*. My version is as bare-bones as it gets: I take all of the dish's traditional vegetables and cut them very thin on a mandoline, fan them out over a thin bed of tomato sauce with seasonings, and bake them until tender. Not only is the resulting dish gorgeous, it comes together quickly.

Nevertheless, the first time I slid layers of it onto a toasted bun, I had my doubts. Surely, it would need some "help" to make it feel hearty—perhaps some goat cheese, maybe even (gasp) a thin layer of prosciutto? Layers of baked vegetables cannot *alone* have the magnitude of orbs of fried meat, smothered with cheese and onions, right? I'm delighted to report that I was absolutely, deliciously wrong.

*　　*　　*

prepare vegetables Preheat your oven to 350 degrees, and prepare the vegetables: Trim the ends from the eggplant, zucchini, and squash, and, with a mandoline, adjustable-blade slicer, or very sharp knife, slice them into pieces approximately 1/16 inch thick. As carefully as you can, trim the ends off the red pepper and remove the core, leaving the flesh intact, like a tube. Thinly slice crosswise. Thinly slice the onion as well.

yield: serves 6 to 8, enough to fill two 8-inch lengths of sub, which can each be divided into hearty 2-inch individual sandwiches

1 long, thin eggplant, such as a Japanese variety

1 long, thin zucchini

1 long, thin yellow squash

1 to 2 red bell peppers, long and narrow if you can find them

½ small yellow onion

1 cup (250 grams) tomato purée (such as Pomi) or canned tomato sauce

1 garlic clove, minced

2 tablespoons (30 ml) olive oil

Salt

Red pepper flakes or piment d'Espelette

1 tablespoon chopped fresh herbs, such as thyme

Two 8-inch sub rolls, or the equivalent length of baguettes

sandwiches, tarts, and pizzas *91*

Spread the tomato purée into a 2-quart baking dish. Stir in the onion slices, minced garlic, 1 tablespoon of the olive oil, a few pinches of salt, and a pinch of pepper flakes. Arrange the slices of eggplant, zucchini, yellow summer squash, and red pepper so that they overlap, with just a smidgen of each flat surface visible. The pepper will give you the most trouble, because it's probably bigger in diameter than the other vegetables, but whether it fans prettily or not, it will bake up nicely. You might not need all of your vegetables. Drizzle remaining tablespoon of olive oil over the vegetables, and sprinkle with thyme. Cover dish with foil, and bake for 45 minutes, until vegetables are almost completely fork-tender.

assemble subs Meanwhile, split your sub rolls. Once the 45 minutes are up, increase heat to 425, remove foil from the baking dish, and bake, uncovered, 15 minutes more. On the other rack, place your sub rolls on a tray to toast for 5 to 10 minutes.

A long, thin offset spatula, like an icing knife, is best for serving here. Carefully slide it under one section of the fanned vegetables, and slide it onto the bottom half of a toasted roll. Keep adding sections until you have covered the bread, and then repeat this so that you have a second layer of fanned vegetables. Scoop up any oniony sauce that was left beneath the vegetables, and lay it over the sub. Close each sub with the top half of the roll, cut into manageable lengths to eat, and serve.

cooking notes

This goes great with soft goat cheese, which can be spread on either side of your toasted roll before adding the ratatouille. You could also forgo the baguette entirely, and serve this over polenta, or couscous or another grain.

I've never noticed any lingering bitterness from the eggplant in this dish, but if you find yourself sensitive to eggplant's nuances, you can preprep the eggplant by tossing the slices with 1 teaspoon table salt and setting them in a colander for 20 minutes to drain while you prepare the other vegetables. Since not all of the salt will run off, you might find you need less elsewhere in the dish.

broccoli rabe panini with mozzarella

My husband is a broccoli rabe fanatic. The more intense, garlicky, and punched with red pepper flakes it is, the happier he is. If he spies it on a menu, he asks if we're sharing sides, and when I tell him there's no need to, he practically does cartwheels, because that means he can guiltlessly have at his favorite. I've been slower to warm to it. I find it . . . harsh. I like moderate bitterness and gentle amounts of garlic; I can be a wimp about red pepper flakes. The usual preparation is awfully amplified for me.

But Alice Waters changed things for me. In a recipe, she cooks broccoli rabe with tender, caramelized bits of onion, and this gives it the balance I always wish it had outside my kitchen. From there, I found that the flavor from a pat of butter stays with the greens long after they are cooked. And fresh, almost sweetly smooth mozzarella allows the rabe's intensity to shine. Piled together in a sandwich, they make a most nontraditional panini—nontraditional in that it's thick and hearty, whereas many panini are thin and restrained. In big wedges, served with a cup of soup, this panini makes a gloomy fall afternoon spent watching October baseball into something utterly perfect.

*　*　*

yield: 2 hearty sandwiches or 4 lighter sandwich halves (see cooking notes)

1 pound (455 grams) broccoli rabe

1 tablespoon butter

1 tablespoon olive oil, plus more for brushing bread

½ medium yellow onion, diced small

Salt and freshly ground black pepper

1 medium garlic clove, minced

Pinch of red pepper flakes

Four ¼-to-½-inch slices of a country bread; or two 4-inch lengths from a flattish ciabatta loaf, halved widthwise

¼ pound (115 grams) mozzarella, thinly sliced

prepare rabe Remove and discard the broccoli rabe's heavy stems. Cut the leaves into ½-inch ribbons. Leave any small florets whole, but halve any larger ones.

Heat the butter and 1 tablespoon olive oil in a large sauté pan over medium heat. Add the onion and a pinch of salt and pepper, and cook until onion is a bit brown at the edges, about 5 to 7 minutes. Increase the heat to medium-high and add the prepared rabe, the garlic, and pepper flakes, and sauté until the greens are tender, about 4 minutes. Season with salt to taste. You should have about 1½ cups of this mixture.

assemble sandwiches Heat a well-seasoned ridged grill pan over moderate heat, or a panini press according to manufacturer's instructions. Brush one side of each slice of bread, or the outsides of your ciabatta sections, with olive oil. Arrange one piece of bread, oiled side down, on grill pan or panini press. Spread with half of rabe mixture and half of mozzarella slices. Arrange second slice of bread, oiled side up, on top. Lower panini-press lid—or an additional frying pan—onto the top of the sandwich, and cook for 4 to 8 minutes, until nicely toasted underneath. Carefully flip sandwiches, and grill on the other side for 3 to 5 minutes.

Cut the sandwiches in half, and eat while still hot.

cooking notes

You don't need a panini press, a special panini grill pan, or a trip to Italy to make panini at home (not that I would mind if the third was a requirement!). You simply need a good skillet (preferably cast-iron, but others will work) and another, smaller heavy cast-iron skillet. The smaller one becomes your "press." Doesn't feel heavy enough? Stack another skillet—carefully! carefully, please!—on top. Sure, it's a little precarious, but it has the same effect as something you might get a lot less use from. Trust me . . .

This recipe makes two very hearty sandwiches—which could be a meal in and of themselves—or four hearty sandwich halves, which would make a good meal with soup and a small salad. If you'd like to make thinner panini, spread the same filling volume over six sandwiches, instead of four, with the thinner-bread-slice option, and then increase the mozzarella a bit, to ensure that you don't miss out on any cheese in a bite.

wild mushroom tart

When I was four years old, my mother was chopping vegetables for a stir-fry one night and introduced me to mushrooms by handing me an uncooked one. I nibbled it, determined it acceptable and myself an Eater of Mushrooms; I would like to tell you that my relationship with mushrooms has been splendid from that day forward, but the next day, in the backyard, it went south.

I was playing with my sister and informed her, all-importantly, that I was a Mushroom Eater now, and proved it by plucking one from the ground and taking a bite. I was quick to learn—as my mother whisked me to the emergency room—that backyard mushrooms and grocery-store mushrooms are not the same. It turned out that, within my small four-year-old, curly-topped packing, there was a stomach—and psyche—of steel, and both were immune to the urgency of the situation. I was later sent home, stomach contents and cheer intact, with the diagnosis that I was probably going to live.

I don't remember mushrooms much after that. It's entirely possible that my parents decided that messing further with their younger daughter's tenuous grip on common sense wasn't worth it and didn't buy them for a while. I next remember mushrooms from the 1990s, when wild mushrooms were all the rage on pizza and pasta, and I loved them as I had once before. This was also around the time I began to fall for savory dinner tarts, quiche compatriots that were a little less about the custard, a lot more about the vegetables. A wedge of one with a big green salad was then and is to this day one of my favorite meals. These days, it's also a bit of a savior, something that I can make on a Sunday and know we can enjoy it for light dinners until Tuesday. This version, packed with as many mushrooms as I could squeeze into a 9-inch shell, takes a haphazard tour of Italy with a cornmeal-enhanced crust and three cheeses. It got a little lost somewhere between Lombardy's mascarpone, Reggio Emilia's Parmesan, and Southern Italy's provolone, and it's not sorry—nor would I be, had I the chance to join it for its whirlwind tour.

yield: one 9-inch round tart, serving 6 to 8 as an entrée with a hearty salad

crust

1 cup plus 2 tablespoons (140 grams) all-purpose flour

¼ cup (30 grams) yellow cornmeal

¼ teaspoon table salt

6 tablespoons (85 grams or ¾ stick) unsalted butter, chilled, diced, plus additional to grease foil

1 large egg

filling

1 tablespoon olive oil

1 tablespoon unsalted butter

2 medium shallots, thinly sliced

1 garlic clove, minced

½ pound (225 grams) cremini or brown mushrooms, thinly sliced

1 teaspoon chopped fresh thyme leaves

1 pound (455 grams) assorted wild mushrooms, such as shiitake, oyster, or chanterelles (if unavailable, use more creminis), sliced or torn into small segments

1 teaspoon table salt

Freshly ground black pepper

* * *

to make crust by hand In a large bowl, combine the flour, cornmeal, and salt. Work the butter into the dry ingredients with a pastry blender, fork, or your fingertips until only tiny bits of it remain visible. Add the egg, and mix with a fork until a dough forms. If this does not happen easily, toss the dough onto the counter and knead it briefly together. This dough can be rather tough, but with a little elbow grease it does come together nicely.

to make crust in food processor Combine the flour, cornmeal, and salt in the work bowl of your food processor. Add the butter, and pulse machine on and off until the butter is in very tiny bits. Add the egg, and run the machine until the dough starts to clump together.

form crust On a lightly floured surface, roll the dough out to a 12-inch circle. I find that rolling this dough between two pieces of plastic wrap makes it a cinch—just keep pulling out wrinkles in the plastic to keep it smooth. Once the dough has been rolled to the correct size, carefully peel back the top sheet of plastic, and invert the dough and bottom piece of plastic over a 9-inch fluted, removable-bottom tart pan. You can use the plastic and your fingers underneath to gently lift and lay the dough down centered in the pan. Once you've got the dough where you want it, carefully peel back the remaining piece of plastic, and press the dough against the bottom and sides. Run your rolling pin firmly over the top edge of your pastry pan to remove the excess dough. Place the tart pan on a baking sheet, and transfer to the freezer for 20 to 30 minutes.

parbake crust If you will be parbaking your crust, preheat your oven to 375 degrees. Once the crust is firm and cold to the touch, lightly butter one side of a 12-inch square of aluminum foil, and press the foil, butter side down, firmly against the base and sides of the crust. Bake with foil (no pie weights needed) for 10 minutes. Carefully remove the foil, and bake for another 5 to 8 minutes, until the crust is firm and lightly golden at the edges. Set tart shell on a cooling rack until needed. Reduce oven temperature to 350 degrees.

make filling If you did not parbake your crust, go ahead and preheat your oven to 350 degrees now. Heat a large sauté pan over medium heat, and add the oil and butter together. Add the shallots, and sauté, stirring

¼ cup (60 grams) mascarpone cheese, at room temperature

¼ cup (60 ml) milk

2 large eggs

½ cup (55 grams) grated provolone or Italian fontina cheese

¼ cup (25 grams) finely grated Parmesan or Romano cheese

cooking note

If you've got the time, you can parbake your crust to ensure it remains crisp. However, if you're in a rush, you can skip this step and just fill the tart shell frozen. Because the dough has no water in it, I find that it keeps fairly firm and unsoggy, even with only a single baking.

dough forms, kneading it once or twice on the counter if needed to bring it together. Pat the dough into a ball, wrap it in plastic, and chill it in the refrigerator for 1 hour or up to 2 days.

prepare squash Preheat your oven to 400 degrees. Peel the squash, then halve and scoop out seeds. Cut into ½-to-¾-inch chunks. Pour 2 tablespoons of the olive oil into one large or two smaller baking sheets, spreading it to an even slick. Lay the squash chunks on the baking sheet in one layer, sprinkle with ½ teaspoon of the salt and freshly ground black pepper, and roast for 30 minutes, or until squash is tender, turning the pieces occasionally so that they brown evenly. Set aside to cool slightly. Leave the oven on.

caramelize onions While the squash is roasting, melt the butter and the remaining tablespoon olive oil in a heavy skillet, and cook the onions over medium-low heat with the sugar and the remaining teaspoon of salt, stirring occasionally, until soft and tender, about 25 minutes. Stir in the cayenne pepper, if you are using it.

Mix the squash, caramelized onions, cheese, and herbs together in a bowl.

assemble the galette On a floured work surface, roll the dough out into a 16-to-17-inch round. Transfer to a parchment-lined baking sheet. Spread the squash-and-cheese mixture over the dough, leaving a 2-to-2½-inch border. Fold the border over the squash and cheese, pleating the edge to make it fit. The center will be open. Brush the outside of crust with the egg-yolk wash, if using.

bake Bake until golden brown, 30 to 40 minutes. Remove the galette from the oven, let stand for 5 minutes, then slide it onto a serving plate. Cut into wedges and serve hot, warm, or at room temperature.

cooking note This recipe can be divided to make two 9-inch galettes.

1 teaspoon chopped fresh thyme, or 2 teaspoons chopped fresh sage

1 egg yolk beaten with 1 teaspoon water, for glaze (optional, but makes for a croissant-looking finish)

pizza dough

When I first moved to New York City, all I wanted was the kind of pizza that I dreamed you might have in Italy: thin, rustic, but subtly elegant in its own way, either served when you were seated with wine and a salad, or cut from a huge pie with scissors, wrapped in brown paper, and eaten as you navigated ancient cobblestoned streets. But New York was a slice town; the slices weighed ½ pound and consisted mostly of stretchy, tasteless cheese. In New York, you were looked at strangely if you didn't take yours to go.

Since then, things have changed for the better. You can barely swing an heirloom tomato without hitting a gourmet pizza restaurant, or a chef's recipe promising authentic pizza at home. Unfortunately, it's within these recipes that it all starts to unravel for me—me, the person who hoped for this pizza revolution!—because these techniques, they stress me out. There are broiler settings and cast-iron pans; fresh tomatoes despite their limited season; fresher mozzarella; and intricate blends of flours. There are 1 to 2 days' fermentations, and insistences on fresh yeast. Peels! Stones! Doppio zero! It's enough to intimidate a pizza-craving home cook right out of the kitchen.

I believe you need none of these things to make good pizza. I am not saying that you won't make good, possibly even excellent, home pizza with them, only that my method doesn't require any special purchases or studies. It incorporates a few of the things I've figured out over the years.

*　　*　　*

* You don't need a bread machine, a dough hook, or a food processor to get pizza dough right. People have been making bread a lot longer than any of these things have been around. Sure, they can knock a few minutes off your kneading, or keep your hands free of the burden of mixing things, but I find it freeing to make everything in one single bowl with a spoon. In a tiny kitchen, saving on complications is key.

* You don't need a pizza stone, paddle, or peel. Got them? Use and enjoy them! Don't have them? Please don't consider this a barrier to homemade pizza. If you have a pizza stone preheating in the oven, you can dust the back of any old baking sheet with cornmeal, prepare the pizza on that surface, and use it to slide the pizza onto the stone. If you don't have a stone, and don't want to mess with preheating a baking sheet, just double up on your baking sheets for a thicker, better-conducting pizza-baking surface. I'm between pizza stones and tiles right now (I have a pesky habit of breaking them), so I bake my pizzas on cold trays and find the crusts to be without fault.

* You don't need a wood-burning pizza oven, sent over brick by brick from Italy, to make gloriously good homemade pizza, but high heat is your friend. Professional pizza ovens often exceed 900 degrees; at home, we're not even close, so don't be scared of cranking your oven's dial all the way up and giving it a good amount of time to preheat before inserting your pizza. You can also finish your pizza under the broiler, especially if you love a blistered-cheese top and your oven doesn't want to cooperate with this request. Is it warm where you are? Do you have a grill on a patio? ~~Can I come over?~~ Crank it up and

cook your pizza right on the grill. Oil it lightly first, though, so it can come back inside with you when it's done. To get even more grilled flavor: Throw the pizza dough down with nothing on it. Once it cooks enough to make a firm base, flip the pizza out onto a plate and *now* cover it with its toppings. Slide it, uncooked size down, onto the pan or pizza stone and finish it up.

* Finally, good pizza adapts to your schedule, not the other way around. Over the years, I've fallen back on two approaches to pizza dough. One is ready—from mixing to rise to rolling out—in 45 minutes flat, if you don't count the time it takes to bake the pizza afterward. It has a spectacular amount of yeast in it for the volume of flour, and will no doubt offend a serious bread-baker, but we find the dough perfect: both stretchy and crisp. And quick. You can make this when you come home from work, prep the toppings while it rises, and have pizza on the table remarkably quickly. The other approach is for when you can or want to plan ahead. You can make it the night before for dinner the following night, or before you leave for work the morning you are dreaming of pizza for dinner, because it takes its time rising in the fridge. With the slower rise comes a more developed flavor, but it takes a little extra time from you on either end.

* Whichever dough approach you choose, the path leads to pizza, so it must be the right one to be on.

rushed pizza dough

* * *

*yield: one 12-ounce dough,
making 1 thin 12-inch round or
9-by-13-inch loosely rectangular pizza*

½ cup warm water (about 110 to 116 degrees)

1¼ teaspoons active dry yeast

1½ cups (190 grams) all-purpose or bread flour,
plus more for counter

1 teaspoon table salt

Olive oil, for coating bowl

Turn your oven on to warm (about 200 to 225 degrees) for 5 minutes; then turn it off.

by hand Pour ½ cup warm water into a large mixing bowl, sprinkle the yeast over the water, and let it stand for 5 minutes. Add the flour, then salt, and mix with a wooden spoon until a rough, craggy mass forms. Turn dough and any loose bits out onto lightly floured counter, and knead for 5 minutes, or until a smooth, elastic dough forms.

in a mixer Pour ½ cup warm water into the bowl of your electric mixer, sprinkle the yeast over the water, and

let it stand for 5 minutes. Add the flour, then salt, and mix with your dough hook at a moderate speed until the mixture starts to form a craggy mass. Reduce the speed to low and mix for 5 minutes, letting the hook knead the mass into a smooth, elastic dough. Remove dough and wipe out bowl.

both methods Coat inside of mixing bowl with olive oil, place dough back in bowl, and cover with plastic wrap. Place in previously warmed oven, and let it sit for 30 minutes, or until doubled. Remove dough from oven (now is a good time to preheat it according to your recipe's instruction).

Turn the dough out onto a floured counter (if you want to roll it out), pizza peel, or prepared baking sheet, and let your recipe take it from here.

leisurely pizza dough

* * *

yield: one 12-ounce dough,
making 1 thin 12-inch round or
9-by-13-inch loosely rectangular pizza

½ cup warm water (about 110 to 116 degrees)

¼ plus ⅛ teaspoon active dry yeast

1½ cups (190 grams) all-purpose or bread flour,
plus more for counter

1 teaspoon table salt

Olive oil, for coating bowl

by hand Pour ½ cup warm water into a large mixing bowl, sprinkle the yeast over the water, and let it stand for 5 minutes. Add the flour, then salt, and mix with a wooden spoon until a rough, craggy mass forms. Turn dough and any loose bits out onto lightly floured counter, and knead for 5 minutes, or until a smooth, elastic dough forms.

in a mixer Pour warm water into the bowl of your electric mixer, sprinkle the yeast over the water, and let it stand for 5 minutes. Add the flour, then salt, and mix with your dough hook at a moderate speed until the mixture starts to form a craggy mass. Reduce the speed to low and mix for 5 minutes, letting the hook knead the mass into a smooth, elastic dough. Remove dough and wipe out bowl.

both methods Coat inside of mixing bowl with olive oil, place dough back in bowl, and cover with plastic wrap. Place in refrigerator for 8 hours or overnight. When you're ready to use it, remove it from the fridge, let it come back to room temperature, and finish doubling in a warm spot.

Once the dough has finished doubling, turn it out onto a floured counter (if you want to roll it out), pizza peel, or prepared baking sheet, and let your recipe take it from here.

cooking note

I routinely use whole-wheat flour for a third or a half of the flour, to make a heartier pizza. You can go further, but I wouldn't advise you to exceed two-thirds (125 grams) in these recipes, or the pizza will get too coarse and crisp.

everyday margarita pizza

Margarita pizza is, as far as I'm concerned, one of the greatest kitchen feats you can pull off, in part because the gap between the Margarita you can make at home and most pizza-shop Margarita pizza is tremendous, and you are on the winning side because you get to make it exactly how you think it should be. It is also the easiest to make; it turns your kitchen from a place unable to produce dinner without a list of special ingredients to a place where a can of tomato purée, a round of cheese, and some flour and yeast stashed in your freezer (presuming you don't use them often, they belong there) will provide stellar homemade pizza with little effort.

With this bare minimum of time and ingredients, I can promise you pizza that you can start when you get home from work and eat less than 90 minutes later. Sometimes, when I'm really showing off, I'll make it in 60, but I still estimate 90 minutes so that, if I have time to kill, I can spend it drinking a glass of wine. (I usually make it in 60.)

I keep this recipe magnetized to my fridge at all times, to remind me that, for the constant question "What the heck can I cook for dinner when I haven't shopped for anything and I feel like being lazy . . . ?" there is always an answer.

*   *   *

Preheat your oven to its highest temperature. Sprinkle a rimmed baking sheet (mine is 9-by-13-inch) with cornmeal, and set aside. In a small bowl, stir together tomatoes, a couple pinches of salt, a pinch of red pepper flakes, and the minced garlic. Taste, and adjust seasonings; a few drops of vinegar or a pinch of sugar can sometimes help bring out the best in processed tomatoes. Stretch your dough out haphazardly to fill your prepared baking sheet—do not worry about making it perfectly rectangular or evenly flat. Pinch together any holes that form. Spread dough with tomatoes, leaving a small margin at edges, then mozzarella. Bake pizza for 7 to 11 minutes until bubbly and a bit brown on top. Sprinkle with basil and Parmesan or Romano, and slice into squares right in the pan.

yield: one 9-by-13-inch loosely rectangular pizza, which, along with a big salad, will serve 2 adults and 1 toddler

Cornmeal, for sprinkling

⅓ cup (85 grams) puréed and strained tomatoes, or ½ cup (130 grams) whole tomatoes in juices, blended until mostly smooth

Salt

Red pepper flakes

1 small garlic clove, minced

Few drops red wine vinegar (optional)

Pinch of sugar (optional)

One ¾-pound pizza dough, ready to go (see preceding recipes)

4 to 5 ounces (115 to 140 grams) mozzarella, grated (about 1 to 1¼ cups), torn, or very thinly sliced

Few fresh basil leaves, torn into bits

Handful finely grated Parmesan or Romano to finish

cooking notes Here are the tenets of shockingly good homemade Margarita pizza, as far as I'm concerned. Just as all the good pizza shops do, you should use an uncooked sauce—just canned puréed, strained tomatoes that you fix up with some garlic, salt, and pepper flakes. My favorite strained tomatoes for pizza are from the brand Pomi, and they're sold in cartons. The sauce cooks in the oven, but not so much that it loses its freshness or natural sweetness. You tear up your mozzarella, and I'm not even going to insist that you use the fanciest stuff, because I find the really soft buffalo mozzarella makes a pizza too watery (though if, poor you, you have only that around, letting it sit out on paper towels helps a lot). The basil stays fresh, just torn on top after it bakes, getting a brief wilt from the residual heat.

And the pizza isn't round. I mean, it can be. But lately I've been stretching it out on a rimmed baking sheet. We cut it in messy squares—sometimes we even use kitchen shears, pizza *al taglio*–style, and pretend we're in Italy.

Want to add toppings? We often thinly slice whatever vegetable we have around—spinach, kale, Brussels sprouts, peppers, broccoli, or even drained canned artichokes—on top. I like to gently sauté mushrooms before using them so they don't dry out in the oven. I go easy on toppings, too, so they don't weigh down the pizza, usually just ½ cup of toppings per recipe. Thin slices of prosciutto or salami are another favorite, since they crisp in the oven.

shaved asparagus pizza

Asparagus has never been hard to cook. You could steam it or blanch it or roast it or grill it, or, if you're tired enough of cooking that day, will it to cook itself with the power of your own mind. Oh, you never do that? Huh. Nevertheless, I don't often tackle asparagus on my website, because I usually feel it's all been done before, and what hasn't been done—well, maybe it shouldn't be (asparagus sorbet, anyone?). But two years ago, I was at a restaurant that served it shaved raw into ribbons, dressed only with lemon, olive oil, and Parmesan, and this changed asparagus for me. Never had it tasted so green and vibrant; never had it looked so little like logs on a plate, but rather an elegant heap of twisted ribbons.

It wasn't long before asparagus landed on a pizza. It's true, if I love something I will eventually make a pizza out of it, which might be why my toddler sometimes looks nervous around me. Throwing things onto a pizza dough with cheese doesn't always make something transcendent (somewhere in my husband's future tell-all, there's a story about chewy white-bean pizza), but this one exceeded expectations: tangled and grassy, bubbly and lightly charred, accented with mild bites of scallion, the raw asparagus wilted from the heat of the baked pizza. It became something to look forward to when the first stalks of asparagus appear after a winter too long, too cold, and too filled with formats of squash and greens, and it never kept you waiting too long, either. Once you've made (or procured) your pizza dough, you can probably get it on your table in 20 minutes. See? Now you're listening.

*   *   *

yield: 1 thin-crust 12-inch pizza

½ pound (225 grams) asparagus

2 teaspoons olive oil

½ teaspoon coarse salt

Several grinds of black pepper

One ¾-pound pizza dough, ready to go (see pages 104 and 105)

¼ cup (¾ ounce or 20 grams) grated Parmesan

½ pound (225 grams) mozzarella, shredded or cut into small cubes

1 scallion, thinly sliced

Preheat your oven to its highest temperature—about 500 degrees in most cases. If you use a pizza stone, place it in the oven.

prepare asparagus No need to snap off the ends; they can be your "handles" as you peel the asparagus. Holding a single asparagus spear by its tough end, lay it flat on a cutting board. Use a vegetable peeler; a Y-shaped peeler works best here, but I've successfully made this with a standard old and dull peeler, so don't fret if you don't have a newer one; a mandoline would also work, in theory, but I found it more difficult to use for this. With your peeler of choice, create long shavings of asparagus by drawing the peeler from the base to the top of the asparagus stalk. Repeat with remaining stalks, and don't fret if some pieces are unevenly thick (such as the end of the stalk, which might be too thin to peel); the mixed textures give the pizza character. Discard the tough ends. Toss the peelings with olive oil, salt, and pepper in a bowl, and be sure to try one—I bet you can hardly believe how good raw asparagus can taste.

assemble and bake pizza Roll or stretch out your pizza dough to a 12-inch round. Transfer either to a floured or cornmeal-dusted pizza peel (if using a pizza stone in the oven) or to a floured or cornmeal-dusted baking sheet. Sprinkle the pizza dough with Parmesan, then mozzarella. Pile the asparagus on top. Bake the pizza for 10 to 15 minutes, or until the edges are browned, the cheese is bubbly, and the asparagus might be lightly charred. Remove from the oven, immediately sprinkle with scallions, then slice and eat.

eggplant and three cheese calzone

When I was growing up in central New Jersey, every strip mall had a pizzeria—a pizzeria that served soft drinks in translucent red plastic cups, where toppings besides pepperoni, mushrooms, or green pepper were met with confusion—and every pizzeria made calzones. But it wasn't until years later that I learned that calzones actually (a) originated in Naples, (b) are supposed to be individual-serving-sized, and (c) are not usually filled with tomato sauce. And now I know why I wasn't the calzone's biggest fan; they were always huge, too big even to be shared by two people, and often gushing with hot tomato sauce and too many fillings, and clumsy, like a large pizza that had been folded in half. I couldn't find their charm.

I couldn't find their charm at the local pizza place, that is. But I did find it in my kitchen, making one the way I always wanted it. I never considered eggplant as a pizza topping (or, in this case, filling) until I had a slice of broiled-eggplant pizza on Arthur Avenue in the Bronx one afternoon. The eggplant was fantastic, all crisp and caramelized and slightly charred, but also bittersweet and heavenly. Dollops of ricotta hovered all around, and there was no skimping on the mozzarella, something I often don't like in excess but found perfect against the eggplant.

This is exactly what I was dreaming about when I tucked the same into my take on a calzone. It has three cheeses in it, but they don't overwhelm the eggplant or the crust. The sauce is on the side. And the portion size . . . well, it's still big, with the goal of feeding all of us for dinner.

*   *   *

prepare eggplant Preheat your oven to 425 degrees. Coat a baking sheet with olive oil. Arrange the eggplant slices in one layer. Season them with salt and freshly ground black pepper. Roast for 20 minutes, flip, then roast for another 10 minutes. Let the eggplant cool slightly. Leave oven on.

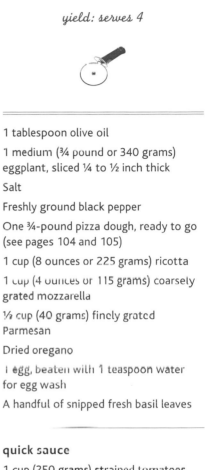

yield: serves 4

1 tablespoon olive oil

1 medium (¾ pound or 340 grams) eggplant, sliced ¼ to ½ inch thick

Salt

Freshly ground black pepper

One ¾-pound pizza dough, ready to go (see pages 104 and 105)

1 cup (8 ounces or 225 grams) ricotta

1 cup (4 ounces or 115 grams) coarsely grated mozzarella

½ cup (40 grams) finely grated Parmesan

Dried oregano

1 egg, beaten with 1 teaspoon water for egg wash

A handful of snipped fresh basil leaves

quick sauce

1 cup (250 grams) strained tomatoes

¼ teaspoon table salt

1 garlic clove, minced

Red pepper flakes

Pinch of sugar (optional)

Few drops of red wine vinegar (optional)

eggplant and three cheese calzone (continued)

assemble calzone Roll the dough into a 12-inch round. Mix together ricotta, mozzarella, and Parmesan, then season the cheese with ½ teaspoon table salt, a pinch of dried oregano (or more to taste), and freshly ground black pepper. Stir the eggplant into the cheese mixture, and then heap it down the center of the dough. Pull the sides of the dough over the center, pressing and crimping a seam down the middle. Brush the outside of calzone with egg wash.

bake Bake the calzone for 15 to 20 minutes, until puffed and golden all over.

make sauce While the calzone bakes, heat the tomatoes, salt, garlic, and a pinch of red pepper flakes in a small saucepan until simmering. Gently simmer for 5 minutes, then taste for seasoning. For extra sweetness or punch, add a pinch of sugar or a few drops of red wine vinegar to taste and simmer for one minute more. Pour into a small dish.

to serve When calzone is finished baking, slide it onto a serving dish and slice into large sections. Garnish with snipped basil and serve with sauce on the side.

the main dish: vegetarian

gnocchi in tomato broth

sweet peas and shells alfredo

linguine with cauliflower pesto

heart-stuffed shells in lemon ricotta béchamel

leek fritters with garlic and lemon

jacob's blintzes, or sweet potato blintzes
with farmer's cheese

corn risotto–stuffed poblanos

slow-cooker black bean ragout

roasted tomatoes and cipollini onions
with white beans

spaghetti squash and black bean tacos
with queso fresco

roasted eggplant with yogurt–tahini sauce
and cumin-crisped chickpeas

wild rice gratin with kale, caramelized onions,
and baby swiss

mushroom bourguignon

gnocchi in tomato broth

*A*ll I ever used to hear about making gnocchi was that it was difficult and that if you hadn't been making it your whole life you'd have trouble pulling it off. For example, the dough is sticky, but you shouldn't overcompensate with flour. Worse, I understood that it required special things, either great skill with a fork to get those telltale ridges, or a gnocchi-rolling board, which, yes, actually exists: It also required a potato ricer. I am staunchly opposed to single-use kitchen objects.

Fortunately, just about everything I knew about gnocchi was wrong. It turns out it doesn't have to have ridges. Sure, they help the sauce adhere and all that, but you can save a lot of trouble by admitting that smooth gnocchi has its own charms, such as taking less time to make and therefore getting to your belly faster. Second, I learned that if you didn't have a potato ricer you could use the large holes of a box grater to a similar effect; this alone turned me from a homemade-gnocchi avoider to a gnocchi embracer. Third, I learned that if you add the flour slowly and carefully, and embrace rather than fight the stickiness inherent in the dough, you won't add too much. Your gnocchi *will* be featherweight. You will *win* at gnocchi, should you secretly care about such things as much as I, not so secretly, do.

But for me, hands down, the best thing about making gnocchi at home was that I could do it my way. For some reason, many restaurants seem to assume that if you're ordering gnocchi, your arteries/girth/sense of meal proportion are already doomed: *Let's just lay on the thick blue-cheese sauce.* I find these heavy preparations unnecessary, and they ruin the delicacy at the heart of perfect gnocchi. In fact, my favorite way to eat gnocchi is in a puddle of tomato broth. Tomato broth is light, gnocchi is light, and they don't fight each other for anything but the chance to be the first thing you taste. I daresay this is even a restrained, overdid-it-in-December, gotta-compensate-in-January kinda meal. That is, if you nix the cheese on top. If you don't, of course, well, you'll hardly question why it belongs there.

yield: 2½ to 3 cups broth and 85 to 100 gnocchi, serving 4

tomato broth

2 tablespoons (30 ml) olive oil

1 medium carrot, chopped

1 medium stalk celery, chopped

1 small yellow onion, chopped

2 garlic cloves, peeled and smashed

½ cup (120 ml) white wine

One 28-ounce (795 grams) can whole or chopped tomatoes with juices

Small handful of fresh basil leaves, plus more for garnish

2 cups (475 ml) chicken or vegetable stock

Salt and freshly ground black pepper, to taste

gnocchi

2 pounds (905 grams) Russet potatoes (3 or 4)

1 large egg, lightly beaten

1 teaspoon table salt

1¼ to 1½ cups (156 to 190 grams) all-purpose flour, plus more for dusting surface

*   *   *

bake potatoes Preheat your oven to 400 degrees. Bake potatoes for 45 minutes to 1 hour, depending on size, until a thin knife can easily pierce through them. Meanwhile, prepare the tomato broth.

make tomato broth Heat the oil in a heavy pot over medium-high heat. Once it's hot, add the carrot, celery, and onion, and cook together for 5 minutes, reducing the heat to medium if they begin to brown. Add the garlic, and cook for 1 minute more. Pour in the wine, and use it to scrape up any browned bits stuck to the bottom of the pan, then cook the wine until it is reduced by half, for several minutes. Stir in the tomatoes, mashing them a bit with a spoon if whole, and the basil and stock, and simmer until the tomato broth thickens slightly, for about 45 minutes. Strain out the vegetables in a fine-mesh colander, and season with salt and pepper to taste. Set aside until needed.

make gnocchi Let the potatoes cool for 10 minutes after baking, then peel them with a knife or peeler. Run the potatoes through a potato ricer, or grate them on the large holes of a box grater. Cool them to lukewarm, about another 10 minutes. Add the egg and salt, mixing to combine. Add ½ cup flour, and mix to combine. Add next ½ cup flour, mixing again. Add ¼ cup flour, and see if this is enough to form a dough that does not easily stick to your hands. If not, add the last ¼ cup of flour, a tablespoon at a time, until the dough is a good consistency—soft and a little sticky, but able to hold its shape enough to be rolled into a rope. Knead the dough together briefly on a counter—just for a minute.

Divide the dough into quarters. Roll each piece into a long rope, about ¾ inch thick. Cut each rope into ¾-inch lengths. At this point, you can use a floured fork or a gnocchi board to give it the traditional ridges, but I never bother. Place the gnocchi in a single layer on a parchment-lined tray. (If you'd like to freeze them for later use, do so on this tray; once they are frozen, drop them into a freezer bag. This ensures that you won't have one enormous gnocchi mass when you are ready to cook them.)

to finish
Fresh ricotta or shaved Parmesan to taste (optional)

cook the gnocchi Place the gnocchi, a quarter-batch at a time, into a pot of boiling, well-salted water. Cook the gnocchi until they float—about 2 minutes—then drain. (Frozen gnocchi will take a minute longer.)

assemble dish Meanwhile, reheat broth to a simmer. Add drained gnocchi and reheat through. Serve gnocchi and broth together, garnished with extra slivers of basil and/or a dollop of fresh ricotta or some Parmesan shavings to taste.

sweet peas and shells alfredo

When I was a kid, I was unwaveringly certain that fettuccine Alfredo was the most glamorous dish on earth and if that didn't give it away, yes, I grew up in the 1980s. Alfredo was on every menu before the low-fat craze eradicated its lushness, as eighties as walnut oil, raspberry vinegar, and me having a very unfortunate set of bangs.

Obviously, given the chance to talk about pasta for a few pages, I had to drag it back here for its renewal (but hopefully not its farewell tour). However, there are a couple things that make this dish especially difficult to construct as an adult, both pertaining to things I didn't know then that I am not sure I am glad I know now. The first is that the thick, creamy Alfredo sauce is as authentically Italian as, well, pizza seasoning blends. The second is that it's much harder as an adult with nagging concerns about arteries and double chins to mindlessly delight in an unapologetic puddle of butter, cream, cheese, and refined flours the way I did as a kid.

But I think if you're going to do something, you should do it right, and if I wanted to find some crystalline sliver of my childhood in a rich bowl of pasta, I was going to have to do it properly—that is, immoderately. And I *almost* pulled it off, but the week I was tinkering with this recipe, I managed to run the little Italian store down the street out of the tiny pasta shells I like best for this dish, leaving only the dreaded whole wheat ones behind. Then, the market by my apartment had fresh shelling peas, and once they landed in the dish, and nested themselves in those little shells, I was too charmed to consider making it without them again. My inner thirteen-year-old might understandably be appalled that I "grown-upped" this with icky fresh vegetables and whole grains, but my outer adult thinks that the sweet, crunchy peas offset the richness perfectly, the heartier pasta is an excellent stage for all the sauce, and that, quite often, pasta dishes (and tastes in bangs, thank goodness) are improved with age.

*   *   *

yield: serves 2 generously or 4 petitely

Salt to taste

½ pound (225 grams) dried small pasta shells, regular, whole wheat, or, if you're a poor planner, a mix

1 cup (455 grams) fresh shelled peas (from about 1 pound in the pod)

1 cup (240 ml) heavy cream

3 tablespoons (40 grams) unsalted butter

Freshly ground black pepper

1 teaspoon finely grated fresh lemon zest

1 cup (115 grams) finely grated Parmesan cheese

2 tablespoons chopped fresh flat-leaf parsley

Bring a large pot of salted water to boil. Add the pasta, and cook according to package instructions. Add peas to cook during the last 30 seconds of pasta cooking time. Reserve ½ cup pasta cooking water, and set aside. Drain the pasta and the peas together.

Dry out the pasta pot, and pour in the heavy cream. Bring the cream to a simmer, and cook it until slightly reduced, about 4 minutes, stirring frequently. Add the butter, and stir it until it has melted. Generously season the sauce with freshly ground black pepper; add a pinch of salt as well as the lemon zest. Add ¾ cup of the Parmesan, and stir it until the sauce is smooth; then toss in the drained pasta and peas. Cook the pasta in sauce for 2 minutes, until the sauce has slightly thickened. Add the reserved pasta water by the spoonful if needed to loosen the sauce.

Divide the pasta among bowls. Garnish with remaining Parmesan and the flat-leaf parsley.

linguine with cauliflower pesto

When my son was about five weeks old, and my every second was devoted to his sweet little squeaks and "beh"s, I realized I hadn't had a real meal in, well, five weeks and that it was becoming hard not to gnaw off his tiny arm from hunger (note: no infants were harmed in the making of this recipe). I came across a cauliflower recipe from a Gramercy Tavern chef that triggered a round of all-consuming hunger so intense that I somehow managed to trick the newborn into letting me put him in the Bjorn long enough to pull it off. I still don't know how I did it—roasting cauliflower rounds, toasting almonds, buttering breadcrumbs, plumping raisins—but it happened, and the results were so good that I stood in the kitchen and ate more than half of it (only dropping a couple raisins on his fuzzy newborn head) before I realized that maybe I should have saved some to share with my husband.

Even if you aren't practicing the art of newborn kitchen negotiation, that recipe probably wasn't intended for people who don't have a lot of free time. So when I returned to it a year later, I was intent on turning the lovely combination of flavors into something more accessible, and closer to a meal that could feed all of us. The results are alarmingly easy to whip up. You don't have to peel and mince garlic cloves and you don't have to chop almonds. The cauliflower is raw and stays that way. The food processor, in stages, does everything for you and all you have to do is stir and toss your way to a fresh and bright fall meal.

*   *   *

Set a large pot of salted water to boil.

prepare pesto Pulse half the cauliflower in a food processor until it looks like mixed sizes of couscous. Transfer the cauliflower to a large bowl, and repeat with the second batch, adding it to the same bowl when you are finished. If your cauliflower looks like the perfect texture but one large chunk insists upon escaping the steel blade's grasp, pick it

yield: serves 6 to 8

Salt

1 small head or ½ large head cauliflower (about 1 pound or 455 grams), trimmed of leaves, cored, and cut into large chunks

1 garlic clove

Generous pinch of red pepper flakes

½ cup (70 grams) almonds or pine nuts, **toasted and cooled**

2-ounce (55-gram) chunk Romano or Parmesan cheese, plus a little more for passing

4 sun-dried tomatoes (dry variety; if oil-packed, be sure to drain them and mince them by hand separately, so the oil doesn't gum up the food-processor mixture, before you add them)

1 tablespoon drained capers

Few tablespoons fresh parsley leaves

⅓ cup (80 ml) olive oil

½ to 1 teaspoon sherry vinegar (to taste)

1 pound (455 grams) linguine

out and pulse it separately. You'll have about 3½ cups of fluffy, delightful cauliflower-couscousc rumbs.

Pulse the garlic, pepper flakes, almonds, cheese, sun-dried tomatoes, capers, and parsley in a food processor until the mixture looks like coarse breadcrumbs. Transfer to the bowl with cauliflower, add the olive oil, the smaller amount of vinegar, and a few pinches of salt, and stir until combined. (If you do this step in the food processor, it becomes an unseemly paste. Best to do it by hand.) Taste and adjust seasoning as needed—either adding more salt, pepper, or remainder of vinegar. I start with about ½ teaspoon salt but often go up to nearly a full teaspoon.

assemble dish Once water is boiling, add the linguine and cook until it is al dente (cooked, but with a tiny bite left). Reserve a cup of the cooking water, then drain the rest. Immediately toss the hot pasta with the cauliflower pesto and half of your reserved cooking water, until everything is nicely dispersed. If the pesto still feels too thick, loosen it with the remaining reserved cooking water. Divide among bowls, and pass with additional Parmesan cheese.

cooking notes

Want to skip the pasta? This is also incredible as a tapenade on olive-oil-brushed toasts.

To make this like an Italian grandmother, or without a food processor: Simply chop everything by hand.

heart-stuffed shells in lemon ricotta béchamel

In restaurants, I have a series of what I call trigger foods—foods I love so much that, if I see them on the menu, I will always order them, no matter how they're made or how good other items might look. At the top of that list is artichokes. Second on the list is any lasagna that promises to exclude ricotta. And the third is any dish that I expect to be made one way—a way I'm not especially fond of—but that has been updated by a chef who clearly shares my tastes.

Which brings me to these stuffed shells, a dish that combines all three of my triggers. Most shell recipes are cheese bombs, stuffed with ricotta until they burst, but with little actual zing. I wanted something brighter, a real surprise to bite into, and attempted to amplify the flavor of my favorite vegetable—the artichoke—in every way I knew how: a slip of browned butter, a hint of white wine, a pile of caramelized onions, Parmesan for flavor, Romano for punch, and lemon juice for brightness. Here, the ricotta is on the outside, a lush complement for the pockets of louder flavor within.

*   *   *

cook the shells Bring a large pot of salted water to boil, and cook shells according to package directions. Drain, and toss with a teaspoon or two of olive oil, to keep them from sticking.

make the filling Melt the butter in a heavy 12-inch skillet (or the bottom of the dried-out pot you used to cook your pasta, if you're into dirtying fewer dishes), and cook it until it turns nutty and brown, stirring occasionally to keep the solids moving on the bottom of the pan. Once it is a nice nutty brown, add 1 tablespoon olive oil, then the onion, and cook until it is lightly brown and caramelized, for about 7 minutes. Add the artichoke hearts, and cook them until they are softened a bit, for about 5 minutes. Add the wine, and cook until it completely disappears.

Remove the pan from the heat, and let it cool slightly; then transfer the artichoke mixture to the bowl of a food processor. Add both cheeses, the

yield: serves 4

shells

18 jumbo pasta shells (about half of a 12-ounce [340-gram] box)

1 to 2 tablespoons (15 to 30 ml) olive oil

3 tablespoons (42 grams) unsalted butter, cut into pieces

1 large onion, diced

12 ounces (340 grams) frozen artichoke hearts (1 package), thawed and patted dry

¼ cup (60 ml) dry white wine

½ cup (1¼ ounces or 35 grams) finely grated Romano cheese

½ cup (1½ ounces or 45 grams) finely grated Parmigiano-Reggiano cheese

2 large egg yolks

1 tablespoon freshly squeezed lemon juice

½ teaspoon table salt, plus more for pasta pot

Freshly ground black pepper to taste

sauce

4 tablespoons (55 grams or ½ stick) unsalted butter

¼ cup (30 grams) all-purpose flour

2 cups (475 ml) whole milk

egg yolks, lemon juice, salt, and black pepper, and pulse in the food processor until well chopped but still a little coarse.

make the sauce Melt the butter in a medium saucepan (or the wiped-out pot you made the artichoke filling in, if you're still into spending less time scrubbing pots) over medium-high heat. Once it's melted, add the flour all at once and whisk it until smooth. Add the milk, a small glug at a time, whisking constantly so that no lumps form. When the mixture has reached a batterlike consistency, you can begin adding the milk in larger pours, whisking the whole time. Once all the milk is added, add the garlic and bring the sauce to a boil, stirring frequently. The sauce will immediately begin to thicken once it boils. Reduce the heat to medium, and simmer for 2 to 3 minutes. Stir in the ricotta, lemon juice, salt, and black pepper. Adjust salt, pepper, and lemon to taste.

assemble the dish Preheat your oven to 350 degrees. Pour 2 cups of sauce (you'll have about 2½ cups total) into the bottom of a 9-by-13-inch baking dish. Scoop 1 tablespoon of artichoke filling inside each cooked shell; this will fill it but still allow the sides to close and neatly hold the filling intact while it bakes. Nest each pasta shell in the sauce, seam up. Dollop a spoonful of the remaining sauce over each shell. Cover the dish with foil, and bake it for 30 minutes, then remove the foil and bake it for a final 15 minutes. Sprinkle with parsley or basil, if using, and serve immediately.

1 clove garlic, minced

½ cup (115 grams) ricotta cheese

2 tablespoons (30 ml) freshly squeezed lemon juice

½ teaspoon table salt

Freshly ground black pepper to taste

2 tablespoons chopped fresh flat-leaf parsley or fresh basil leaves, for garnish (optional)

leek fritters with garlic and lemon

At some point in the last few years, fritters became my favorite things to cook, and by fritters I really just mean latkes but without potatoes. I've made them with everything from zucchini to apples, and I'm not even close to tiring of the format.

What I like about fritters is that they come together fairly quickly but they won't rush you. It's easy to keep them warm in the oven while you're working your way through the batter, or for another hour after they're all done, until you're ready to eat them. They hold up in the fridge for a few days, and they freeze well too—you only need to rewarm and crisp them in the oven to bring them back to day-one-level perfection. And they've got a great balance of indulgence—they're fried and crispy, after all—and good deed, because they include shredded wholesome vegetables. The first part gets me excited about dinner, the second part keeps me from feeling too bad about it after I eat.

I made leek fritters one day on a whim, since I'm a little obsessed with leeks. First, they're gorgeous. A cross section appears like the rings of a tree, with gradients from Shamrock Green to Unmellow Yellow (or so says my son's box of crayons), and I want to wear it. I know that leeks are part of the onion family, but they're also mild; a sauté of them always reminds me of potatoes and chives—i.e., a perfect dish. In fritter format, their bite is especially tame, so tame that a tart lemon–garlic–sour cream dollop on top should not be skipped. They're as good with a fried egg on top for dinner as they are when made even tinier, for a party snack.

* * *

prepare the batter Trim the leeks, leaving only the white and pale-green parts. Halve them lengthwise, and if they look gritty or dirty, plunge them into cold water and fan the layers about to remove any dirt and grit. On a cutting board, slice the leeks crosswise into ¼-inch strips. Bring a pot of salted water to a boil, and cook them for 3 to 4 minutes, until they are

yield: about ten 2½-inch fritters

2 pounds (905 grams) leeks
(about 3 very large ones)

½ teaspoon table salt, plus more for pot

2 scallions, trimmed, halved lengthwise, and thinly sliced

¼ cup (30 grams) all-purpose flour

1 teaspoon baking powder

Freshly ground black pepper

Pinch of cayenne pepper (optional)

1 large egg

Olive or vegetable oil, for frying

garlic lemon cream

½ cup (120 grams) sour cream

1 tablespoon freshly squeezed lemon juice

Few gratings of fresh lemon zest

Pinches of salt

1 small garlic clove, minced or crushed

slightly softened but not limp. Drain, and wring them out in a dish towel or a piece of cheesecloth.

Transfer the wrung-out leeks to a large bowl, and stir in the scallions. In a small dish, whisk together the flour, salt, baking powder, freshly ground black pepper, and cayenne pepper, if you're using it. Stir the dry ingredients into the leek mixture, then stir in the egg until the mixture is evenly coated.

cook the fritters Preheat your oven to 250 degrees, and place a baking sheet covered in foil inside. Stack a few paper towels on a large plate. In a large, heavy skillet—cast iron is dreamy here—heat 2 tablespoons oil over medium heat until it shimmers. Drop small bunches of the leek mixture onto the skillet—only a few at a time, so they don't become crowded—and lightly nudge them flatter with the back of your spatula. Cook the fritters until they are golden underneath, about 3 minutes. If you find this is happening too quickly, reduce the heat to medium-low; I find I have to jump the heat back and forth a lot to keep it even. Flip fritters, and cook for another 3 minutes on the other side.

Drain the fritters on paper towels, and transfer them to warm oven while you make the remaining fritters.

I like to let the fritters hang out in the oven for at least 10 minutes after the last one is cooked—they stay crisp, and this ensures that they're cooked through, even if they finished quickly on the stove.

to serve Whisk together the garlic lemon cream ingredients until smooth. Dollop on each fritter before serving. These fritters are also delicious with a poached or fried egg on top. Trust me.

do ahead Fritters keep well, either chilled in the fridge for the better part of a week, or frozen in a well-sealed package for months. When you're ready to use them, simply spread them out on a tray in a 325-degree oven and heat until they're hot and crisp again.

jacob's blintzes, or sweet potato blintzes with farmer's cheese

*M*y eating-habits-of-the-under-three-set studies are limited to a sample population of one, so I cannot tell you what other toddlers like to eat for dinner. But my two-year-old is half Russian, and the grandmother on the Russian side has been making him cheese blintzes to eat since he was a year old, and my child, he really loves cheese blintzes. Preferably with a dollop of yogurt or a bit of berry jam on top. I think he has excellent taste.

In fact, about the only thing I can say he's enjoyed more consistently than blintzes is sweet potatoes, and I decided last fall to create a blintz recipe just for him, with a little of everything that he likes. I'm not going to lie. The more balanced approach to crepe fillings appeals to me—vegetable, farmer's cheese, and a sauce I could make quickly from berries that keeps fantastically in the freezer. Okay, if I'm *really* not going to lie, I will also tell you that leftover cranberry syrup goes nicely in a glass with club soda and vodka. But—ahem!—the children. We must focus on the children.

The only thing I have learned so far about feeding my sample population of one is that things never go the way you think they will. One day your kid will be so crazy for raspberries that he'll inhale an entire container, and the next day you'll buy three containers on sale and he'll get all poltergeist in the offending berries' presence: "Berries! Yuck! How *could* you?!" So, even though I worked hard on Jacob's blintzes, and even though he eagerly eats them every time I make them, we must pretend I never discussed this with you or the winds of toddler will might change and his father and I will be stuck making rounds of vodka cocktails with the leftovers. And that would be terrible.

*   *   *

yield: 16 blintzes

wrappers

1½ cups (355 ml) milk (I use whole milk, but other fat levels work, so use what you have)

6 large eggs

1½ cups (190 grams) all-purpose flour

¼ teaspoon table salt

1 tablespoon melted butter or neutral oil, for brushing the pan, plus additional for cooking blintzes

filling

About 4 medium sweet potatoes

2 cups (455 grams or 16 ounces) farmer's cheese

2 large egg yolks

¼ cup (50 grams) sugar

½ teaspoon ground cinnamon

Few fresh gratings of nutmeg

Pinch of salt

cranberry syrup

2 cups (225 grams) fresh or frozen cranberries

make wrapper batter In a blender, combine all the wrapper ingredients except butter or oil. (Alternatively, combine them in a bowl with an immersion blender.) Pour the batter into a bowl, cover with plastic wrap, and refrigerate for an hour or up to 2 days.

prepare sweet potato Preheat your oven to 400 degrees. Bake the sweet potatoes on a tray for about 40 minutes, until soft. Let them cool in their skins. Once they're cool, peel the sweet potatoes, and mash them or run them through a potato ricer.

cook wrappers Preheat a medium skillet or crepe pan over medium-high heat. Once it's heated, brush the pan lightly with melted butter or oil. Pour ¼ cup batter into the skillet, swirling it until it evenly coats the bottom, and cook, undisturbed, until the bottom is golden and the top is set, about 2 minutes. No need to flip them. Transfer the wrapper to a paper-towel-covered plate, cooked side down. Continue with remaining batter.

prepare filling Once sweet potato puree is cool, stir in the farmer's cheese, egg yolks, sugar, cinnamon, nutmeg, and salt.

make blintzes Preheat your oven to 200 degrees. Put an ever-so-slightly heaped ¼ cup of filling in the center of each wrapper, and fold the opposite sides of wrapper over filling until they barely touch. Pull the end of

¼ cup (60 ml) orange juice

½ cup (100 grams) sugar

Sour cream or cranberry syrup, for serving

the crepe nearest to you up over the filling, and roll the rest of the way, to completely enclose filling, forming elongated, egg-roll-shaped packets. Repeat with the remaining blintzes and filling. Reheat your crepe skillet—or a larger one, if you want to cook more blintzes at a time—over medium heat and add more butter or oil to coat the pan. Place a few blintzes, seam side down, in skillet, and cook them until they are golden brown and crisp, for about 5 minutes on each side. Transfer them to a baking sheet, and keep them warm in the oven until they are ready to serve.

make syrup In a saucepan, over medium heat, simmer the cranberries, orange juice, and sugar together until the berries burst, about 7 to 10 minutes. Reduce the heat to medium-low, and simmer for 5 minutes more. Strain the syrup into a bowl.

Serve blintzes warm with a drizzle of cranberry syrup and/or a dollop of sour cream.

do ahead

The crepe batter can be made 1 day ahead of time. The cooked crepes keep in the fridge for 2 days, unfilled or filled. You can also freeze prepared blintzes before or after browning them, but we prefer doing so before they are browned, so they always taste fresh and crisp when they are served.

corn risotto–stuffed poblanos

This is the recipe equivalent of a misheard song lyric. Whether you've crooned, "Hold Me Closer, Tony Danza" to the tune of Elton John's "Tiny Dancer" or, as I did for years, sung "my food is yours, son" instead of "my foolish notion" when George Michael's "Faith" came on the radio, we've all been there.

In this case it was at a Mexican restaurant in my old neighborhood and it was an order of poblanos, stuffed with what I was absolutely certain was a perfect risotto, punctuated with sweet kernels of crunchy summer corn, right off the cob. Now I realize in hindsight that it was unlikely that a Mexican restaurant was filling poblanos with a classic Italian preparation of starchy short-grained rice. I realize that it might have actually been a rich, creamy combination of rice, corn, onions, and cheese. But as it turned out, I didn't care because I was more in love with what I thought it was than what it might have actually been.

What I mean to say is, I want this food to be totally yours, son.

And so I went home and started making it the way I thought it had been, actual ~~lyrics~~ *ingredients* be damned. Fiddling with the classic risotto formula, I used olive oil instead of butter, a Mexican cerveza instead of Italian wine, a mixture of Monterey Jack and queso fresco instead of Parmesan. Then, of course, I stuffed this mixture into poblanos, finishing it with a Mexican crema and cilantro and serving it with lime wedges. And even though this dish would likely be as lost in Italy as it would be in Mexico, it lives happily on our dinner table in New York City every summer, and soon, I hope, yours as well.

*   *   *

prepare peppers Lay several chiles at a time on their sides on the racks atop a gas burner, and turn the flame to high. Using tongs, rotate the chiles frequently until their skins are blistered, about 4 to 6 minutes each. Transfer the peppers to a bowl, and cover them with foil or plastic wrap. Repeat with the remaining chiles. Should you not have a gas burner, you

yield: serves 4 generously

8 large fresh poblano peppers

6 cups (1422 ml) chicken or vegetable stock

2 tablespoons (30 ml) olive oil

1 small onion, finely chopped

1 garlic clove, minced

2 cups (400 grams) short-grained rice such as arborio or carnaroli

½ cup (120 ml) beer, preferably light or medium in color

1½ cups (200 grams) fresh corn kernels (from about 2 cobs) or 1½ cups frozen and defrosted kernels

¾ cup (70 grams) grated Monterey Jack cheese

½ teaspoon table salt

Freshly ground black pepper

¼ cup (30 grams) crumbled queso fresco, ricotta salata, or another crumbly cheese

3 tablespoons (45 grams) sour cream mixed with 1 tablespoon milk and a pinch of salt for serving

3 tablespoons chopped fresh cilantro leaves or flat-leaf parsley

can do this under a broiler. Or you can skip this step altogether if the pepper skins don't bother you.

make risotto In a medium saucepan, heat the stock to a low simmer. On a separate burner, heat a larger saucepan over medium heat. Once the saucepan is hot, add the oil and heat through; then add the onion, and sauté until it is softened and translucent, about 8 minutes. Add the garlic, and cook for 1 minute more. Add the rice to the pot, and stir it for a minute or two, until it becomes lightly toasty. Pour in the beer, scraping up any stuck bits from the bottom of the pan. Let beer simmer for roughly a minute—it will mostly disappear.

Ladle 1 cup of warm stock into rice mixture, and simmer until it has been absorbed, stirring frequently. Add the remaining stock, ½ cup at a time, allowing stock to absorb before adding more, and stirring often. Along with the final addition of stock, add the corn. The total cooking time for the rice is about 30 minutes, after which it should be creamy and tender. Though risotto is traditionally supposed to be on the loose side, you can leave this one ever-so-slightly thicker, so it can be easily stuffed into peppers. Once the stock is added and the risotto is tender, stir in the Monterey Jack cheese, the salt, and many grinds of black pepper. Adjust seasonings to taste. Remove risotto from the heat.

corn risotto–stuffed poblanos (continued)

assemble and cook poblanos Preheat your oven to 400 degrees. Remove chiles from bowl, and gently rub off the skins, which should now remove easily. Cut a slit lengthwise in each chile, and remove the seeds and membranes as best as you can. Leave the stems on—they're cute. Fill each chile with risotto through the slit. Arrange the chiles tightly in a baking dish, and sprinkle the space between them with crumbled cheese. Bake the chiles for 10 to 15 minutes, until bronzed a bit on top.

to serve In a small dish, whisk together the sour cream mixed with milk and salt. Drizzle the mixture over hot chiles. Garnish with cilantro. Eat them while they're hot.

slow-cooker black bean ragout

I am a black bean thief. Don't ever go to a Tex-Mex restaurant—the kind that has strung chile lights over the bar, margarita glasses with cacti for stems, and enough salty tortilla chips and salsa on the table that you will keep ordering refills in said glasses—with me, because I will steal your black beans. You see, eventually we'll realize that we should order some quesadillas or fajitas to offset the tequila damage and they'll arrive with a little puddle of black beans on the side and I will eat mine and yours, too.

The thing is, I could never get them right at home. The situation was so bad that, in recipes on my website that went with black beans, I'd advise people to pick up a can of black-bean soup, drain off a few spoonfuls of liquid, and use that instead. I was that black-bean-impaired. (But seriously, in a pinch, try it.)

It was a glorious day when I realized two things: one, that my inability to make black beans to my liking had to do with the fact that I was starting with already cooked beans, which cook into a mushy mass before you get any flavor back into them; and, two, that if I used the slow-cooker, I didn't even have to do any work. From there, I starting loading them up with all of my favorite flavors, cumin and smoked paprika, oregano and tomato paste, a finely diced onion and a few smashed cloves of garlic, and, for the very best slow-cooked suggestion of heat, a dried chile.

I realize that, for most people, black beans are a side dish. But for me, they're my very favorite stuck-inside-on-a-bleary-weekday lunch, and I put them together just like this. And should it be noon *somewhere*—and ahem, it always is—they go down especially well with a glass of beer fitted with a lime wedge.

*   *   *

to cook the beans:

slow-cooker Put all the bean ragout ingredients except lime juice or vinegar in a 6-quart slow-cooker (the slow-cooker doesn't care how you

yield: about 6 cups ragout

bean ragout

1 large onion, finely chopped

3 garlic cloves, minced

1 tablespoon ground cumin

½ teaspoon dried oregano

2 teaspoons smoked paprika

1 pound (455 grams or 2¼ cups) dried black beans, rinsed if not already soaked

1 dried chile

2 tablespoons (35 grams) tomato paste

2 teaspoons table salt

9 to 10 cups (2 to 2½ liters) water or unsalted vegetable or chicken stock

1 tablespoon lime juice or sherry vinegar

garlicky toast

1-inch-thick slices of bread, such as country or ciabatta loaf

Olive oil

Table salt

1 large garlic clove, halved

cumin crema

1 teaspoon ground cumin

1 cup (240 grams) sour cream, crème fraîche, or crema mexicana

layer your ingredients). Cover and cook at high setting until beans are very tender, about 3 hours (in my super-speedy slow-cooker) to 6 hours.

stovetop Put all the bean ragout ingredients except lime juice or vinegar in a large pot, and bring to a boil. Reduce to a very low simmer and cook for approximately 3 hours, until the beans are tender.

to make toasts Brush bread with olive oil, and sprinkle lightly with salt. Toast bread under the broiler, and as soon as you take it out of the oven, rub it with the raw garlic clove.

to make crema Stir together 1 teaspoon ground cumin with sour cream and set aside.

to make lime-pickled red onions Mix the lime juice, onion, and a pinch or two of salt in a small dish, and let stand for 15 minutes, stirring occasionally. Use to garnish black-bean ragout.

Once the beans are cooked, stir in the lime juice or vinegar. Adjust seasonings to taste. Ladle over garlicky toasts and sprinkle with chopped cilantro, cumin crema, and lime-pickled red onions. Serve with avocado wedges.

cooking notes No need to presoak your black beans, but if you do, you can cut down your cooking time a bit. Please use the bean soaking liquid as your cooking water; it would be a terrible shame to let its wonderful flavor go down the drain.

For a thicker ragout, transfer 1 cup of the cooked bean mixture to the blender, then return the purée to the ragout.

Eat your black beans over rice, in tacos or huevos rancheros, as a filling for quesadillas, or as a side for arroz con pollo.

lime-pickled red onions

2 tablespoons (30 ml) freshly squeezed lime juice

¼ medium red onion, finely diced

Table salt

Chopped fresh cilantro leaves (or flat-leaf parsley, if you're cilantro-averse)

Avocado wedges

roasted tomatoes and cipollini onions
with white beans

This is my desert-island dish. And, yes, I know you're probably going to point out that I'm not likely to find tiny cipollini onions on a desert island, or seasonal tomatoes, let alone garlic cloves and basil. So, basically, I'm not really talking about a desert island, I'm talking about Italy. Can you blame me?

You take the simplest of things—tiny boiling onions, smallish tomatoes, olive oil, and coarse salt—and you roast the heck out of them, to use fancy cooking terminology. What comes out of the oven is something completely different. The onions emerge charred in spots, semi-tender, and sweet. The tomatoes slump and intensify, their flavor as pronounced as can be. But neither of those things is the reason I'm so obsessed with this dish, although even looking at photos of it in February makes me a little sniffly that tomato season is so far off.

What really gets me is the gravy. What collects at the bottom of the pan is as close to manna as I think I'll experience in my lifetime, on a desert island or elsewhere. This puddle in the pan is everything great about cooking, and I need you to promise—no, really, *promise* me—that you will not eat this dish without using a soft spatula to remove every drop of it from the pan. It will help if you bury a thick garlicky crouton at the bottom of your bowl, to catch the drippings before the bowl does. I like to add some white beans to the mix as well, because the pan juices make an excellent dressing, and they help turn this into a full meal. I pile the onions and tomatoes on top, garnish it with a few slivers of basil, and then lie to my husband and pretend I never made it, because I don't want to share what's left.

* * *

Preheat your oven to 375 degrees. Boil a small pot of water, and blanch the cipollini onions for 10 seconds, then plunge them into cold water. Use a paring knife to make a small slit in each onion, and slide them out of their skins and their outer layer.

*yield: serves 4 as a small dish,
2 as a main*

1 pound cipollini onions

1½ pounds (680 grams) small Roma or large cherry tomatoes

¼ cup (60 ml) olive oil

Coarse salt

Four 1 inch thick slices country or ciabatta bread

Garlic clove (optional)

One 15-ounce (425-gram) can of large white beans, such as Great Northern, drained and rinsed, or 1½ cups cooked beans of your choice

Few fresh basil leaves, slivered

roasted tomatoes and cipollini onions with white beans (continued)

Spread the peeled onions and the tomatoes in a roasting pan. Drizzle them with olive oil and a few good pinches of coarse salt. Toss everything together until well coated, and roast in preheated oven for 45 to 55 minutes, reaching in every 15 minutes with a spatula to roll the tomatoes and onions around to ensure all sides get blistered.

Just before you take the tomatoes and onions out, place your bread slices on the oven rack (or on a tray, if you're more refined than we are) and let them toast lightly. You can rub the toasts with a halved garlic clove, if you like, while still hot. Use tongs to arrange the toasts in one layer on a serving platter. Dump the white beans over the bread, and, using a pot holder, scrape the entire contents of the tomato-and-onion roasting pan, still hot, over the white beans. Do not skimp on the juices that have collected, all of them—don't leave any in the pan. They could make a religious person out of you.

Sprinkle the dish with the basil, and eat at once.

spaghetti squash and black bean tacos with queso fresco

*E*veryone has their culinary pet peeves, and this is one of mine: I don't like it when a recipe tries to convince me that spaghetti squash, with its noodle-sounding name, is an acceptable substitute for spaghetti itself. Eating spaghetti squash treated as spaghetti—tangled in tomato sauce, as a nest for meatballs—only makes a large commotion of the gap between them, and, no, squash does not come out ahead.

This doesn't mean that I am not a hypocrite, however, because I'm sure you read this recipe's title and thought, Spaghetti squash tacos? *Tacos?* That's just *weird*. But I can't help it, spaghetti squash occasionally reminds me of pork shoulder—yes, pork shoulder—in that it starts out as a heavy, solid mass but, when cooked right, breaks into shards with the encouragement of a fork. And from that place, I knew I had to get some spaghetti squash in my tacos.

It doesn't hurt that squash is no foreigner to Mexican cooking. The mild sweetness of squash plays excellently off the sharp lime, spices, onion, and herbs in a good taco, and couches the ferocity of a favorite hot sauce. I know I haven't sold you yet on spaghetti squash as a taco filling—heck, I hadn't even sold myself or the friend who was around the day I made these. But that plate over there? It was gone, wiped clean, not 10 minutes after I took the photo.

*   *   *

to cook the squash in a microwave Pierce squash (about an inch deep) all over with a small sharp knife to prevent it from bursting. Cook at high power for 6 to 7 minutes. Turn the squash over, and microwave it until it feels slightly soft when pressed, 8 to 10 minutes more. Cool the squash for 5 minutes.

to roast the squash in an oven Cut the squash in half lengthwise, scoop out the seeds, and roast the halves facedown in an oiled baking pan for about 40 minutes in a 375-degree oven.

yield: sixteen 6-inch tacos, serving 4 generously or 8 modestly

3 pounds (1360 grams) spaghetti squash (either 1 large or 2 small)

2 tablespoons (30 ml) freshly squeezed lime juice (from about 1 lime)

1 teaspoon chili powder

½ teaspoon ground cumin

½ teaspoon ground coriander

½ teaspoon coarse salt

Sixteen 6-inch corn tortillas

One 15-ounce (425-gram) can black beans, rinsed and drained very well

4 ounces (115 grams) crumbled queso fresco, feta, or Cotija cheese

¼ cup (35 grams) finely diced red or white onion

¼ cup chopped fresh cilantro leaves (the cilantro-averse can use flat-leaf parsley)

optional finishes
Dashes of hot sauce
Lime wedges

spaghetti squash and black bean tacos with queso fresco (continued)

When the squash has finished cooking and cooled slightly, working over a bowl, scrape the squash flesh with a fork, loosening and separating the strands as you remove it from the skin. Discard the skin. In a small dish, whisk lime juice with chili powder, cumin, coriander, and salt. Pour over the squash strands, and gently toss them together. Taste the squash, and adjust seasonings as you wish.

assemble tacos Heat a dry, heavy skillet over medium-high heat. Warm and slightly blister each tortilla, about 30 seconds per side. Transfer with tongs or a spatula to platter, and sprinkle each with 2 tablespoons of black beans, 2 tablespoons of spiced squash mixture, 2 teaspoons of crumbled or finely chopped cheese, and a couple pinches of onion and cilantro. Dash each with hot sauce, if that's your thing. Serve with lime wedges and extra hot sauce.

A LITTLE SOMETHING EXTRA

The seeds from spaghetti squash can be rinsed and toasted as you would pumpkin seeds. On an oiled baking sheet, spread out cleaned seeds (it's okay if they're still damp), and sprinkle them generously with chili powder and a few pinches of fine salt. Roast at 375 degrees for 7 to 10 minutes, tossing them about halfway through so that they cook evenly.

roasted eggplant with yogurt-tahini sauce and cumin-crisped chickpeas

Becoming a mom made me an expert on roasting vegetables. What, you thought I was going somewhere else with that? That maybe I'd have become an expert on Tantrum Management, or Getting Child to Sleep Through Night or Love Turnips? Ha. No, I save my expertise for crisping vegetables for easy release. Around the time my son took an interest in vegetables, I realized that my roasting technique had a lot of kinks in it. Like most people, I'd toss vegetables in oil, often more than I wanted to use, in hopes of keeping them from sticking to the pan while cooking. They always did anyway, while mocking my oiling efforts by tasting heavy and a bit greasy even though they cemented themselves to the pan. Eggplant was the worst of these, and the least pleasant to scrub off later. I found that I could keep vegetables from sticking without sopping them in oil the same way I'd keep an egg from adhering to a skillet—by oiling the pan first. The roasting pan becomes a frying pan, and the released vegetables—eggplant *especially*—get a gorgeous bronzed skin on the outside, and immense tenderness within.

From there, it was just a matter of dressing. I make this eggplant two ways, sometimes with a sprinkling of seasoned and browned ground lamb, and other times with oven-crisped chickpeas, which are as addictive apart from the eggplant as they are buried in the yogurt-tahini dressing (so I've given you plenty extra to snack on). As with many of my favorite dishes, I like the way it turns a classic approach to a meal on its head, with vegetables as the "main" course and meat or other protein as the side dish, and we all end up a lot more balanced for it.

*   *   *

yield: serves 4 to 6

1¾ cups (from a 15.5-ounce or 425-gram can) cooked chickpeas, drained, patted dry on paper towels

5 tablespoons (45 ml) olive oil

Coarse or kosher salt

Freshly ground black pepper

½ teaspoon ground cumin

3 pounds small eggplants (Italian-style eggplants if you can find them, 4 to 7 ounces [115 to 200 grams] each)

yogurt-tahini sauce

⅓ cup (45 grams) tahini paste

⅔ cup (150 grams) full-fat, thick plain yogurt

3 tablespoons (45 ml) freshly squeezed lemon juice

2 garlic cloves, minced

½ teaspoon table salt

About ⅓ cup (80 ml) cold water

2 tablespoons coarsely chopped fresh flat-leaf parsley

crisp chickpeas Preheat your oven to 425 degrees. Toss the chickpeas with 2 tablespoons olive oil, ¼ teaspoon coarse salt, freshly ground black pepper, and ground cumin. Spread them on a baking sheet, and roast on top rack for 30 to 40 minutes, rolling them around on the tray from time to time, until they are browned and crisp. I find that freshly cooked chickpeas crisp faster, so you may need less time for them to crisp if not canned.

roast eggplant Brush a large baking sheet or roasting pan with a generous tablespoon of oil. Halve the eggplants lengthwise, arrange them, cut side up, in one layer on oiled sheet. Brush the cut sides lightly with a tiny amount additional oil (which I know I just told you wouldn't be necessary, but I like using an extra "insurance plan" with vegetables that are especially unpleasant to scrub from pans), and sprinkle them generously with salt and freshly ground black pepper. Roast for 15 minutes, until lightly browned on top. Carefully flip the eggplants so that their cut sides are against the pan, and roast for another 15 minutes, until they are bronzed underneath and tender throughout. (If you are using larger eggplants, you may need up to 5 minutes additional roasting time.)

meanwhile, make yogurt-tahini sauce Whisk together tahini, yogurt, lemon juice, garlic, and salt; the mixture will become very thick and stiff. Add water, a tablespoon at a time, until mixture is smooth, with a thick but pourable consistency. I find that about 5 tablespoons (a little shy of ⅓ cup) water does the trick.

to serve Arrange the eggplant sections, cut side up, on a large platter. Dollop each piece generously with yogurt-tahini sauce. Sprinkle with crisped chickpeas and parsley. Serve immediately, passing extra chickpeas and yogurt-tahini sauce.

meatier riff About 10 minutes before eggplants are done roasting, heat 1 tablespoon butter with 1 tablespoon olive oil in a large, heavy skillet over medium-high heat. Add ½ small onion, finely chopped, and cook until it begins to brown. Add a minced clove of garlic and a pinch of chili flakes, and heat through for another minute. Add 1 pound ground lamb and cook, breaking up lumps, until no longer pink, about 5 minutes. Season with salt, sprinkle mixture over eggplant, and dollop with yogurt-tahini sauce.

This also pairs well with Sesame-Spiced Turkey Meatballs (see page 167).

wild rice gratin with kale, caramelized onions, and baby swiss

One of the most perplexing things to me as a parent thus far was discovering that I'd given birth to someone who disliked cheese so intensely he wouldn't even eat macaroni and cheese. Didn't he know that's like a breach of toddler contract? But the thing is, it was hard to be overly bummed about a kid's not liking something that's hardly good for him to begin with. In fact, if he'd liked macaroni and cheese, I'd never have been forced to reconsider ways to make a deep, crusty, and cheesy gratin that he would find acceptable.

My first attempt was a homemade spaetzle gratin. See how tricky I was? Not macaroni, but an *elongated dumplinglike noodle*—he'd never know! But every time I went to retest the recipe, I found something more interesting to do. For example, the curtains needed to be lint-rolled. The baby's sock drawer was a mess. Fact is, any recipe that starts with making batter, then spaetzle dumplings, then caramelized onions, then sautéed greens, and then assembling it in a gratin with cheese and baking it in the oven, involves (a) a ridiculous amount of labor and (b) more dishes than I can fit in my dishwasher. Both are dealbreakers.

The wild rice whim came out of a pantry cleanup, when I realized I had four types of couscous, countless pasta shapes, three bags of unsweetened coconut flakes, eight pounds of dried Rancho Gordo beans, and not a single bag of rice. No rice! Who doesn't have rice? This set me off on a wild-rice hunt, and when I found one that made us swoon, swoon to the point where we wondered why we'd ever wasted our time with white rice, this rice sneaked its way into the gratin one night. And although wild rice takes a bit of time to cook, you can get everything ready and even read a few board books while it does. What comes out of the oven is astoundingly delicious: hearty, bubbly, loud with flavor, a great thing to serve alongside a roast at a holiday meal, or a meal itself if you're a toddler who has been recently, unknowingly converted to cheese.

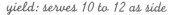

yield: serves 10 to 12 as side

wild rice

5 cups cooked wild rice (from 1⅔ cups, 10.5 ounces or 300 grams uncooked)

caramelized onions

1 tablespoon butter

1 tablespoon olive oil

2 large sweet onions, halved and thinly sliced

½ teaspoon table salt

Freshly ground black pepper

4 cups stemmed, ribboned kale leaves (from an 8-ounce or 225-gram bundle)

assembly

2 cups (8 ounces or 225 grams) coarsely grated Emmentaler or another Swiss cheese

2 tablespoons unsalted butter (1 tablespoon to grease dish; 1 tablespoon, melted, for crumbs)

¾ cup (180 ml) chicken or vegetable broth

1 cup (60 grams) fine, dry breadcrumbs

Table salt

Freshly ground black pepper

*   *   *

cook the rice according to package directions.

Preheat your oven to 375 degrees.

meanwhile, caramelize the onions Heat the butter and olive oil in
a large, heavy skillet over medium-low heat. Add onions, sprinkle with salt
and a little pepper, and cook until they're tender and sweet, stirring occasionally, about 30 minutes. Add the kale ribbons, and cook until they wilt
a bit, about 5 minutes. Stir together the onion-kale mixture, wild rice, and
1 cup grated cheese in a large bowl. Season to taste with additional salt
and pepper, if needed.

assemble the gratin Use 1 tablespoon butter to generously coat a
2-quart baking dish. Spread the wild-rice mixture into prepared gratin and
pour broth over it. Sprinkle remaining cheese over gratin. Toss breadcrumbs
with 1 tablespoon melted butter and salt and pepper to taste; sprinkle over
cheese.

Bake for 30 to 35 minutes, or until a little bubbly and beginning to brown
on top.

mushroom bourguignon

*B*efore I decided that a life without pulled pork was no longer one I wanted to participate in, I was a vegetarian for more than a decade. An unwavering one. I resolutely believed that the things people believed they liked about meat dishes had nothing to do with meat itself, but the flavors and techniques used to cook them. Fried chicken was about the crisp coating, and bacon about the holy matrimony of smoke, salt, and fat. And although these days I gleefully indulge in all food groups, I'm still applying elements of one side of the food chain to the other.

Why should beef have all of the bourguignoning fun? Mushrooms are aptly "meaty," take well to longer cooking times, and delight in drinking up rich sauces around them. The hearty flavor of layered onions, wine, broth, and tomatoes is not lost when you leave out the beef. Yet this dish is about more than substitutions and shortcuts—it's about getting one of the best classically complex French flavors in your kitchen on a weekday night with only a moderate amount of effort and minimal cooking time.

* * *

Heat 1 tablespoon olive oil and 1 tablespoon butter in a medium-sized Dutch oven or heavy saucepan over high heat. Sear the mushrooms and pearl onions until they begin to take on a little color—your mushrooms will make a delightful "squeak-squeak" as they're pushed around the hot pan—but the mushrooms do not yet release any liquid, about 3 or 4 minutes. Remove mushrooms and onions from the pan and set aside.

Lower the flame to medium, and add the second tablespoon of olive oil. Toss the carrot, onion, thyme, a few good pinches of salt, and several grinds of black pepper in the pan, and cook for 5 minutes, stirring occasionally, until the onion is lightly browned. Add the garlic, and cook for just 1 more minute. Season with more salt and pepper.

Add the wine to the pot, scraping any stuck bits off the bottom, then turn the heat all the way up and reduce it by half, which will take about 4 to

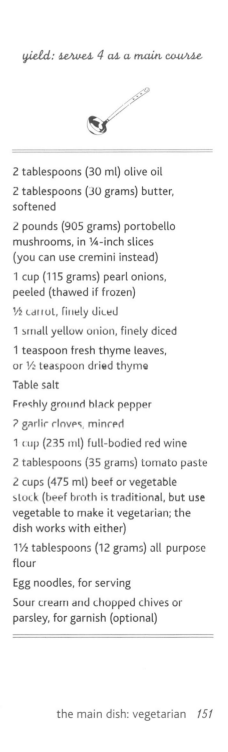

yield: serves 4 as a main course

2 tablespoons (30 ml) olive oil

2 tablespoons (30 grams) butter, softened

2 pounds (905 grams) portobello mushrooms, in ¼-inch slices (you can use cremini instead)

1 cup (115 grams) pearl onions, peeled (thawed if frozen)

½ carrot, finely diced

1 small yellow onion, finely diced

1 teaspoon fresh thyme leaves, or ½ teaspoon dried thyme

Table salt

Freshly ground black pepper

2 garlic cloves, minced

1 cup (235 ml) full-bodied red wine

2 tablespoons (35 grams) tomato paste

2 cups (475 ml) beef or vegetable stock (beef broth is traditional, but use vegetable to make it vegetarian; the dish works with either)

1½ tablespoons (12 grams) all purpose flour

Egg noodles, for serving

Sour cream and chopped chives or parsley, for garnish (optional)

5 minutes. Stir in the tomato paste and the stock. Add back the mushrooms and pearl onions with any juices that have collected, and bring the mixture to a boil; reduce the temperature so it simmers for 10 to 15 minutes, or until both the mushrooms and onions are very tender.

Combine the flour and the remaining butter with a fork; stir this into the stew. Season to taste with salt and pepper. Lower the heat, and simmer for 10 more minutes. If the sauce is too thin, boil it down to reduce to a "coating" consistency. Season with additional salt and pepper if needed.

To serve, spoon the stew over a bowl of egg noodles, dollop with sour cream, if using, and sprinkle with optional chives or parsley.

do ahead   The mushroom stew reheats very well on the second and third days, in a large saucepan over low heat.

the main dish: seafood, poultry, and meat

vermouth mussels with tarragon oven fries

seared halibut and gazpacho salsa with
tomato vinaigrette

pancetta, white bean, and swiss chard pot pies

sesame-spiced turkey meatballs and
smashed chickpea salad

mustard milanese with an arugula fennel salad

flat roasted chicken with tiny potatoes

harvest roast chicken with grapes,
olives, and rosemary

pork chops with cider, horseradish, and dill

balsamic and beer–braised short ribs
with parsnip purée

maya's sweet and sour holiday brisket and
roasted fingerling and carrot coins

tomato-glazed meatloaves with
brown butter mashed potatoes

pistachio masala lamb chops with
cucumber mint raita

vermouth mussels with tarragon oven fries

As a gateway seafood, there's nothing less obvious to people than mussels. "Really? You didn't start with shrimp? Lobster? Not even lobster dipped in butter and lemon?" But I didn't, and I know why: the best mussels are steamed open with wine, shallots, and butter and served with French fries; shrimp cocktail has *nothing* on that. Please, don't even try to argue it. Yes, husband, I'm talking to you.

They're also one of my favorite things to make as an "Oh, this? I just threw this together!" kind of weekday-night surprise-visitor meal. And you wouldn't even be lying. You do have to "just throw them" together; in fact, you have no choice, because you have to buy the mussels on your way home and you have to cook them quickly. With a big green salad and a crusty baguette (your friends should bring the wine; you are, after all, making them dinner), people will feel as if they've hit the jackpot. It was because of this that I discovered that mussels are great cooked in wine, but even better with vermouth (an aromatic fortified wine with herbs). I discovered this because I don't always have wine around, but vermouth keeps, and therefore it stays.

But the real clincher for me, as someone who takes French fries seriously enough to consider them one of her five favorite foods, was cracking the oven-fries code. Not even someone as insane as me is going to deep-fry on a weekday night for a quick meal. I find most oven fries tough and hollow, more of an apology for not being deep-fried until golden and crisp than an acceptable substitution. It wasn't until I was watching the Food Network one day and saw Michael Chiarello first parboil his fries that I had my *Aha!* moment. The thing is, the best French fries are cooked twice: once to cook them throughout, and a second time to brown and crisp their edges. Oven fries rarely follow this formula. But by boiling them first, you lock in a ton of moisture; by roasting them to finish, you get that toasty exterior and light crunch. I fiddled with his formula many ways over the years—I boil mine for less time, so they're less likely to fall apart when drained; I always use Yukon Golds; I use less olive oil

yield: serves 2 to 4

tarragon oven fries

3 tablespoons (45 ml) olive oil

1½ pounds (680 grams) Yukon Gold potatoes, peeled if you so desire

Coarse salt

Freshly ground black pepper

1½ tablespoons minced fresh tarragon

vermouth mussels

2 pounds (905 grams) mussels

2 tablespoons (30 grams) unsalted butter

¼ cup minced shallots (2 large) or minced white onion

½ cup (118 ml) dry white vermouth

2 teaspoons chopped fresh tarragon

by oiling the pan, not the fries; and I preheat the pan, so the potatoes land on it with a sizzle—but that first step makes all the difference. Just ask the taste tester.

*   *   *

make the oven fries Preheat your oven to 450 degrees. Coat a large baking sheet with 2 tablespoons olive oil. Slice the potatoes into ⅜-inch-thick matchsticks. Transfer them to a pot, and cover them with cold water. Bring the potatoes to a simmer, and let them cook until they are halfway done, about 5 minutes (a paring knife will resist going all the way through the potato). Carefully drain them (they'll want to break, so removing them with a slotted spoon might make it easier) and pat them dry on paper towels.

Set the prepared baking sheet in the oven before you drain the potatoes, and let it heat for 3 to 4 minutes. Remove the baking sheet with a pot holder. Spread the fries on sheet. Drizzle them with remaining tablespoon olive oil; sprinkle with coarse salt and freshly ground black pepper. Roast them for 25 minutes, tossing the tray about to redistribute and turn the fries after 10 and then 20 minutes.

Remove the tray from the oven, then toss the fries with additional seasoning, if needed, and fresh tarragon.

clean your mussels There are a zillion ways to do this, and this is mine: I put them in a big bowl of very cold water for about 10 minutes. This encourages the mussels to expel their sand. Scoop the mussels out (not dump; if you dump the sandy water over them, it defeats the purpose) one by one, and scrub them under running water. Most cultivated mussels have the bissus (beard) removed, but if one lingers, yank it toward the hinge (if you do it away from the hinge, it can kill the mussel prematurely) or cut it with a knife. Discard any mussels with chipped shells, or mussels that are not completely shut; they are more than likely dead, and it's not worth finding out if it may or may not make you sick, right?

cook mussels Bring the butter, shallots, and vermouth to a boil together in a medium pot. Add the mussels, cover, and steam them over high heat until they open. You can start checking at 3 minutes, but it can take up to 6. I like to use the lid and pot holders and shake them around a little from time to time, to make sure they're getting equal access to the vermouth and heat.

Once the mussels have swung open (discard any that have not), transfer them to bowls with a slotted spoon. Turn the heat all the way up, and boil the cooking broth for 1 minute, then ladle this over the mussels. Garnish with tarragon, serve with the fries, and eat immediately.

seared halibut and gazpacho salsa
with tomato vinaigrette

I 'm a closet picky eater, and it rarely takes long into a restaurant meal for someone to unearth one of my many, many forms of food fussiness. More or less, people like me have to learn how to cook or they might not eat.

Take soup, for example. I don't like it cold. I cannot get my head around the idea of cold vegetables puréed in a bowl. This means I miss out on gazpacho—or would, had I not hacked it into a summery salsa a long time ago. I know gazpacho-eaters are on to something, because this stuff tastes really good as a salad.

But the biggest of my dark eating secrets is my relationship with fish: It's not a good one. I don't like it—not broiled, not baked, not wrapped *en papillote*, and not even breaded and fried and served with lemon and hot sauce. To my credit, I routinely try to get myself to love fish, but I rarely get past a bite. "Well, that was tasty," I'll say politely. And I mean it; I just don't reach for more.

Fortunately, I have a friend who loves fish. Most of my friends do, actually; I suppose they're normal and well adjusted and *overrated* things like that. But my friend Angie in particular also loves cooking and has a sixth sense about food. Without her, this would be a fish-free book. With her, however, I discovered halibut, which, it turns out, is a great gateway fish. It's delicate but sturdy, flaky but minimally, you know, "fishy." And it goes spectacularly well with a light summer salad, like one modeled after a cold soup. It might also be good alongside a cup of gazpacho, but I'll never find out, because . . . Look, I ate fish. One new thing at a time, please.

*   *   *

make tomato vinaigrette In a blender or food processor, purée the tomato until smooth. Add sherry vinegar. With machine running, drizzle in olive oil slowly, in a very thin stream. Season with salt and pepper. Set aside.

yield: serves 4

tomato vinaigrette
1 medium tomato, peeled (if desired), seeded, and chopped

2 tablespoons (30 ml) sherry vinegar

¼ cup (60 ml) olive oil

Table salt

Freshly ground black pepper

fish
Four 6 to 8 ounce (70 to 225 gram) halibut fillets

Olive oil to coat pan

Table salt

Freshly ground black pepper

salsa
2 large beefsteak or 4 medium Roma tomatoes (about 1 pound or 905 grams), seeded (if desired) and diced

½ English cucumber (½ pound or 225 grams), diced

2 bell peppers, red or a combination of colors if available

½ small sweet onion, such as Vidalia, diced

3 tablespoons minced fresh parsley (optional, for garnish)

seared halibut and gazpacho salsa with tomato vinaigrette (continued)

cook fish Bring the halibut to room temperature. Season generously with salt and freshly ground black pepper on both sides. Heat a large sauté pan over medium-high heat. Once the pan is hot, coat it evenly with olive oil. Once oil is hot, lay fish in the pan (depending on the size of your pan and how much fish you are cooking, you may need to cook this in multiple batches) and cook for 3 to 4 minutes, until the fish is golden underneath but not sticking to the pan. Carefully flip the fillets. Cook for a few more minutes, until a fork cuts through easily and the meat is opaque white and flaky.

assemble salsa Toss salsa ingredients together on a plate. Arrange the halibut on top. Drizzle on the vinaigrette to taste. Serve with additional vinaigrette on the side.

cooking note Can't get halibut? Try using another flaky white fish, such as cod.

pancetta, white bean, and swiss chard pot pies

Over the years, we've had a lot of dinner parties. I've made mussels and fries and red pepper soup; I've made meatballs and spaghetti repeatedly; brisket and noodles were on repeat until I got the kinks ironed out of the recipe in this chapter, and there was this one time when I decided to make nothing but delicate flatbreads for dinner. It was a terrible idea. Don't do this unless you want to spend three days making doughs and mincing vegetables, only to have everyone leave hungry.

I'm pretty sure if you asked my friends what the very best thing I've ever served them was, they'd still go on about chicken pot pies I made from an Ina Garten recipe all those years ago. People, it turns out, go berserk for comfort food—especially comfort food with a flaky pastry lid—doubly so on a rainy night. I liked them too, but the chicken—which often ends up getting cooked twice—has always been my least favorite part. What I do like is the buttery velouté that forms the sauce, and it was from there that I decided to make a pot pie I'd choose over chicken, peas, and carrots any night of the week.

You really have to try this for a dinner party, especially if your guests were expecting something fancy. The crust and stews can be made up to 24 hours in advance, and need only to be baked to come to the table; this means that you could spend that time getting cute, or at least making pudding for dessert. And if people are expecting the same old same old beneath the lid, this will be a good surprise—the lid is so flaky, it's closer to a croissant than a pie crust, and the pancetta, beans, and greens make a perfect stew, one you'd enjoy even without a bronzed crust. But, you know, it helps.

*   *   *

make lids In a large, wide bowl (preferably one that you can get your hands into), combine the flour and salt. Add the butter and, using a pastry blender, cut it up and into the flour mixture until it resembles little pebbles. Keep breaking up the bits of butter until the texture is like uncooked couscous. In a small dish, whisk together the sour cream, vinegar, and water, and

yield: serves 4

lid

2 cups (250 grams) all-purpose flour

½ teaspoon table salt

13 tablespoons (185 grams or 1 stick plus 5 tablespoons) unsalted butter

6 tablespoons (90 grams) sour cream or whole Greek yogurt (i.e., a strained yogurt)

1 tablespoon (15 ml) white wine vinegar

¼ cup (60 ml) ice water

1 egg, beaten with 1 tablespoon water, for egg wash

filling

2 tablespoons (30 ml) olive oil

4 ounces (115 grams or ¾ to 1 cup) ¼-inch-diced pancetta

1 large or 2 small onions, finely chopped

1 large carrot, finely chopped

1 large stalk celery, finely chopped

Pinch of red pepper flakes

Salt and freshly ground black pepper

2 garlic cloves, minced

Thinly sliced Swiss chard leaves from an 8-to-10-ounce (225-to-285-gram) bundle (4 cups); if leaves are very wide, you can halve them lengthwise

combine it with the butter-flour mixture. Using a flexible spatula, stir the wet and the dry together until a craggy dough forms. If needed, get your hands into the bowl to knead it a few times into one big ball. Pat it into a flattish ball, wrap it in plastic wrap, and chill it in the fridge for 1 hour or up to 2 days.

make filling Heat 1 tablespoon olive oil over medium-high heat in a large, wide saucepan, and then add the pancetta. Brown the pancetta, turning it frequently, so that it colors and crisps on all sides; this takes about 10 minutes. Remove it with a slotted spoon, and drain it on paper towels before transferring to a medium bowl. Leave the heat on and the renderings in the pan. Add an additional tablespoon of olive oil if needed and heat it until it is shimmering. Add onions, carrot, celery, red pepper flakes, and a few pinches of salt, and cook over medium heat until the vegetables are softened and begin to take on color, about 7 to 8 minutes. Add the garlic, and cook for 1 minute more. Add the greens and cook until wilted, about 2 to 3 minutes. Season with the additional salt and freshly ground black pepper to taste. Transfer all of the cooked vegetables to the bowl with the pancetta, and set aside.

make sauce Wipe out the large saucepan; don't worry if any bits remain stuck to the bottom. Then melt the butter in the saucepan over medium-low heat. Add the flour, and stir with a whisk until combined. Continue cook-

3½ tablespoons (50 grams) butter

3½ tablespoons (25 grams) all-purpose flour

3¼ cups (765 ml) sodium-free or low-sodium chicken or vegetable broth

2 cups white beans, cooked and drained, or from one and a third 15.5-ounce (440-gram) cans

do ahead

The dough, wrapped twice in plastic wrap and slipped into a freezer bag, will keep for up to 2 days in the fridge, and for a couple months in the freezer. The filling can be made up to a day in advance and stored in a covered container in the fridge.

cooking note

For a vegetarian version, skip the pancetta and cook your vegetables in 2 tablespoons olive oil instead of 1.

ing for 2 minutes, stirring the whole time, until it begins to take on a little color. Whisk in the broth, one ladleful at a time, mixing completely between additions. Once you've added one third of the broth, you can begin to add the rest more quickly, two to three ladlefuls at a time; at this point you can scrape up any bits that were stuck to the bottom—they'll add great flavor. Once all of the broth is added, stirring the whole time, bring the mixture to a boil and reduce it to a simmer. Cook the sauce until it is thickened and gravylike, about 10 minutes. Season with salt and pepper. Stir the white beans and reserved vegetables into the sauce.

Preheat your oven to 375 degrees.

assemble and cook pot pies. Divide the filling between four oven-proof 2 cup bowls (you'll have about 1½ cups filling in each) and arrange them on a baking sheet or roasting pan. Divide the dough into four pieces, and roll it out into rounds that will cover your bowls with an overhang, or about 1 inch wider in diameter than your bowls. Whisk the egg wash and brush it lightly around the top rim of your bowls (to keep the lid glued on; nobody likes losing their lid!) and drape the pastry over each, pressing gently to adhere it. Brush the lids with egg wash, then cut decorative vents in each to help steam escape.

Bake until crust is lightly bronzed and filling is bubbling, about 30 to 35 minutes.

sesame-spiced turkey meatballs
and smashed chickpea salad

I'd like to tell you that I'm just brimming with self-awareness, but, alas, there's just so much evidence to the contrary—pretty much every boyfriend I had from eighteen to twenty-seven and a shiny orange duvet that burned our eyeballs for six weeks before I admitted what a bad purchase it was and stuffed it in a closet where it still lives today—that I won't bother.

And I'd like to tell you that at the wise old age of "But didn't we just celebrate your thirtieth birthday last year?" I've become much more insightful as to my motives in and out of the kitchen, but here are these meatballs, telling me otherwise. I pulled the idea out of what I thought was thin air: tiny, intensely spiced turkey meatballs with a crisp edge. I knew they needed cumin, and coriander, and Aleppo pepper. I thought toasted sesame seeds would add a light crunch and nutty flavor. And I knew that, above all else, they'd sit on a bed of crushed chickpeas dressed with lemon and garlic and spices. . . . Maybe you'd even serve them in pitas. And it took me weeks, longer even, until I was going over the recipe and photos, to realize that, duh, "thin air" was actually a falafel stand. I turned one of the most beloved vegetarian meals on the planet into meatballs.

You know, mostly. But what I really think we should talk about is this salad. I've had my share of chickpea salads, most of which are, you know, chickpea-flavored, but this one, one I devised mostly as a complement to spicy meatballs, became my instant favorite. Sumac is a dark-red ground powder that tastes almost like a sour paprika and is used a lot in Middle Eastern cooking. Here, it's dreamy, and adds an extra dimension to the tart lemon-garlic dressing.

* * *

form meatballs Preheat your oven to 400 degrees. Combine all of the meatball ingredients in a medium bowl with a fork, breaking up the clumps of meat until the ingredients are evenly distributed. Form turkey mixture

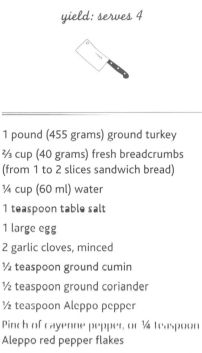

yield: serves 4

1 pound (455 grams) ground turkey

⅔ cup (40 grams) fresh breadcrumbs (from 1 to 2 slices sandwich bread)

¼ cup (60 ml) water

1 teaspoon table salt

1 large egg

2 garlic cloves, minced

½ teaspoon ground cumin

½ teaspoon ground coriander

½ teaspoon Aleppo pepper

Pinch of cayenne pepper, or ¼ teaspoon Aleppo red pepper flakes

2 tablespoons (15 grams) sesame seeds, toasted

Olive oil, to coat pan

into 1½-inch, or golf-ball-sized, meatballs, and arrange them on a tray. I find wet hands make it easier to form the meatballs and keep them from getting sticky.

cook meatballs Heat a generous slick of oil in a large ovenproof sauté pan with a lid. Brown the meatballs in batches, being careful not to crowd the pan or nudge them before they are nicely browned. These meatballs are soft, so use a gentle hand. Transfer the meatballs to a paper-towel-lined tray, and continue cooking in more batches until they are all browned.

Discard the oil, and wipe all but a thin layer from the pan. Return all of the meatballs to the pan, and transfer to preheated oven. Bake until a thermometer reads an internal temperature of 160 to 165 degrees, or about 10 to 15 minutes.

Serve with smashed chickpeas (below).

smashed chickpea salad with lemon and sumac

*   *   *

yield: about 2 cups salad

1¾ cups (440 grams) cooked chickpeas, drained and rinsed

Handful of pitted, halved, and very thinly sliced green olives

½ teaspoon ground sumac, plus more for garnish

Chopped fresh parsley

2 tablespoons (30 ml) freshly squeezed lemon juice

1 small garlic clove, minced

Pinch of cayenne pepper

¼ teaspoon table salt

Olive oil

Mix everything but the olive oil in a small to mid-sized bowl. Very lightly smash the chickpea mixture with the back of a fork or a potato masher. You're not looking for a hummuslike purée, but something closer to a coarse chop, with a few smaller bits to hold it together. Dress the chickpeas with a drizzle of olive oil and stir to combine. Adjust seasoning to taste.

cooking note
These meatballs are also excellent made with ground lamb.

mustard milanese with an arugula fennel salad

Were I a different kind of person—perhaps the kind who always has loaves of homemade bread and bags of homemade chicken stock in the freezer and never, ever has glare-offs with sinks full of dirty dishes—it might not have taken me most of my lifetime to accept that boneless, skinless chicken breasts are possibly not the worst food on earth.

However, in my actual life, the one where I walk by the basket of unfolded laundry for so many days that by the time the clothes are folded they look like they came from the hamper, I considered boneless, skinless chicken breasts to be the bane of my cooking existence. They were always dry and overcooked—like "pressed sawdust," I'd tell people—their popularity made them wasteful (since most people weren't buying the remaining parts of the bird), and I made every effort to avoid them, which was amusing at times, because I was certain I was the only person on earth who didn't delight in white chicken cubes on a salad.

Then I discovered—like generations of cooks before me—that, no matter how little you like an ingredient, you will change your mind when you have it pounded thin, breaded, and deep-fried. You might actually fall in love. These thin and crisp slices of chicken are moist and crunchy and packed with one of my favorite flavors, Dijon mustard, which makes things like chicken and salad sing.

*   *   *

prepare chicken On a cutting board with a very sharp knife, butterfly your chicken breasts, and slice them all the way through, so that you end up with four thin cutlets. With a meat pounder (not a tenderizer), pound your cutlets out between two pieces of plastic wrap to ¼-inch thickness. Season the chicken on both sides with salt and pepper.

Grab three big plates, and line them up on your counter. Pour the flour into the first one. In a small dish, whisk together the egg white, smooth Dijon, garlic, oregano, and lemon zest. Pour half of this mixture into the bottom of the second plate. In the third plate, spread out the breadcrumbs.

yield: serves 4

for the chicken

2 boneless, skinless chicken breasts

Table salt

Freshly ground black pepper

½ cup (65 grams) all-purpose flour

1 large egg white

2 tablespoons (45 grams) smooth Dijon mustard

2 garlic cloves, minced

1 teaspoon dried oregano

½ teaspoon freshly grated lemon zest

1½ cups (80 grams) coarse, lightweight breadcrumbs, such as panko (see cooking note)

Mix of vegetable and olive oil, for frying

for the salad

3 tablespoons (45 ml) freshly squeezed lemon juice (from 1 large lemon)

2 tablespoons (30 grams) whole seed or coarse Dijon mustard

1 tablespoon smooth Dijon mustard

¼ cup (80 ml) olive oil

5 ounces (140 grams) baby arugula leaves

Small fennel bulb (5 ounces or 140 grams)

Dredge each piece of chicken lightly in flour, then heavily in the egg-white–mustard mixture, and generously in the breadcrumbs. Repeat with second piece of chicken, then refill egg-white–mustard plate, and repeat with final two pieces of chicken. Arrange the breaded cutlets on a large tray, and chill them in the fridge for 1 hour, or up to 1 day (covered with plastic wrap). This helps the coating set.

Preheat your oven to 175 degrees.

cook chicken Pour ½ inch of oil—use a mixture of olive and vegetable oil, or the frying oil of your choice—in a large pan, and heat over medium-high heat. Test the heat with a flick of water—if it hisses, you're good to go. Cook the chicken until golden brown on both sides, about 3 to 4 minutes on the first and 2 to 3 minutes on the second. Remove the chicken from heat, and salt and pepper on both sides while draining on paper towels. Once it's drained, transfer the chicken to a tray to keep in the warm oven. Repeat with additional oil and remaining pieces of chicken.

meanwhile, prepare salad In a small bowl, whisk lemon juice and mustards together, then whisk in olive oil in a thin stream. Pour three-quarters of this into a large bowl. Add arugula to bowl. Thinly shave your fennel bulb on a mandoline, or cut it as thinly as you can with a sharp knife, and add this to the arugula.

to serve When you're ready to serve it, toss the salad. Arrange one piece of chicken from the warm oven on a plate. Drizzle a few drops of the reserved salad dressing directly onto the chicken (you'll thank me when you try it), and pile the salad on top. Season with salt and pepper, and eat immediately.

cooking note
Can't find panko breadcrumbs? Here's how I fake it when I run out: Preheat your oven to 350 degrees. Tear one or two slices of soft, crustless white bread into 1-inch pieces, and pulse them in the food processor until they are coarsely ground. This will make a generous ½ cup. Transfer the crumbs to a rimmed baking sheet, and bake them until they are golden brown and dry, for about 15 minutes, stirring occasionally. Cool the breadcrumbs before using them.

flat roasted chicken with tiny potatoes

I became a roast chicken person while visiting as fine a place to fall in love as any: the streets of Paris. It wasn't my first visit to Paris with my husband, but it was the first time we stayed at a real, actual Parisian apartment, with a kitchen at our disposal. At a nearby market, I discovered green olives so mild they still tasted vegetal. I bought fleur de sel that didn't cost an arm or a leg. I learned that in Paris people wait patiently in line for their turn at stands, and never touch the produce, just trust the sellers to choose the right apple for them. And I discovered what has to be one of the universe's top ten foods, the small yellow potatoes that roast under the racks of small rotisserie chickens they sell all over Paris. Yes, they roast *in* the chicken drippings. We brought a chicken and an unglamorous shovelful of potatoes home in a foil-lined bag and have not stopped gushing over it since.

Upon returning home, I studied hard the doctrine of Popular Roast Chicken. From *The Zuni Café Cookbook*, I learned to have faith that the chicken skin will crisp itself in a high-heat oven, and not to load it with oils and rubs. From Thomas Keller, I learned to rain the salt down on the outside of a bird, and to trust that it manages to never leave the chicken too salty, just perfect. From buying birds at the greenmarket, I learned that smaller, cleaner birds taste incredible—they have enough fat so they don't need anything extra to taste rich, enough flavor so you can rely on the simplest of preparations, and a compact enough size so they bake evenly without your forcing them to do handstands. And from being crunched for time, I learned that taking out the backbone from a chicken—spatchcocking, it's delightfully called—meant that we could have roasted chicken with the maximum amount of crispy skin in a minimum of time. And, yes, it is always roasted on a bed of small yellow potatoes.

This dish is a win-win for me, and if I don't dawdle, I can get it on the table in only an hour. Did you hear that? You're 1 hour from glossy, crackly-skinned chicken, perfectly complemented by wee potatoes browned in drippings, and a side of green beans. I honestly don't even know why you're still reading this. Get thee to the kitchen!

yield: serves 4

One 3-to-3½-pound (1⅓-to-1½-kg) chicken

Table salt

Freshly ground black pepper

1½ pounds (680 grams) tiny yellow potatoes, peeled

2 tablespoons (30 ml) melted butter or olive oil, for potatoes

1 lemon, to finish

1 tablespoon minced fresh thyme leaves, to finish

*   *   *

Preheat your oven to 450 degrees. Using a pair of sharp kitchen shears, remove the backbone of the chicken and discard it (or freeze and save it for making stock). Season the cavity generously with salt and freshly ground black pepper. Lay the chicken, breast side up, in a roasting pan (I adore my 12-inch cast-iron skillet for this; it works best with 3-pound birds), and gently pat the breast skin dry with a paper towel. Generously season the top of the bird with more salt and freshly ground black pepper. Nestle the potatoes around the chicken, and drizzle them lightly with butter or olive oil. Sprinkle the potatoes with salt and pepper.

Roast the chicken for 30 to 45 minutes, or until a thermometer inserted into the thigh registers 165 degrees. Toss the potatoes after about 20 minutes, so that they cook evenly. When the chicken has finished cooking, transfer potatoes to a large serving platter. Remove the legs, thighs, wings, and breasts from the spatchcocked chicken, and arrange them with potatoes. Squeeze juice of entire lemon over dish, then sprinkle with thyme. Serve with simply cooked vegetables. Eat at once.

harvest roast chicken with grapes, olives, and rosemary

This is my absolutely favorite example of why I—and possibly you—should never listen to myself. Because I couldn't have been further off in my guess that this dish would be an epic disaster.

You're probably wondering why I made it anyway. The thing is, I think browning and then oven-roasting chicken, making a sauce from the pan drippings, is one of the greatest ways you can cook a bird—it's quick, so it totally passes muster on a weekday night. It's not terribly expensive, especially if you cut up a whole bird yourself. But, because it's cooked in pieces, it can accommodate any arrangement of pickiness—say, a husband who only likes white meat, a wife who only likes dark meat, and a child who insists he doesn't like chicken while chewing on a drumstick. You can use whatever mix of parts you wish. So I was eager to include a recipe with this method in the lineup. From there, though, I hit a wall, marching my way through all of my crutch ingredients one summer—leeks! Dijon! tomatoes!—and coming up, well, bored.

Then, one day, the temperature dropped, and I could smell September in the air. Let nobody tell you otherwise: Fall is the very best time to roast a chicken. It's no longer so hot that you resent turning on the oven, and not yet so cold that you crave only soups, stews, and braises. I started wondering how olives, grapes, and rosemary would taste roasted together and immediately rejected it, because I find most table grapes too sweet and most readily available olives too salty, and rosemary doesn't always cook into a dish the way I want it to. And then I made it anyway, with the menu for pizza delivery pulled up on my laptop, because I was in a huge rush and clearly it wasn't going to work out anyway, and proceeded to be blown away by how obvious it was that these things were meant to be together.

The saltiness of the olives muted the sweetness of the grapes; the sweetness of the grapes made the overly salty olives delightful; and the rosemary, it's just home. My husband, who insists to this day

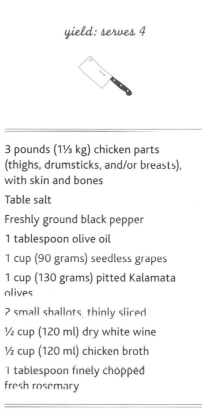

yield: serves 4

3 pounds (1⅓ kg) chicken parts (thighs, drumsticks, and/or breasts), with skin and bones

Table salt

Freshly ground black pepper

1 tablespoon olive oil

1 cup (90 grams) seedless grapes

1 cup (130 grams) pitted Kalamata olives

2 small shallots, thinly sliced

½ cup (120 ml) dry white wine

½ cup (120 ml) chicken broth

1 tablespoon finely chopped fresh rosemary

that he doesn't like fruit in savory dishes, had seconds. Since then, I have made it highbrow (with local grapes and imported olives) and low (street cart grapes and sad olives scavenged from the back of the fridge) and have never found it less than perfect.

* * *

Preheat your oven to 450 degrees with a rack in middle. Pat chicken dry, and season generously with salt and freshly ground black pepper. Heat oil in an ovenproof 12-inch heavy skillet (use a cast-iron skillet if you've got one) over medium-high heat until it shimmers. Working in two batches, brown the chicken, skin side down first and turning them over once, about 5 minutes per batch. I like to take a lot of care in this step, not moving the chicken until the skin releases itself and has a nice bronze on it.

Return the pieces to the pan, skin side up, and surround the pieces with grapes, olives, and shallots. Roast the chicken in the oven until it has just cooked through and the juices run clear, about 20 minutes. Transfer the chicken, grapes, and olives to a platter, then add wine and chicken broth to the pan juices in skillet. Bring liquid to a boil, scraping up any brown bits, until it has reduced by half, for 2 to 3 minutes. Strain sauce, if desired, then pour it over the chicken. Garnish with rosemary and see how long it takes guests to offer to slurp the sauce up with a spoon.

pork chops with cider, horseradish, and dill

Although I didn't grow up in a kosher home, I would not say that my family embraced *treif* with any vigor. There weren't any pork tenderloins or braised shoulders for barbecue. Baked hams really weren't a thing when I was growing up. My parents might have had shrimp egg rolls at Chinese restaurants and nobody raised an eyebrow if you had bacon with your eggs at a diner, but pork chops just never came up in conversation. I won't attempt to explain these idiosyncrasies, I only wanted to set the stage for how strange I found it that my Jewish husband loved pork chops, something that when we met I wouldn't even have recognized at the butcher's counter.

And so it wasn't long before I started occasionally bringing them home for dinner, but it did take some time before I found them as appealing as he did. I found my favorites not in the thick, hearty chops boasted on restaurant menus but thinner chops, and I loved them with apple cider, dill, and horseradish, the liking for which I suspect originated deep within my Germanic/Eastern European blood (though I imagine nobody in my lineage previously applied them to pork).

Cooked together, these flavors are my happy place: tangy, sweet, and salty with a mellow, clearing bite. They're hardly the prettiest dish—being brown against beige—but they disappear too quickly for anyone to notice.

*   *   *

Whisk the glaze ingredients together in a small dish, and set aside.

Trim any excess fat around chops until it is but a thin ribbon, no more than ⅛ inch thick. Pat the chops dry with a paper towel, and generously season them with salt and pepper. Heat the oil in a heavy 12-inch skillet over medium-high heat until the oil starts to smoke. Add the pork chops to the skillet, and cook them until they are well browned, about 3 minutes. Turn the chops, and cook 1 minute longer; then transfer chops to a plate and pour off any fat in skillet.

yield: serves 2 to 4

glaze

½ cup (120 ml) cider vinegar

½ cup (120 ml) hard or pressed apple cider

2 tablespoons (30 grams) freshly grated or prepared horseradish

½ teaspoon table salt

Pinch of cayenne pepper

chops

4 bone-in loin pork chops, ½ inch thick (1½ pounds/680 grams total), preferably at room temperature

Table salt

Freshly ground black pepper

1 tablespoon olive oil

1 tablespoon chopped fresh dill

Pour glaze mixture into the emptied skillet. Bring it to a simmer, and cook until mixture thickens enough so your spatula leaves a trail when scraped across the pan, about 2 to 4 minutes. Return the chops and any accumulated juices from their plate to skillet; turn to coat both sides with glaze. Cook them over medium heat in the glaze until the center of the chops registers 140 degrees on instant-read thermometer, about 5 minutes. Adjust the seasonings to taste. Transfer the chops to a serving platter and pour the glaze from the pan over them. Sprinkle with dill, and eat immediately.

balsamic and beer–braised short ribs with parsnip purée

$\mathcal{I}$ was not a cooking wunderkind. I did not braise my first cuttlefish at eight or roast a chicken at twelve. When I was twenty-eight, I decided to make short ribs for the very first time, and when our families came over for dinner that night, I was in a tizzy because I was convinced I'd wrecked the dish. The bones, they were all falling out of the ribs! It was my mother-in-law who gently informed me that meat so tender that it falls off the bone is a good thing.

This began my ongoing love affair with short ribs. They are one of the most perfect dinner-party foods, because their cooking time is flexible enough that if people show up late your short ribs don't mind. If everyone cancels, it's cool, because they're better the next day. They're fairly inexpensive, which is helpful when that one friend brings another friend to dinner who also has two friends in town and you don't mind, right?

Finally, it's really hard to mess ribs up; pretty much any combination of wine or beer, something from the onion family and something tomatoish makes them weepingly delicious. Still, this version, which I like to call "midnight short ribs," is my favorite since I have a soft spot for foods such as dark ales and syrupy vinegars, and here, together, they make a pitch-dark, intensely flavored, infallible braise that drapes gorgeously over buttery mashed parsnips with a little kick of horseradish.

* * *

prepare the braise Season the short ribs generously and on all sides with salt and freshly ground pepper. Heat a large Dutch oven (7 to 8 quarts) over high heat, and add enough olive oil to coat the bottom. Once the oil is hot, brown the short ribs on all sides, in batches. I take my sweet time in this stage, making sure I get a nice brown sear on all six sides. A single batch can take me 10 to 15 minutes to brown. Transfer the browned ribs to a plate, and then repeat with remaining ribs.

yield: serves 4 to 6

5 pounds (about 2¼ kg) bone-in short ribs (English-style—i.e., separated; about 6 large or up to 10 smaller ones), at room temperature, trimmed of excess fat

Kosher salt

Freshly ground black pepper

2 tablespoons (30 ml) olive oil

1 large red onion, chopped

4 garlic cloves, smashed and peeled

2 tablespoons (35 grams) tomato paste

½ cup (120 ml) balsamic vinegar (no need to use your best aged balsamic here)

3 tablespoons (45 ml) Worcestershire sauce

2 bottles (24 ounces or 710 ml) dark beer, such as a black lager

2 to 3 cups (475 to 710 ml) beef stock

Minced fresh flat-leaf parsley, to serve (optional)

braise the ribs Preheat your oven to 325 degrees. Once all the ribs are browned and removed from pot, turn heat down to medium-high and pour off all but 1 tablespoon of the oil and fat. Add the onion, season with salt and pepper, and cook until softened and a little brown, about 10 minutes. Add the garlic cloves, and sauté for 3 minutes more. Add the tomato paste, and cook for another few minutes, until thickened; then add the vinegar, Worcestershire sauce, and beer, scraping up any bits stuck to the bottom. Return the browned ribs to the pot. If you can, arrange them all with their meatiest sides facedown. If you have too many ribs and not enough surface area, stand them up on their sides, with the bones vertical. Add enough beef stock just to cover the ribs. Bring the liquid to a simmer, then turn off heat. Cover the pot tightly with foil, then with a lid—I find when I don't use foil the liquid evaporates too much in the oven, leaving the ribs exposed and a bit dry.

Bake for 3 hours, or until the meat can easily be pierced with a knife, or pieces can be torn back with a fork. If the bones look as if they don't want to stay in much longer, that's another good sign. Remove from the oven and let the ribs rest for 15 minutes, uncovered. Skim as much fat as you can off the top.

to serve There are two ways to finish the dish. The first is the simplest route from oven to table; the second provides a little more texture and elegance.

option 1 Simply serve the short ribs as they are, with a side of the parsnip purée.

option 2 Preheat your oven to 420 degrees. Remove ribs from braise and spread them out on a large baking sheet. Roast them for 15 minutes, or until the edges start to crisp. Meanwhile, strain the braising liquid into a saucepan and simmer it over high heat for 10 to 15 minutes, until reduced by a third. The sauce should be fairly opaque and have more body to it. Arrange the roasted ribs on a serving platter and drape them generously with half the sauce. To serve, generously mound some parsnip purée on each serving plate or shallow bowl. Arrange 1 to 2 short ribs on the parsnips and ladle with additional sauce. Garnish with parsley, if using.

do ahead

When you are letting the ribs rest after cooking, it's a great time to take a break. You can chill the entire dish in its braising liquid in the fridge for up to one day. The advantage of this is that it will be very easy to remove the fat from the dish, as it will separate and firm up. Plus, ribs taste wonderful on day 2, and you'll look even better at your dinner party, having only had to reheat dinner, not cook it from scratch.

parsnip purée

*   *   *

2 pounds (905 grams) parsnips (about 6 medium), peeled, sliced into medium-sized chunks

4 tablespoons (55 grams or ½ stick) unsalted butter

⅓ cup (80 ml) heavy cream

1 tablespoon prepared horseradish sauce or freshly grated horseradish

½ teaspoon table salt

Freshly ground black pepper

In large, heavy pot, combine parsnips with enough cold water to cover. Place over moderately high heat, cover, and bring to a boil. Once boiling, reduce to a simmer and cook until tender, about 20 to 30 minutes, then drain.

Purée hot parsnips, butter, heavy cream, horseradish, salt, and freshly ground black pepper until smooth.

maya's sweet and sour holiday brisket and roasted fingerling and carrot coins

I just lied to you. This is not actually my mother-in-law's High Holiday brisket. My mother-in-law does indeed make the best brisket I've ever eaten, but what goes into the slow-cooker is a bottle of None of Your Business, a few spoonfuls of Also Not Going to Tell You, and a packet of So Many Questions Today! How Is My Beautiful Grandson? What you need to know is that the final result will repeatedly transcend your highest hopes for brisket and erase from your taste memory any recollection of grainy, dry, and bland failed brisket efforts.

So suffice to say that I have spent a ridiculous amount of time reverse-engineering those bottles and packets to create a brisket that, I promise, will turn you into something of a hero among friends scrounging for a palatable brisket recipe like clockwork every September, or on cold February evenings like the one when we served this dish for dinner. My version includes things you already have in your pantry while keeping the best part of the flavor intact—that is, the sweet and-sour flavor—think "Jewish barbecue sauce," not Chinese take-out. It works every time. It converts people who previously didn't consider brisket and noodles a dish that can easily become one of a cook's highest callings.

*   *   *

yield: serves 10 to 12

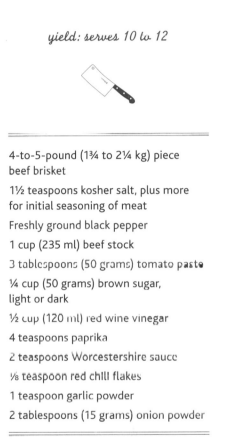

4-to-5-pound (1¾ to 2¼ kg) piece beef brisket

1½ teaspoons kosher salt, plus more for initial seasoning of meat

Freshly ground black pepper

1 cup (235 ml) beef stock

3 tablespoons (50 grams) tomato paste

¼ cup (50 grams) brown sugar, light or dark

½ cup (120 ml) red wine vinegar

4 teaspoons paprika

2 teaspoons Worcestershire sauce

⅛ teaspoon red chili flakes

1 teaspoon garlic powder

2 tablespoons (15 grams) onion powder

cook brisket Season the meat generously on both sides with kosher salt and freshly ground black pepper.

Whisk all of the remaining ingredients together in a medium bowl.

to make brisket in a slow-cooker Place meat in slow-cooker, pour sauce over it, and set it to cook at low setting for 10 hours.

to make in the oven Preheat your oven to 350 degrees. Place the meat in a baking dish or Dutch oven, and pour the sauce over it. Cover tightly

maya's sweet and sour holiday brisket (continued)

with foil or a tight-fitting lid. Bake for 3 hours, until tender enough to pull apart with a fork.

When the brisket is cooked but still hot, use a spoon to scrape off any large fat deposits around the edges of the meat.

If you're using a slow-cooker, transfer the brisket and all of its sauce to a baking dish. If you've baked it in the oven, you can continue in that same dish.

rest brisket Chill the entire dish in the fridge for several hours and up to one day; this resting time will enhance the flavor and texture of the meat. An hour before you are ready to serve it, preheat your oven to 300 degrees, and then remove the dish from the fridge. For a less oily final dish, you can remove all of the fat that has solidified with a slotted spoon.

to serve Carefully remove the meat from its sauce, and place on a large cutting board. Cut the brisket into ¼-to-½-inch slices, and carefully place the sliced meat (moving it in large sections with a spatula helps keep it together) back into the sauce. Spoon the sauce over the meat. Replace the lid, and reheat in the oven until bubbling at the edge; serve immediately.

do ahead

The entire brisket dish can be made over a day in advance. The leftovers, kept submerged in the sauce, reheat extremely well. The schedule I usually follow is to set it up in the slow-cooker right before I go to bed. The next morning, I move it to the fridge and forget about it until an hour before I need to serve it. Dinner for a crowd should always be this easy.

cooking note

Though this brisket can be made "low and slow" in an oven, a slow-cooker—yes, that seventies thing collecting dust in the far reaches of your most inaccessible cabinet—is a dream come true for fork-tender, flawlessly cooked brisket. If you have one, by all means use it; set it up the night before, and wake up with the centerpiece to your dinner party already cooked and ready to rest for a day. Brisket is always best on the second day.

roasted fingerling and carrot coins

* * *

2 pounds (905 grams) fingerling potatoes, sliced into ½-inch "coins"

2 pounds (905 grams) large carrots (about 4 to 5),
sliced into ½-inch "coins"

¼ cup (60 ml) olive oil

1½ teaspoons kosher salt

Freshly ground black pepper

2 tablespoons minced fresh dill, or herb of your choice

Preheat your oven to 400 degrees. Generously coat two large baking sheets with olive oil. Spread the vegetables out on the prepared sheets and drizzle them with any remaining oil before seasoning them with salt and freshly ground black pepper. Roast for 20 minutes before using a large spatula to flip the vegetables.

Resume roasting for another 10 to 15 minutes, until they are brown and crisp at the edges. The potatoes should be soft and tender inside, the carrots soft but not mushy.

Remove from the oven. Season with additional salt and pepper if necessary, then sprinkle with fresh dill and transfer to a serving dish.

tomato-glazed meatloaves with brown butter mashed potatoes

I'm a sucker for a good meatball. Something happens when you mix otherwise one-dimensional ground meats up with fresh breadcrumbs, herbs, seasonings, and bits of extra ingredients—and that thing is that I will swat your fork away to get at them first. However, it had always been my belief that I held no such adoration for meatloaf. I cleared my throat, stepped up on my invisible soapbox, and pronounced as much on my website one day. And one by one, readers gently whispered to me in the comments, "Deb, you do realize that meatloaf is like one giant meatball?"

Well, no. No, I had not. From that point on, it became my personal mission to retract my hasty remarks by finding meatloaf nirvana, especially once I realized that meatloaves were like meatballs with *even more flavor*. My version is busy with everything—a fine mirepoix, garlic, smoked paprika, piercing Dijon mustard, steak sauce, and a tangy tomato glaze—but I still couldn't get past the typical loglike meatloaf shape. So I decided not to. These little meatloaves masquerading as big meatballs fool nobody except maybe the meatloafphobic.

* * *

make glaze Combine glaze ingredients in a small saucepan, and simmer, whisking constantly, for 2 minutes. Set aside.

make meatloaves Preheat your oven to 350 degrees. Tear the bread into chunks and then blend it, in a food processor, into breadcrumbs. Place the breadcrumbs in a large bowl. Add the onion, garlic, celery, and carrot to the food processor, and pulse it until they are finely chopped.

Heat a large skillet over medium heat. Once the skillet is hot, coat the bottom with olive oil, and heat the oil for a minute; add the finely chopped vegetables. Season with salt and pepper, and cook, stirring frequently, until they begin to brown, about 10 to 15 minutes.

yield: serves 6

glaze
4 teaspoons vegetable oil

¼ cup (65 grams) tomato paste

2 tablespoons (30 ml) cider vinegar

2 teaspoons honey

2 teaspoons Worcestershire sauce

1 tablespoon Dijon mustard

¼ teaspoon table salt

meatballs
2 slices sandwich bread

1 medium onion, finely chopped

1 garlic clove, minced

1 medium stalk celery, finely chopped

1 medium carrot, finely chopped

Olive oil, for cooking

1 teaspoon table salt, plus more for vegetables

Freshly ground black pepper

2 pounds (905 grams) ground beef

1 tablespoon tomato paste

1 teaspoon smoked paprika

1 teaspoon Dijon mustard

2 tablespoons (30 ml) Worcestershire sauce

Add the vegetables to the large bowl with breadcrumbs, then add the remaining ingredients. Stir the ingredients together with a fork. With wet hands, form the mixture into twelve 3-inch meatballs; each will weigh about 4 ounces.

bake meatloaves Space meatballs so that they are not touching, in a baking dish. Drizzle or brush each meatball with a teaspoon or so of the tomato glaze you made earlier, and bake until cooked through, about 20 minutes. (An instant-read thermometer inserted into the center of a cooked meatball will register 160 to 165.)

to serve Serve with additional glaze on a bed of brown butter mashed potatoes.

½ cup (120 ml) milk
¼ cup finely chopped fresh flat-leaf parsley
2 large eggs

brown butter mashed potatoes

*   *   *

2 pounds (905 grams) Yukon Gold potatoes

8 tablespoons unsalted butter (4 ounces, 115 grams, or 1 stick), melted and browned (see page 201)

1 cup (235 ml) buttermilk

1 to 2 teaspoons table salt

Freshly ground black pepper

Place the potatoes in a medium saucepan, and cover with cold water. Bring to a boil over high heat, and once it's boiling, reduce the heat to a simmer. Cook for 20 to 30 minutes, depending on your potato size; the potatoes are ready when a paring knife or cake tester can be inserted into the center with little resistance. Drain the potatoes, and wipe the pot dry.

Peel the potatoes—I find that holding one in a pot-holdered hand and using a paring knife with the other is easiest. Repeat with remaining potatoes until they are completely peeled. Run the potatoes through a food mill or potato ricer, then return the mashed potatoes to your emptied saucepan. Add browned butter, buttermilk, salt, and black pepper to taste. Do your best not to eat it all before guests arrive.

pistachio masala lamb chops
with cucumber mint raita

These lamb chops are an homage to one of my favorite foods on earth, which I had as often as possible at one of my favorite restaurants on earth until it closed before its time—meaning, I wasn't done with it yet. I went to Tabla the first time in 2000. It led to more than a decade of regular visits so I could get my fix of their obsessively good bhoondhi raita (a yogurt dish with chickpea dumplings and hot and cool spices), saag paneer pizza (with spinach and homemade cheese), and apple and potato chaat salad (modeled on an Indian street snack). But for me, it always came back to my favorite dish at the restaurant, and likely the most overlooked one: the bowls of popcorn on the downstairs bar.

Yes, *popcorn*. This wasn't any old popcorn but popcorn that was dusted with an intense mix of Indian spices that I tried endlessly and ineffectively to re-create at home. I begged the chef for the recipe but it was apparently a trademarked blend of spices. And then the restaurant closed, and my husband and I were popcorn and Masala Mary (an Indian-spiced Bloody Mary) bereft until one afternoon at Kalustyan's, a packed-to-the-rafters wonderland of an ethnic grocery store on Lexington Avenue, on a tip, I picked up a spice mix called chaat masala and was reunited, at last, with the intricate play of flavors (loud, soft, bright, pale, snappy, sour, hot! All at once!) I'd missed so much.

I immediately started sprinkling it on everything, from melon to, of course, bowls of popcorn. I mixed it into yogurt and dipped toasted pita wedges into it. But I always wanted more. And so I created a special-occasion dinner dish just to show it off. Here, small lamb chops are browned, then coated generously with a blend of the chaat masala, ground pistachios, and other spices before they're briefly baked; you eat them with a cucumber and mint raita and reminisce about all the great meals that led to this one.

yield: serves 3 to 4

raita

1 cup (230 grams) full-fat plain yogurt

¼ teaspoon table salt

¼ teaspoon ground cumin

2 tablespoons minced fresh mint leaves

¼ cup minced English cucumber

Pinch of cayenne pepper

Pinch of sugar

chops

½ cup (60 grams) shelled pistachios

2 to 3 teaspoons chaat masala (see cooking note)

½ teaspoon ground cumin

2 teaspoons paprika

Pinch of cayenne pepper

6 small lamb chops (about 3 to 4 ounces, or 85 to 115 grams each)

Table salt, for lamb chops

Freshly ground black pepper

Olive oil

*   *   *

make raita Mix all ingredients in a bowl. Adjust seasonings to taste. (Easy, right?)

make lamb chops Grind the nuts and spices in a food processor in short pulses until it resembles breadcrumbs. Pile them on a small plate, and set aside.

Season your lamb chops generously on either side with salt and freshly ground black pepper. Allow them to sit for 10 to 15 minutes before cooking. Preheat your oven to 425 degrees. Coat a large sauté pan generously with olive oil and heat over medium-high heat. When the oil is hot but not smoking, add the lamb chops (three at a time), and sear them for about 2 minutes on each side. Lower the heat if the pan begins to smoke.

Holding the bone end, dip the seared sides of each chop in the nut-spice mixture. Arrange the chops on a baking sheet or roasting pan and roast for another 4 to 5 minutes in preheated oven. Remove the chops from oven, and let rest for 5 minutes. Serve with the raita.

cooking note One of my cooking pet peeves is when a recipe says, "And first, you must go buy this obscure food product." Because the recipe is clearly begging never to be used in anyone's home. Although I usually delight in reverse-engineering packaged ingredients—see homemade panko (page 170)—chaat masala (available at most ethnic and Indian grocery stores, as well as on the Web; my favorite is from the MDH brand) has an ingredient list nearly as long as this book's index. Okay, I embellish, but I'm not going to assume you keep dried mango, dried ground pomegranate seeds, and black salt around your kitchen and if you do, may I please come over to play? So, if you like Indian spices that are so elaborate they're tangy, sour, and hot (but not overly so) at once, you should track down chaat masala. And when you do, buy two boxes because it's pretty inexpensive and more than a little habit-forming.

sweets

cookies

pies and tarts

cakes

puddings and candy

cookies

buttered popcorn cookies

rhubarb hamantaschen

salted brown butter crispy treats

chocolate peanut butter cookies

cranberry crumb bars with mulling spices

gooey cinnamon squares

brownie roll-out cookies

alex's chocolate raspberry rugelach

buttered popcorn cookies

I recently found out that a friend of mine hates popcorn. And it's funny, because, whereas most people's food dislikes generally seem harmless but mildly understandable—tomatoes, eggs, broccoli rabe, fish (ahem)—who doesn't like popcorn? *Popcorn?*

I harassed her for a while about this. She talked about hating how the shell-like kernels scratched her mouth, about the taste of the fake-buttery slick of the packaged stuff and the steaminess that comes out of the bag when it's opened, and how nightmarish movie theaters are for people like her. She said she'd fallen in the past for powdery "cheddar"-dusted popcorn, and caramel popcorn mixed with nuts, but she knew you could also cover cardboard with that stuff and it would taste good. She insisted that nobody liked popcorn plain—you either admitted that it smelled funky or you were lying—that they just liked the stuff you put on it, and that stuff was like a chemistry set. She went on and on. I was impressed by how much thought she'd put into it.

Still, I decided we couldn't be friends after that. Um, just kidding! No, I decided that the only thing I could possibly love more than buttered popcorn would be to take that buttered popcorn and put it into a cookie. It follows basic snack math, which is that two forms of junk food together always exceed the greatness of them separately, especially when you mix the salty and the sweet. It's like chocolate-covered pretzels, salted chocolate caramel sauce, or potato chips crushed inside a peanut-butter-and-jelly sandwich (don't look at me like that; those kids at the second grade lunch table were geniuses).

Popcorn inside a cookie, however, it's different. In some bites it provides a little extra buttery crunch, and in others, a soft cloud to break up the crispness of the cookie. It's spectacular against a brown-sugar-and-vanilla base, and downright pretty in the puddle of a toasted buttery cookie.

* * *

yield: 24 cookies

---

2 tablespoons (30 ml) vegetable oil

¼ cup (45 grams) popcorn kernels

¼ teaspoon table salt

1 tablespoon butter, melted

½ cup (115 grams or 1 stick) butter, softened

½ cup (95 grams) packed light brown sugar

⅓ cup (65 grams) granulated sugar

1 large egg

½ teaspoon vanilla extract

1¼ cups (155 grams) all-purpose flour

½ teaspoon baking soda

---

make popcorn Pour the oil over the bottom of a large saucepan that has a lid, and add the popcorn kernels, shimmying the pan around so the kernels land in one layer. Cover the pot, heat it over medium-high heat, and, once the kernels begin to pop, keep the saucepan moving until all of the kernels have popped, about 5 to 7 minutes total. Toss the table salt and then the melted butter over the popcorn, then transfer it to a bowl so that you can fish out any unpopped kernels. You should have about 4 to 4½ cups popcorn. Let cool.

mix dough Preheat your oven to 350 degrees. In a large bowl, cream together the softened butter, brown sugar, granulated sugar, egg, and vanilla until smooth. In a separate bowl, whisk the flour and baking soda together. Stir the combined dry ingredients into the butter-sugar mixture. Fold in the cooled popcorn so that it is evenly distributed through the batter, which will seem like a ridiculous instruction because there is so much popcorn and so little cookie batter, but it works. Don't worry if the popcorn breaks up a bit. The mixed-size pieces are part of the cookie's charm.

bake cookies Scoop heaping-tablespoon-sized mounds 2 inches apart onto a parchment-lined baking sheet. Bake the cookies for 10 to 12 minutes, until the edges are light brown. Let them sit on the hot baking sheet for a few minutes to firm up before transferring them to a rack to cool.

rhubarb hamantaschen

I like a lot of things about rhubarb, the first being that it's still relatively new to me. I don't remember hearing a thing about it growing up but have been making up for lost time since a co-worker introduced me to it several years ago. She said it grew almost uncontrollably in her backyard in Seattle (a place I've since imagined as a veritable rhubarb wonderland; please do not tell me if this is incorrect), so she quickly learned how to cook with it. I like that it's a vegetable masquerading as a fruit. I like that it's shiny and pearly and fuchsia and green at once, and can hardly think of another thing in nature that pretty. Unlike the color of so many purple carrots and the swirly pink cranberry beans I fall for at the market, rhubarb's blush holds up once it's cooked. I like the way it may seem mundane, but every time you eat it you're living on the edge: The leaves at the top of those alluring stalks are actually, well, deadly. And I like the fact that it's kind of a grandma thing; rhubarb pies have an old-time-y thing going on, something people have baked for generations before you. I'm all for grandmas.

Hamantaschen are traditionally brought out during the Jewish holiday of Purim, which is an early-spring festival. (It is often considered the Jewish Halloween, but without TP-ed houses and wicked pumpkins, I'm sorry, it's just not the same.) Early spring, if you're real lucky, will provide you with rhubarb, one of the first things to emerge from the defrosted winter ground, and that is why it makes the very best cookie filling possible.

Also, it's pink, which, if you tell me doesn't charm you, well, I won't believe you.

I learned the rhubarb cooking technique you see here from *Good to the Grain*, one of the very best baking books I've bought in this decade. From Kim Boyce, I learned that you could simply cook fruit dry—no liquids, no water—over low heat, coax out its juices within, and make the kind of fruit filling that doesn't run all over the place from you when it hits the oven. I doubt she was dreaming of hamantaschen when she made it, but it's saved me from burned jammy puddles every time.

yield: thirty 2-inch hamantaschen

filling

1 pound (905 grams) rhubarb stalks
(to make 3 cups chunks)

⅔ cup (130 grams) sugar

cookie

½ cup (50 grams) finely ground almonds, almond meal, or heaping ½ cup sliced almonds

2 cups (250 grams) all-purpose flour

⅓ cup (65 grams) sugar

¾ teaspoon table salt

8 tablespoons (115 grams or 1 stick) unsalted butter, chilled, cut into small pieces

1 large egg

⅛ teaspoon almond extract

to slice cookies Slice each log of frozen cookie dough into just shy of ¼-inch slices. I like to hold the end of the log gently with two fingers as I slice the cookies, because they are so prone to breaking.

to roll out cookies First, promise me you know what you're getting into. These cookies are crumbly and the dough, it will not want to be rolled out. It helps to let it warm up a little and use as little flour as possible. And again, accept that the dough will be crumbly and keep nudging it back together until the cutouts resemble cookies. The upside of all of this crumbliness is that the cookies hold their shapes nicely in the oven.

Roll out one dough disc at a time until it is a little shy of ¼ inch thick. Cut into desired shapes—I used a 1⅓-inch fluted square for mine and encourage something equally petite as the peanut butter cookies are intense, especially in sandwiched pairs. Gather your scraps, attempting to pick up as little flour as possible, and knead them back into something resembling a ball of dough. It will be fragile. Roll the dough again into the same thickness and cut into cookies.

bake cookies Transfer the formed cookies to prepared baking sheets with a thin spatula and bake for 10 to 12 minutes. They should be a little puffed and faintly golden at the edges when they are finished. Transfer the cookies to cooling racks and cool completely before filling.

make the filling In the top of a double boiler or in a bowl set over simmering water, combine the chocolate, peanut butter, butter, and a pinch of sea salt, whisking together until they are melted and smooth. Let the mixture cool until it is thick but spreadable. You can speed this process up in the fridge or by setting the bowl in another bowl of ice water, but for both methods, be sure to stir frequently so that it chills evenly.

finish the cookies Dollop half the cookies with about 1 teaspoon of chocolate peanut butter filling each. You can do this with a butter knife or, if you wish to be more precise, you can use a pastry bag with a round tip, or a sandwich bag with the corner snipped off. Place a second cookie over the chocolate mixture, and press the cookies gently together so that the filling approaches the edges. Repeat with the remaining cookies. Let the cookies set until the chocolate is mostly firm.

do ahead
The unbaked cookie dough will keep, well wrapped, for up to 3 days in the fridge and up to two months in the freezer. The cookies will keep in an airtight container at room temperature for a week and for two months in the freezer. At room temperature, they will soften after the first day.

cranberry crumb bars with mulling spices

When you really think about it, whoever invented the cookie wasn't really on our team. Between the butter that needs to be softened and whipped *just so* to the chilling, scooping, and arranging of dough on trays upon trays, only to rearrange cookies on cooling racks a short while later . . . Wait, why do we make cookies again? They're like the breakfast pancake of the dessert course, the maximum amount of labor one can squeeze from a single bowl of batter.

But the bar cookie, oh, the bar cookie is your friend. They're pressed and crumbled in pans; they feed a crowd and rarely take more than an hour, from beginning to end. The absolutely best bar cookies remind us of pie in flavor, but have none of the rolling, lifting, crimping, filling, lidding, eternal baking times, and shamelessly sloppy servings of the real deal. If you're lucky, there's buttery shortbread on either side of the fruit. These cranberry bars are the winter companion to a blueberry crumb bar on my site. A buttery cookie with a whiff of winter spice sandwiches a tart candy-red filling and the whole thing is so insanely simple to throw together that you might kiss your exacting #128 1.5-teaspoon cookie scoop good-bye forever.

*　　*　　*

Preheat your oven to 375 degrees. Line the bottom of a 9-by-13-inch baking pan with parchment paper, and butter the sides and the parchment. In a large, widish bowl, whisk together the flour, sugar, salt, baking powder, and spices. With a pastry blender or fork, work the chilled butter and the egg into the flour mixture until the mixture resembles a coarse meal. Pat half the crumb base into the bottom of your prepared pan; it will be thin.

In the bowl of a food processor or blender, briefly pulse the filling ingredients until the berries are coarsely chopped but not puréed. Spread the filling over the crumb base. Sprinkle the remaining crumbs evenly over the cranberry mixture.

Bake cookies for 30 to 35 minutes, or until lightly brown on top. Cool completely before cutting into squares.

yield: 36 smallish rectangles

crumb

16 tablespoons unsalted butter (225 grams or 2 sticks), chilled, plus more at room temperature for the pan

3 cups (375 grams) all-purpose flour

1 cup (200 grams) sugar

½ teaspoon table salt

1 teaspoon baking powder

½ teaspoon ground cinnamon

¼ teaspoon ground nutmeg

⅛ teaspoon ground cloves

⅛ teaspoon ground allspice

1 large egg

filling

½ teaspoon freshly grated orange zest

1½ tablespoons (25 ml) orange juice

3 cups fresh cranberries (340 grams or 12-ounce bag)

½ cup (100 grams) sugar

1 tablespoon cornstarch

gooey cinnamon squares

9 was eighteen when I had my first snickerdoodle—a cinnamon-sugar-dusted soft butter cookie straight from the heavens—and I am still trying to make up for lost time. I believe that snickerdoodles have powers of coercion, of will-bending and heartwarming—powers that were once previously limited to brown sugar and chocolate chips. I know this because I made them ~~to bribe~~ as a gift for the Labor & Delivery nurses working when I had my son. And boy, were those nurses sweet to me.

That kid was but five months old when I had my first St. Louis Gooey Butter Cake, possibly all of two hours after reading about it in *The New York Times*. I became consumed with sadness that I hadn't grown up in St. Louis, where I imagine I never would have had to spend thirty-two years denied the understanding that if you mix just the right amount (read: a lot) of butter, sugar, flour, and egg together and spread it over a cake batter, it will not bake into, say, more cake, but something akin to spun sugar or the burnt sugar lid of the best crème brûlée you've ever had.

The problem with gooey butter cake, if there could be one (and believe me, I had to think really hard to come up with a limitation), is that once you realize how utterly delicious a layer of sugary manna is on top of a simple cake, you start to wonder why it cannot be used as a topping for everything that goes in an oven—gooey butter baked French toast? Gooey butter breakfast muffins?

And this is what happens when snickerdoodles go to St. Louis, meet some gooey butter cake, and have little buttery, golden-squared children. You could say their meeting was inevitable, but I know the truth, which is that I wanted to make both for a party and didn't have time, so I mashed them up. The base is slightly more cake than cookie, the topping is a cross between a toasted marshmallow and cinnamon toast, and if you just read that and haven't shut this book to make this happen in your kitchen immediately, I've failed.

And, lo, I haven't separated them since. I hope you'll see why, soon enough.

yield: about 7 dozen 1-inch squares

soft cookie base

8 tablespoons (115 grams or 1 stick) unsalted butter, at room temperature, plus more for the pan

1½ cups (188 grams) all-purpose flour

1 teaspoon cream of tartar

½ teaspoon baking soda

¼ teaspoon table salt

¾ cup (150 grams) sugar

1 large egg

¼ cup (60 ml) milk

gooey layer

¼ cup (60 ml) light corn syrup, golden syrup, or honey

¼ cup (60 ml) milk, half-and-half, or heavy cream

1 tablespoon vanilla extract

12 tablespoons (170 grams or 1½ sticks) butter, at room temperature

1 cup plus 2 tablespoons (225 grams) sugar

¼ teaspoon table salt

1 large egg

1¼ cups (155 grams) all-purpose flour

* * *

Preheat your oven to 350 degrees. Line the bottom of a 9-by-13-inch cake pan with at least 2-inch sides with parchment paper and either butter the paper and sides of the pan or coat them with a nonstick spray. Set aside.

prepare the cookie base Whisk together the flour, cream of tartar, baking soda, and salt in a medium bowl. In the bowl of an electric mixer, beat the 8 tablespoons butter with sugar until light and fluffy. Add the egg and the milk, and beat until combined, scraping down bowl and then beating for 10 seconds more. Beat in dry ingredients until just combined.

Dollop cookie base over the bottom of the prepared pan and spread it into an even layer with a butter knife or offset spatula. Set pan aside.

prepare the gooey layer Whisk liquid sweetener, milk, and vanilla together in a small bowl and set aside. In the bowl of an electric mixer, cream the butter, sugar, and salt until light and fluffy. Beat in the egg, scrape down sides of bowl, and mix for 10 seconds more. Add ⅓ of flour and mix, then ½ of vanilla mixture and mix. Repeat again, twice, until all of the flour has been mixed until just combined. Dollop over the cookie base and spread carefully with an offset spatula or butter knife.

make the topping Mix the sugar and cinnamon in a tiny dish and sprinkle it over the entire gooey layer. It will be thick but will come out of the oven *almost* like a crème brûlée lid, i.e., awesomely.

to bake and serve Bake for 25 to 30 minutes until the cookies have bronzed on top. The gooey layer will rise and fall in the oven but will still be a bit liquidy under the cinnamon crust when the squares are done. Let cool completely on a rack, then cut into 1-inch squares.

do ahead The squares keep at room temperature for at least a week, although never in my apartment.

topping
2 tablespoons (25 grams) sugar
1½ teaspoons ground cinnamon

cooking notes
Traditional snickerdoodles have always been a slightly soft, cakey cookie. The base of these is even more so—and also, easier to spread in a pan—due to the addition of some milk. Snickerdoodle purists insist that they include cream of tartar as part of the leavening formula, essentially a homemade baking power holdover from a time when you couldn't buy it at the store. If you don't have and don't feel like purchasing cream of tartar (you'll find it in the spice aisle), you can replace *both* the tartar and the baking soda with 2 teaspoons baking powder.

The topping is a mash-up between several gooey butter cake toppings I have known and loved, plus a bit of milk to keep it even softer. Traditionally, corn syrup is used but I've found that both honey and golden syrup work equally well. You'll put a lot of cinnamon sugar on top of this and question the logic of it until you discover the cinnamon-crunched lid it creates in the oven.

brownie roll-out cookies

When I was growing up, these were our Hanukkah cookies. We made them with blue plastic cookie cutters that attempted to stamp dreidels, menorahs, and Stars of David into the tops of the cookies but mostly just took chunks of the dough back with them. The cookies had absolutely nothing otherwise to do with Hanukkah, and I think that rescuing them from the month of December was a brilliant move on my part. Not to eschew a fine family holiday tradition, but these cookies are too good to eat only once a year.

My mother's yellowed recipe card calls them "Chocolate Sugar Cookies," but I think they taste like brownies that someone has compressed with a rolling pin—that is, firm but also tender, immensely rich, with a substantial chocolate flavor for such a small package. I cannot tell you how many cookie recipes I've seen that audaciously suggest that a chocolate-lover, the kind who dreams of Willy Wonka's Fudge Room only, would be satisfied with the mere *suggestion* of cocoa. Here, the chocolate is no afterthought.

They're good rolled thin—especially if you, say, are into home-made ice-cream sandwiches—but I think that they are best at ¼ inch high. At that thickness, they are at their brownie-est; the edges are firm and the centers are soft, and you will immediately reach for a glass of milk. They're a fine dunking cookie as well, but I trust you will figure that out on your own.

*   *   *

Preheat your oven to 350 degrees. Whisk the flour, cocoa, salt, and baking powder together in a bowl, and set aside. Beat butter and sugar with electric mixer until fluffy. Add eggs, one at a time, scraping down bowl. Mix in vanilla. Gradually mix in the dry ingredients. Wrap in plastic, and chill for at least 1 hour.

Roll out the cookie dough on a floured counter. Cut into desired shapes, brushing extra deposits of flour off the top. (It does disappear once baked, though, so don't overly fret if they go into the oven looking white.) Bake

yield: sixty-five 1½-to-1¾-inch cookies, from ¼-inch-thick dough

3 cups (375 grams) all-purpose flour, plus more for counter

⅔ cup (55 grams) unsweetened cocoa

¾ teaspoon table salt

½ teaspoon baking powder

16 tablespoons (225 grams or 2 sticks) unsalted butter, softened

1½ cups (300 grams) sugar

2 large eggs

1 teaspoon vanilla extract

on a parchment-lined baking sheet for 8 to 11 minutes (the former for ⅛-inch-thick cookies, the latter for ¼-inch cookies), until the edges are firm and the centers are slightly soft and puffed.

Transfer to a wire rack to cool.

cooking note

I use fancy Dutch cocoa when I make them these days, but my mother made them then and now with Hershey's old-school natural cocoa, and we were never disappointed in their flavor.

alex's chocolate raspberry rugelach

When you first meet the person you're going to spend the rest of your life with, you usually cannot stop talking about them. You don't mean to be so annoying, it's just that you're thinking about them constantly and it gives you away. But as time passes, there's less to talk about, not because nothing happens anymore but because you've nested so neatly together that the edges between where each of your interests begin and end are blurred. It's pretty wonderful.

This is why, in the early days of my site, there's a lot of "Alex thinks we should pickle more things!" and "Don't you love this photo Alex took?" and other swoonish blather . . . and nowadays, it's more like "Jacob was so happy when his dad got home and his mama finally stopped caterwauling 'Santa Baby.'" It's a shame, though, because Alex is the great voice of food reason behind the site, always suggesting one of the following when I ask what a recipe would benefit from: bacon, peanut butter, chocolate, or salt. "You're welcome," says Alex.

And these are his rugelach, exactly as he thinks they should be. Most rugelach are filled with cinnamon-sugar, nuts and dried fruit, sometimes jam as well, and all too infrequently, chocolate. Most rugelach force you to choose an aisle. "Nonsense," said Alex, in regard to this unjust segregation. Instead he gently encouraged me to see what happened if they all tangled together in one twist of cream cheese pastry genius. What happened was the very best damned rugelach we've ever had. They're like rugelach with "the works" but as compact, tender, and flaky as the originals.

*   *   *

make the dough In the bowl of an electric mixer, beat butter and cream cheese together until they are light and fluffy. In a medium bowl, combine the salt and flour, then pour flour mixture into the mixer. Beat on a lower speed until the flour just disappears. Scrape dough onto a large piece of plastic wrap and shape as best as you can into a flatish packet. Wrap well

yield: forty-eight 2½-to-3-inch rugelach

dough

16 tablespoons (230 grams or 2 sticks) unsalted butter, at room temperature

8 ounces (230 grams or 1 brick) cream cheese, at room temperature

½ teaspoon table salt

2 cups (250 grams) all-purpose flour

fillings

⅔ cup (215 grams) raspberry jam (preferably seedless)

⅔ cup (135 grams) sugar

1 tablespoon ground cinnamon

3 tablespoons (1½ ounces or 41 grams) pecans, toasted and finely chopped (walnuts and almonds work as well)

½ cup (3 ounces or 85 grams) finely chopped bittersweet chocolate or miniature chocolate chips

glaze

1 large egg yolk

1 teaspoon water

Coarse or sanding sugar, for sprinkling, or additional cinnamon-sugar

in plastic and chill in fridge for two hours or up to three days. The dough can also be frozen for up to two months.

note I have also made this dough successfully in the food processor. Just like with a stand mixer, you want to be careful not to overmix the flour—just do so in pulses until it is no longer visible.

While the dough is chilling, you could go take a nap or read a gossip website—not that I ever do anything like that—but I usually regret it if I don't use the time to prepare the fillings, because it always takes longer than I anticipated.

prepare the baking sheets Line three large baking sheets with parchment paper.

prepare the fillings Heat your jam in a small saucepan until it simmers. This will loosen it, so it will be easier to spread thinly. If your jam has seeds and you, like me, find raspberry seeds incredibly annoying, you can push the warm jam through a fine-mesh strainer to remove them. Set the warm jam aside.

Grab four small dishes. Stir together your sugar and cinnamon in one and set it aside. In your second dish, put the pecans. In your third bowl, put the chocolate. In the last one, whisk together your egg yolk and water until it is smooth. While you're getting organized, you'll also want to take out a rolling pin, flour for the counter, a small offset spatula or butter knife for spreading the jam, a knife or pastry wheel for cutting the dough, a spoon for the dry toppings, a large piece of waxed paper to help set the fillings, and a brush for the egg wash. See how that dough-chilling time flew?

assemble the rugelach Divide your chilled dough into thirds. On a well-floured counter, roll the first third (the remaining two can go back into the fridge until needed) into a large, thin circle about 12 inches in diameter—but please, no reason to trim the edges or fuss if it is slightly larger or smaller. I usually make my first one really neat, remember that it doesn't matter, and then make the rest into oblong, roundish shapes.

Spread two to three tablespoons of jam thinly over your dough. (See cooking note about jam levels.) Sprinkle with 3 tablespoons cinnamon-sugar, 2 tablespoons chopped chocolate, and 1 tablespoon chopped nuts. Use your piece of waxed paper to gently press the toppings into the dough

do ahead
Rugelach keep in an airtight container at room temperature for three to four days and frozen between layers of waxed paper in an airtight container for up to two months.

cooking note
The best rugelach make a terrible mess on baking sheets. I find that the two-tablespoon level of jam per round of dough has the smallest amount of jam-spill when baked and the three-tablespoon level almost always creates a puddle. Logically, one would then recommend the smaller amount, but I like the extra jam-miness of the larger amount. (Alex thinks both levels are just fine.) That said, if you line your baking sheets with parchment paper—even if you have a nonstick baking mat, you'll probably appreciate using something disposable here—cleanup will be a breeze and nobody will be the wiser in the final cookie.

so that they spill out less once rolled. You can set the paper aside for the remaining batches. Use your knife to divide the dough into 16 wedges. Roll each wedge tightly from the outside to the center. Transfer the rugelach to the prepared baking sheet—keeping the pointed end of each rugelach tucked underneath—and space them 1 inch apart. Pop the tray in the freezer for 15 minutes before baking.

Meanwhile, preheat your oven to 350 degrees. Repeat the rugelach-making process with remaining filling and two pieces of dough, then chill the trays in the freezer.

bake the rugelach Before baking, brush the rugelach with the egg yolk wash. Sprinkle with coarse sugar or extra cinnamon sugar. Bake the rugelach for 20 to 25 minutes, until they are puffed and golden brown. Transfer the rugelach to cooling racks while they are still hot—this is important because the jam that spills out will harden as it cools, making the cookies harder to remove from the paper. Serve cooled or lukewarm.

pies and tarts

whole lemon bars

butterscotch banana tarte tatin

chocolate silk pie

marbled pumpkin gingersnap tart

all butter, really flaky pie dough

almond and sweet cherry galette

deepest dish apple pie

peach dumplings with bourbon hard sauce

whole lemon bars

$\mathcal{I}$n the early seventies, when my sister was still a wee thing and I wasn't yet on the horizon, my mother won first prize in a regional cooking contest for her lemon bars. A two-layer affair, you first parbaked a shortbread base, then beat a mixture of lemon juice, lemon zest, butter, eggs, sugar, and then some and poured it over the cookie crust and baked it again. They're delightful. I love them. These are not them.

What? Look, I've decided that every generation should have her chance to make her mark on the lemon bar, and these are, well, more me: lazier, louder, and lush with butter. The whole of this recipe can be completed in the single bowl of a food processor. And instead of zesting and juicing many lemons, you just use one. All of it: the zest, the skin, *and* the flesh. Ground with sugar, butter, eggs, salt, and a bit of cornstarch, it bakes into the very best layer of lemon custard you could possibly imagine. I may not have won any prizes for these, but my mother, the lemon bar expert herself, tried one the other day and declared them "very, very good," which is all the blue ribbon I need.

*　　*　　*

Place a rack in middle of the oven and preheat your oven to 350 degrees. Cut two 12-inch lengths of parchment paper, and trim each to fit the bottom of an 8-inch square baking pan. Press the first sheet into the bottom and up the sides of your pan in one direction, then use the second sheet to line the rest of the pan, running it perpendicular to the first sheet. Lightly butter exposed parts of parchment or coat them with a nonstick cooking spray. Set the pan aside.

make the crust Blend the flour, sugar, and salt together in the work bowl of a food processor. Add the butter and pulse until the mixture is powdery, but if firmly pinched, will hold the pinched shape. Turn the dough crumbs into the prepared baking pan and press the dough evenly across the bottom and about ½ inch up the sides. Prick the dough all over with a fork and bake for 20 minutes, or until lightly browned. Should any parts bubble up, gently prick them again with a fork. Leave the oven on.

crust

1 cup (125 grams) all-purpose flour

⅓ cup (65 grams) sugar

¼ teaspoon table salt

8 tablespoons (115 grams or 1 stick) unsalted butter, cut into chunks, plus extra for greasing pan

filling

1 small-to-medium-sized lemon (about 4½ ounces or 130 grams, or about 3 inches long)

1⅓ cups (265 grams) sugar

8 tablespoons (115 grams or 1 stick) unsalted butter, cut into chunks

4 large eggs

2 tablespoons (15 grams) cornstarch

¼ teaspoon table salt

make your filling Cut your lemon in half, and here's where I need us all to be, briefly, quite fussy. Is the white part of the skin especially thick? If the widest part of the white is ¼ inch thick or less, continue on to the next step; your lemon is good to go. If any part of it is *thicker* than ¼ inch, however, I find it safest to remove the skin from half the lemon or the bitterness of the pith can overwhelm the bars. To remove the skin, place half the lemon cut-side-down on the cutting board, and remove the skin and pith from the entire half in downward cuts and discard it. The second half, even if just as thick, can be used as is.

Cut your lemon halves into thin rings and discard any seeds. Toss the lemon rounds—lemon flesh *and* peel—in the bowl of your food processor, add the sugar, and run the machine until the lemon is thoroughly puréed, about 2 minutes. Add the butter and again run the machine until the mixture is smooth, scraping down the sides of the work bowl as needed. Add the eggs, cornstarch, and salt and pulse the machine in short bursts until the mixture is evenly combined.

Pour the lemon mixture over the crust and bake it for 35 to 40 minutes, or until the filling is set. You can test this by bumping the pan a little; it should only jiggle slightly. In my oven, I find that the point at which the filling is set is also when the lemon bars start to get very light brown on top.

Let the pan cool completely on rack or in the fridge. Gently cut around the outside of the parchment paper to make sure no sides have stuck, then gently use the parchment "sling" to transfer bars from pan to cutting board. Cut into 16 squares.

cooking notes

Most recipes for whole lemon desserts recommend Meyer lemons. I actually prefer these with regular old grocery store lemons; with some modifications (described above) should their skins be extra thick, I find that they have the perfect balance of tart and fragrance. Nevertheless, to make these bars with Meyer lemons, use just one (of similar size and weight) and reduce the sugar in the filling to 1 cup (200 grams).

You can double the recipe and bake it in a 9-by-13-inch pan as well.

butterscotch banana tarte tatin

I know there are a lot of sitcoms about New Yorkers and their close quarters and the way their living situations lead them to get to know their neighbors, who are always wacky, and never, say, overworked accountants who use their ovens to store sweaters . . . but I lived in my moderate-sized apartment building for what I swear was half a year before I met a single one of my neighbors. Meanwhile, because my cooking smells up the hallway daily, I have to imagine what my neighbors think of me, but I don't really know, because usually no one knocks on the door.

I would say that the hallway-invading-est recipes I've made are french onion soup—if I smelled that in the hallway, I would scratch at a stranger's door until I was let in. My mother's apple cake makes October explode on the floor—apples and cinnamon mingle loudly enough that you might check for colorful leaves to crunch under your feet as you make your way from the elevator to the door, but somehow it has yet to draw a curious nose to our doorbell.

The day I devised this recipe, well, I had doubts about it. Would it be too sweet, too gooey, or just hideous? My track record with tartes Tatin is terrible, especially those made with pesky apples that always want to burn before they cook through. But long before I had even tasted it—really, just five minutes after it hit the oven—I knew that it would be one of the most delicious things in this book, because the aroma of bubbling butterscotch *climbs* the walls. It quickly escapes its confines. Shortly thereafter, when I went to take the trash to the basement, I bumped into a neighbor who said, "Wow. What are you guys cooking?" ~~and I won!~~ Ahem. No, I said as curtly and calmly as possible, "Oh, just a dessert for something." It's New York, after all, and probably best not to get to know your neighbors too well.

* * *

yield: serves 6 to 8

All-purpose flour, for work surface

1 sheet frozen puff-pastry dough (my favorite brand is Dufour), thawed in the refrigerator for 1 day

3 tablespoons (42 grams) unsalted butter

½ cup (95 grams) packed dark-brown sugar

½ teaspoon sea salt flakes, such as Maldon

5 large ripe bananas (preferably without speckles), peeled, halved lengthwise

1 teaspoon vanilla extract

1 tablespoon bourbon or Scotch (optional)

Vanilla ice cream, for serving

For this recipe, you'll need a 9-inch skillet heavy enough so you fear dropping it on your toes. Preheat your oven to 400 degrees. Roll out your puff pastry on a floured surface to a 9-inch circle, and trim if necessary. Transfer the pastry to the fridge until needed.

Melt the butter in the 9-inch skillet over medium-high heat. Stir in the sugar and salt. Cook, swirling the skillet occasionally, until the mixture turns medium amber, about 3 minutes.

Arrange the bananas in the skillet, overlapping them slightly. Cook, without stirring, for 3 minutes. Drizzle the vanilla and the alcohol of your choice (if using) over the bananas, and cook them until most of the liquor has evaporated and the liquid has thickened, about 1½ minutes. Remove the bananas from heat.

Place the pastry round on top of the bananas, and transfer it to the oven. Bake until the pastry is golden brown and puffed, about 25 minutes. Remove the tarte from the oven, and carefully invert the tarte onto a serving plate. Don't even think about serving this without vanilla ice cream.

chocolate silk pie

The problem with having a microbiologist for a mother is that you never get to eat raw eggs. Thus, it was absolutely inevitable that I would fall in love with some forbidden fruit or, perhaps, non–FDA-recommended protein-cooking temperatures when I was at a friend's house one afternoon—some extraordinary glorification of piles of whipped butter, melted chocolate, and three entire raw eggs. When my mother came to pick me up, I demanded she get the recipe from the friend's mom and then went home and nagged her to make it every single day for the rest of, well, at least fourth grade.

To her credit, she caved a few times. It is, after all, chocolate and butter and other good things. But those raw eggs never felt right to her, and mostly she dodged our requests, trying to ply us with chocolate pudding and Breyer's Neapolitan ice cream instead. But I think if you get your eggs from a place you trust, and rein in your horror over the butter volume, life is too short to miss out on this puddle of mousselike pie. Though it contains only a small amount of chocolate, it has a richness and intensity that will make it worth dismissing every single thing you learned in your dog-eared copy of *Man and Microbes* for the sake of a most excellent slice of a good time.

*   *   *

make crust Preheat your oven to 350 degrees. In a medium bowl, stir together cookie crumbs, sugar, and salt. Stir in melted butter until evenly dispersed. Press crumbs evenly across bottom and up sides of a standard 9-inch pie dish. Bake in preheated oven for 10 minutes, then let cool completely (the fridge can speed this up) before using.

make filling In a large stand mixer, whip butter and sugar together until pale and fluffy. While mixer is running, drizzle in melted chocolate. Add eggs one at a time, beating mixture at medium speed for 5 minutes after each addition, and scraping down the bowl. Add vanilla, and blend well. Spread chocolate filling in prepared crust, and smooth the top. Set pie in the fridge until fully chilled, at least 6 hours.

yield: 1 profoundly rich 9-inch pie

chocolate crust

1½ cups (130 grams) chocolate-wafer crumbs

2 tablespoons (25 grams) sugar

Pinch of salt

5 tablespoons (70 grams) unsalted butter, melted

filling

12 tablespoons (170 grams or 1½ sticks) butter, at room temperature

1 cup (200 grams) sugar

3 ounces (85 grams) unsweetened chocolate, melted and cooled

3 large eggs

1 teaspoon vanilla extract

garnish

1 cup (235 ml) heavy or whipping cream

1 tablespoon sugar

Chocolate curls shaved from a bittersweet bar with a peeler (optional) *to finish* Just before serving, beat cream with sugar until it just holds soft peaks. Spoon onto pie and garnish with bittersweet chocolate shavings, if you're feeling fancy.

cooking note This pie recipe has pretty fun origins. While my mother got the recipe from my friend's mom in the mid-1980s, the friend's mom picked it up at a cooking class she took in the early 1970s, where it appears to have been a riff on a runner-up in the 1951 Pillsbury Bake-Off, a "French Chocolate Silk Pie." It's changed twofold since then—this one uses fewer eggs and less butter for the same amount of chocolate—but the effect is similar: decadent and unforgettable. The bake-off winner used a regular single pie crust (such as my All Butter, etc. p. 226), but I like it even more with the chocolate crumb base shared here.

marbled pumpkin gingersnap tart

This is my all-in-one Thanksgiving/fall dessert, an earnest attempt to find a singular pumpkin dessert that would please my whole family. You see, I love pumpkin pie as much as any red-blooded American—it smells like fall blew up in your kitchen, it tastes as cozy as a marshmallow-topped mug of cocoa in front of the fireplace—but I never like the proportions. The filling always feels a little thick to me, a little out of whack with the base, so I started making a thinner pie in a tart pan. When my toddler developed an affection for gingersnaps, I started using them as a cookie-crumb crust instead of rolled or pressed. And when my husband lamented that I only make pumpkin cheesecake once a year, when he'd like it once a month, I swirled in some cheesecake batter, the way you would on a marbled brownie. (You marble your brownies, don't you?)

Together, this is the perfect marriage of pumpkin preferences, and also impatience—it comes together in no time. Because, to unforgivably botch a quote from one of my favorite movies, when you find the pumpkin pie you want to spend the rest of your life with, you want the rest of your life to start as soon as possible.

* * *

make crust Preheat your oven to 425 degrees. Remove any children sensitive to loud noises from the premises, and finely grind the gingersnaps and graham crackers in a food processor (yielding 1½ cups). Add the melted butter, and process until the cookie-crumb mixture is moistened. Press the mixture firmly into the bottom and up the sides of a 9-inch-diameter tart pan with removable bottom. (I like to use the bottom and outer side of a measuring cup to help pack the crumbs into the base and neatly up the walls of my crumb crusts.) Place pan on rimmed baking sheet.

make cheesecake batter Mix together the ingredients in a small bowl until smooth.

yield: one 9-inch tart, serving 8

crust

4 ounces (115 grams) gingersnap cookies (about 16 cookies), coarsely broken

3 ounces (85 grams) graham crackers (five and a half 2½-by-4⅞-inch graham-cracker sheets)

4 tablespoons (55 grams or ½ stick) salted butter, melted

cheesecake batter

4 ounces (115 grams) cream cheese, well softened

3 tablespoons (40 grams) granulated sugar

1 large egg yolk

pumpkin batter

1 large egg

1 large egg white

1¼ cups (10½ ounces or 300 grams, about ½ to ¾ of a 15-ounce can) pumpkin purée

¼ cup (50 grams) granulated sugar

¼ cup (50 grams) brown sugar

½ teaspoon table salt

¾ teaspoon ground cinnamon

make pumpkin batter Beat the egg and the egg white lightly in a large bowl. Whisk in the pumpkin, sugars, salt, cinnamon, ginger, cloves, and nutmeg. Gradually whisk in the cream.

assemble tart Pour the pumpkin batter into gingersnap-graham crust. Dollop the cheesecake batter over pumpkin batter, then marble the two together decoratively with a knife. Try not to pierce the bottom crust as you do. Bake for 10 minutes, then reduce temperature to 350 degrees and bake for another 30 to 40 minutes, or until a knife or toothpick inserted into the center comes out clean.

to serve Cool the tart completely on a rack, or in the fridge if you, like me, prefer it cold. Serve immediately, and refrigerate any leftovers. Theoretically, it keeps for several days, but the crumb crust will get a little soft on the bottom after day one.

¼ teaspoon ground ginger
¼ teaspoon ground cloves
Few fresh gratings of nutmeg
1 cup (235 ml) heavy cream

all butter, really flaky pie dough

About seven years ago, I realized that there were people who could whip up a pie at a moment's notice and people who could not, that I'd fallen on the latter side of the divide, and that I didn't want to be there anymore. I know this sounds strange; I know that when most people decide to up and change their life's direction it's because they realized they hadn't read enough classic literature or seen the Himalayas or they decided it was about time they learned Senegalese. Well, my thing was pie. I wanted to be a person who could whip up a pie because you were coming over or because it was high blueberry season or because *my goodness, do I really have to explain to you why pie for dessert is a very good thing?* No, I didn't think so.

And so I decided to make pie until making pie wasn't scary anymore. You'd be surprised how easy this is to do. Try this: End any conversation you have today with "I made some pie, if you'd like to come over tonight and have some" or "Can I bring you a pie I made?" and it turns out you actually have no excuse not to make pie because someone, *someone* will always valiantly intercede before that pie can negatively impact your chin count.

Seeing as mixing 6 cups of berries with sugar and cornstarch is hardly an obstacle, I am pretty sure that most FOP (fear of pie) is driven by the crust, as it was for me. And it took me a few pie seasons to fine-tune my technique. I spent time distracted by shortening, vodka, grating frozen sticks of butter, and, frankly, making things way more complicated than they needed to be before ditching the long-winded techniques for a single bowl, a pastry blender, and half a pound of butter, and I haven't looked back since. The only thing standing between you and the golden flaky pie dough of magazine pages, the kind that puffs up like mille-feuilles in the oven, is butter size and temperature management, which I will hopefully keep really simple below. And, if you make it in a big wide bowl—that is, by hand—you can later use that same bowl to make your filling. That's right: 1-bowl pies. Which means: Pie more often. Which means: Everyone wins.

yield: enough dough for 1 double- or 2 single-crust standard pies, 1 batch of Peach Dumplings with Bourbon Hard Sauce (p. 235) or Deepest Dish Apple Pie (p. 231), or 2 Almond and Sweet Cherry Galettes (p. 229)

2½ cups (315 grams) all-purpose flour
1 tablespoon sugar
1 teaspoon table salt
16 tablespoons (225 grams or 2 sticks) unsalted butter, very cold
½ cup (120 ml) ice-cold water

do ahead
Dough will keep in the fridge for a week, and the freezer for longer. To slowly defrost dough, move it to the fridge the day before you will need it.

* * *

by hand In a large, widish bowl, stir together your flour, sugar, and salt. Cut the butter into a medium-sized dice and scatter the pieces over the flour. Using your pastry blender (my first choice) or fingertips, work the butter into the flour mixture until the largest pieces of butter are the size of tiny peas.

in a food processor Combine flour, sugar, and salt in the work bowl of your food processor with a few quick pulses. Cut the butter into a small dice and scatter the pieces over the flour. In quick pulses, let the machine work the butter into the flour, stopping as soon as the largest pieces of butter are the size of small peas. Transfer the flour-butter mixture to a large bowl.

both methods If the butter has warmed up a bit, place the bowl in the freezer for 5 minutes to quickly cool it down again. Drizzle the water over the flour-butter mixture and use a flexible spatula to gently stir it together until a craggy, uneven mass forms. Knead the dough and any loose bits together, working quickly so as to warm it as little as possible. If your bowl is wide enough, you might be able to get your hands in and work the dough together there; otherwise, dump all the flour bits on the counter and do so there.

If your recipe (such as the Deepest Dish Apple Pie, p. 231, or Peach Dumplings, p. 235) calls for the dough all at once, wrap it tightly in a large piece

of plastic wrap. For a traditional 2-crust pie, divide the dough and wrap it in two separate pieces. Chill it in the fridge at least 1 hour for a halved dough and 2 hours for a full one before rolling it out.

roll out the dough When you're ready to make your pie, dust your counter generously with flour, place your piece of dough on it, sprinkle the top with additional flour, and begin to roll it out into a large round. I like to keep the pie dough moving at all times, rolling it twice, lifting it, and rotating it a quarter turn, repeating until it's the desired size and shape. Keep a bench scraper or long thin spatula handy and if the dough ever sticks to the counter, shimmy the spatula underneath and lift the dough enough that you can dust the counter with more flour. If the pie dough becomes soft, it will be harder to roll, more likely to stick and to break up those flake-inducing bits of butter—don't even try to fight it. Just slide the dough onto the back of a baking sheet and into the freezer for a few minutes until it firms up again.

If the dough is intended for a pie pan, I like to fold it into *uncreased* quarters and gently transfer it so that the inner corner meets the center of the bottom of my pie pan. Then, gently unfold the dough, letting it drape against the inner sides of the pie tin, and trim the overhang. Let your recipe take it from here.

cooking note

My favorite method for making pie dough is with a pastry blender. It's delightfully lo-fi—both clutter- and dish-reducing—and I find it to be the easiest way to control the temperature of the dough and the size of your bits of butter. Nevertheless, I have included instructions for how I'd make it in the food processor and still avoid these pitfalls. If you use the food processor, you'll find that it saves a couple minutes' work.

almond and sweet cherry galette

One of my favorite things to do in the summer, on the kind of day when there's not a single good reason to be inside, is to wander over to one of the greenmarkets with no agenda, no recipe in mind, and no real dinner cravings to speak of, and buy whatever looks pretty. In my fantasy life, I would do this every day. I'd wear a brimmed hat and flowing sundress, and I'd put all my purchases—including, of course, a brown paper bundle of wildflowers—in my weathered French market tote and, I suspect, soar home on a cloud of earthy bliss. In reality, I tend to bring home things that are, indeed, lookers—a bundle of rainbow carrots, two marbled zucchini—but rarely amount to dinner for three.

But I had no such trouble finding an application for the baskets I found one day of every imaginable color of sweet cherry. Most people save their gushing for sour cherries—their tartness makes baked goods sing, after all—but think that sweet cherries can be too easily overlooked for anything but snacking. The key is contrast; limiting the sweetness around them with a mostly unsweetened crust and minimal sprinkling of sugar on top. I also like showing off some of their best traits with an almond base. Cherries and almonds taste almost as if they were separated at birth; they were meant to be reunited. This lazy galette with a slick of almond frangipane keeps the cherries in place and might just have been dinner that night, along with some carrot sticks. It happens sometimes around here.

*   *   *

make pastry   See page 226. The dough should be refrigerated for at least an hour before you use it in this recipe.

make filling   Finely grind almonds and flour in a food processor. Mix in sugar, butter, and extract, then egg white. Blend until smooth. Cover, and chill until needed.

prepare galette   Preheat your oven to 400 degrees. On a floured work surface, roll the dough out into a 12-inch round. Transfer to a baking sheet

yield: makes 1 freeform galette; serves 8

pastry
½ recipe All Butter, Really Flaky Pie Dough (see page 226)

filling
⅓ cup (30 grams) sliced, slivered, or coarsely chopped almonds, blanched if you can get them

1½ teaspoons all-purpose flour

3 tablespoons (40 grams) granulated sugar

1 tablespoon butter (warm it to room temperature if you will be mixing your filling by hand)

¼ teaspoon almond extract

1 large egg white

1 pound (455 grams) sweet cherries, any variety or a mix of varieties

to finish
1 large egg yolk

1 teaspoon water

1 tablespoon coarse sugar

Confectioners' sugar, for dusting

lined with parchment paper. Spread the almond filling evenly over the bottom of the galette dough, leaving a 2-inch border. Scatter the cherries on top. Fold the border over the filling, pleating the edge to make it fit; the center will be open. Whisk egg yolk with water, and brush crust with mixture. Sprinkle crust with coarse sugar.

Bake the galette until the filling is puffed and the crust is golden brown, about 30 to 40 minutes, rotating the galette front to back halfway through for even browning. Cool, and serve dusted with powdered sugar.

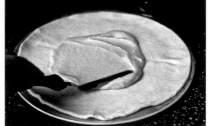

do ahead

The pastry dough can be made up to 2 days ahead and stored in the fridge, longer if stored in the freezer. Almond filling can be made up to 2 days ahead and stored in fridge.

TO PIT OR NOT TO PIT

I am sure most of you are looking at me like I am nuts right now: Why would you not pit cherries? Well, in France it is very common to make cherry clafoutis, a pancakelike cake, with the pits left in, the theory being that the pits impart a beguiling almond flavor.

deepest dish apple pie

I devised this pie as a solution to the greatest Apple Pie Crisis of my family's time—that is, that we never have enough of it at the Thanksgiving table. My clan, we gather in masses that routinely exceed twenty, and pie, you see, generally serves eight. I started making two apple pies instead of one a while back, but even that never felt like enough, especially if you celebrate (and, oh, you really should) one of my other favorite days of the year: National Pie for Breakfast Day, the day after Thanksgiving. I briefly considered lobbying my family to accept the slab pie (a large flat pie made in a quarter sheet pan, kind of like a giant Pop-Tart—yes, *really*), which is the original pie for dozens, but the slab pie increases the crust-to-filling ratio, and my family, we're filling people.

Out of ideas—and, yes, I really spent so much time thinking about it, and I'm okay with what that says about me—I came up with this fantastic monstrosity of a pie: over 3 inches tall, 5 pounds of apple within, and a baking time of the better part of 2 hours. It's apple pie for big families, for people for whom there is never enough apple pie.

My husband jokes that every other comment left on my site in the month of October is "Help! I went apple picking last weekend and we brought home an entire bushel of apples and I need recipes to help me use them up!"

. . . Thus, it's apple pie for you too.

*　　*　　*

prepare crust Lightly coat a 9-inch springform pan with 3-inch sides with oil and set aside.

Roll the dough on a floured surface to a 16-inch round. (More thorough rolling instructions are on p. 228.)

Fold the dough gently (making no crease) in half and then gently in half again, then lift it into prepared springform pan. Unfold the dough, draping it into the center from the sides, lowering enough dough to fill the springform's cavity. Press it against the sides, trim the overhang to 1 inch, and

yield: serves 12 to 16

crust

1 recipe All Butter, Really Flaky Pie Dough (see page 226), chilled for at least 2 hours

Butter or neutral oil, for greasing the springform pan

streusel topping

¾ cup (150 grams) granulated sugar

¼ teaspoon ground cinnamon

¼ teaspoon table salt

1¼ cups (165 grams) all-purpose flour

1 teaspoon baking powder

8 tablespoons (115 grams or 1 stick) butter, melted

filling

5 pounds (2¼ kg, or about 13 or 14 medium) apples (3 pounds Golden Delicious; 2 pounds baking apples of your choosing)

1 tablespoon freshly squeezed lemon juice

1 cup (200 grams) granulated sugar

¼ cup (30 grams) all-purpose flour

½ teaspoon table salt

use the scraps to patch any tears or holes. Let crust chill in fridge while you prepare the apples.

make streusel Stir together sugar, cinnamon, salt, flour, and baking powder in a medium bowl. Pour in melted butter, and stir until large clumps form. Set streusel aside.

Preheat your oven to 375 degrees.

make filling Peel, core, and chop each apple into eight wedges. Thinly slice each wedge crosswise into pieces no more than ¼ inch thick. These thin small pieces are more important in this pie than in most, because you really want them to fill the crust, edge to edge, as fully as possible. Sprinkle them into your largest bowl (in my tiny kitchen, I need to use two) with the lemon juice. Whisk sugar, flour, salt, cinnamon, and nutmeg in a small bowl, and sprinkle this over the apples, tossing gently to coat. Add apple filling to prepared crust, a quarter at a time, using a spatula to spread the apples as flat and evenly as possible. (This will also ensure that you can fit all of the apples in.)

bake the pie Bake for 30 minutes, then remove pie just long enough to sprinkle prepared streusel over top of pie, pressing it into apple mound if needed. Reduce temperature to 325 and bake for another hour. If streusel begins to brown too soon, cover it with foil, removing it only for the last 2 minutes of baking.

to finish Let pie cool to lukewarm in springform. (You can hasten this process in the fridge—in fact, the pie cuts most cleanly from the fridge.) When ready to serve, gently cut away any part of the crust that has stuck to the outside of the springform ring, then loosen the clamp of the ring and remove it. Slide the pie onto a serving plate and into the fridge overnight, or serve immediately.

cooking note There's a bit less sugar than you'd expect in this pie, 1 cup instead of a typical amount for 5 pounds of apples, which can be closer to 1¾ cups. Adjust it if you're nervous about its not being sweet enough. This pie delights in a nap in the fridge overnight. Those hours of chilling really gel the juices so that you can get the clean slice the photo promises. This makes it especially fitting for the planning ahead that is inevitable when feeding a crowd.

1 teaspoon ground cinnamon

¼ teaspoon freshly grated nutmeg

peach dumplings with bourbon hard sauce

I'm perfectly aware that most people spend their time in the shower, waiting in line at the coffee shop, or trying to avoid a stranger's gaze on the subway thinking about normal things, like errands they need to run, or that they should call their mother. But I spend the better part of summer dreaming about peaches, and things one can make with them. I think about crumbles you could bake right on top of peaches, I dream about pecan toffees that you could shatter with a mallet and sprinkle over roasted peaches, I imagine brushing them with honey, grilling them until they are charred, and dolloping them with a sweetened lemon mascarpone. But I couldn't come to a conclusion about what kind of peach dessert I wanted to include here until one morning when I was awakened by an irate, nonsleeping toddler at 4 a.m. and afterward could not fall back asleep myself. Suddenly it was so obvious: apples. Why don't we do to peaches what we do to apples? Have you tried peach sauce (i.e., peaches cooked as you would applesauce)? It's amazing. Peach butter on biscuits? Deadly delicious, I promise. Country peach dumplings?

Ding! Ding-ding-ding! I hadn't even made them yet and I already wondered where they'd been my whole life. I was tempted to get out of bed right then and start a pie dough; it sounded more enjoyable than willing the Sleep Fairy to come back to me. But, sure enough, she did, and visions of flaky pastry-wrapped peaches, their bellies puddled with a buttery brown-sugar caramel, danced in my head—and twelve hours later, in our bellies.

The dumplings are packets of slow summer perfection. The pie dough, unhindered by a heavy filling, expands and flakes like puff pastry. As you tear in, your first impression will likely be an unenthusiastic "Oh, huh, it's a peach half . . . ," until you cut into the peach half and a trickle of buttery brown-sugar caramel floods your bowl. (You're welcome.) From there, the dessert is a fantastic mess—chunks of peach, buttery layers of dough, and a mingled puddle of sweet bourbon and a dark caramel—and easily one of the best summer desserts I've ever made.

yield: makes 6 large peach dumplings

crust
1 recipe All Butter, Really Flaky Pie Dough (see page 226)

filling
3 large peaches

⅓ cup (65 grams) light or dark brown sugar

Pinch of salt

¼ teaspoon ground cinnamon

Few fresh gratings of nutmeg, or a pinch of ground

1 tablespoon butter, cut into 6 pieces, kept cold

1 large egg, for glaze

hard sauce
4 tablespoons (55 grams or ½ stick) butter, at room temperature

¾ cup (95 grams) confectioners' sugar

1 tablespoon bourbon

*   *   *

make crust See page 226.

Roll crust to a 12-by-18-inch rectangle, and divide into six 6-inch squares. If dough gets too soft or warm while you're rolling it, continue to the square stage, but then transfer the squares to a parchment-lined baking sheet and chill them in the freezer for a couple minutes, until they firm up again.

make filling Halve peaches, and cross your fingers that you've gotten freestone ones, because it makes life much easier. Remove pits. I like to scoop a little tiny extra out of the pit indentation with a melon baller (larger side) or knife, so that there is more room in the "belly button" to pack the filling.

assemble dumplings Mix brown sugar, salt, cinnamon, and nutmeg together in a little dish. Spoon 1 lightly packed tablespoon on top of each peach, smooshing as much of the sugar mixture as you can into the center. Dot the top of each with a piece of the cold butter. Center a peach half, cut side up, in your first pastry square. Bring corners up to meet each other over the center—if it feels tight, or as if you're short of dough, make sure that the dough underneath is flush with the peach curve; it tends to get slack—and seal the seams together, pinching with your fingertips.

bake dumplings Arrange peach dumplings in a buttered 9-by-13-inch baking dish, and chill for 30 minutes. Meanwhile, preheat your oven to 375 degrees.

Whisk egg together with 1 teaspoon water to form a glaze. Brush glaze over the tops and exposed sides of dumplings. Bake for 30 to 40 minutes, until pastries are puffed and bronzed on top.

to finish While baking, make the hard sauce. Beat softened butter, confectioners' sugar, and bourbon until smooth. Scrape into a serving dish. When pastries come out of oven, dollop each (or at least the ones that will not be served to children) with a heaping spoonful of the hard sauce, and serve pastries with the sauce melting over the sides.

Traditionally, apple dumplings are not cooked dry but in a bath of hard sauce, loads of it. I found that I preferred to go easier on the hard sauce and spoon it over the dry dumplings, so you could get the most flavor (and flakiness) out of this dessert.

The 6-inch squares suggested for each dumpling are based on an estimate that your peach half will be 3 inches in diameter, which is a fairly big peach. If it's smaller, you can reduce the size of the square accordingly.

If you don't wish to use the bourbon in the sauce, you could use a few dashes of vanilla extract, filling the rest of the tablespoon with water.

cakes

mom's apple cake

grapefruit olive oil pound cake

blueberry cornmeal butter cake

olive oil ricotta cake with concord grape coulis

tiny but intense chocolate cake

golden sheet cake with berry buttercream

chocolate hazelnut crepe cake

s'more layer cake

red wine velvet cake with whipped mascarpone

mom's apple cake

*E*very year, my mother asks me what she should bake for Rosh Hashanah dinner, as if she doesn't already know the answer. I am always assigned baking tasks, you see, not because I can't pull off a brisket or matzo-ball soup; it's just that, when you know how to whip up an excellent cake, that's pretty much what people want you to do, again and again. (Nobody gets tired of excellent cake.) So, every year, my mother calls me and asks what she should bake, and I become immediately exasperated—she is my mother, after all—and likely say in my most bershon adolescent voice, "Have you seen my *Internet website*, Mom? I bet there are fifty casual cakes for you to choose from." And then, "But you know you should just make your apple cake." "Oh, that thing?" she says, because I think she's bored with baking it. But that's the way it is with showstopping dishes: The people have chosen. It's no longer up to you.

So consider yourself warned: Should you bake this cake once, you will bake it again. And I know you're thinking, "Apple cake? Apple cake is delicious. But it's not showstopping." But this one is. It's ludicrously moist; days after it is baked, it only gets better. It contains nearly as many apples as a pie, and yet is clearly, unwaveringly, a cake. And it's enormous—it feeds a crowd, in fact, which is important, because it always draws one.

But beyond the High Holidays, this is a cake that will make you a good friend. It's perfect for housewarmings, for new babies, for co-workers and coffee. It looks humble, but it keeps well on a counter, and nobody, nobody who comes by will be bummed if you offer them a slice and a cup of tea.

*   *   *

Preheat your oven to 350 degrees. Butter a 10-inch tube pan, or coat it with nonstick spray. Peel, core, and chop the apples into ½-to-¾-inch chunks. Toss them with all of the cinnamon and the 5 tablespoons granulated sugar, and set them aside.

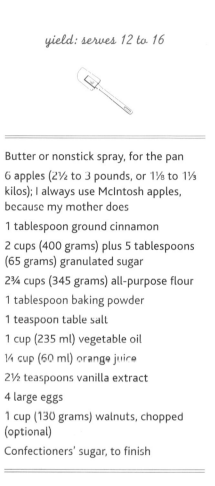

yield: serves 12 to 16

Butter or nonstick spray, for the pan

6 apples (2½ to 3 pounds, or 1⅛ to 1⅓ kilos); I always use McIntosh apples, because my mother does

1 tablespoon ground cinnamon

2 cups (400 grams) plus 5 tablespoons (65 grams) granulated sugar

2¾ cups (345 grams) all-purpose flour

1 tablespoon baking powder

1 teaspoon table salt

1 cup (235 ml) vegetable oil

¼ cup (60 ml) orange juice

2½ teaspoons vanilla extract

4 large eggs

1 cup (130 grams) walnuts, chopped (optional)

Confectioners' sugar, to finish

Sift the flour, baking powder, and salt together in a large bowl. In a medium bowl, whisk together the oil, orange juice, remaining 2 cups of granulated sugar, vanilla, and eggs. Stir the wet ingredients into the dry ones, then scrape down the bowl to make sure all the ingredients are evenly incorporated. Stir in the walnuts, if you are using them.

Pour half of the batter into the prepared pan. Spread half the apple chunks over it. Pour the remaining batter over the apples, and arrange the remaining apples on top. Bake for about 1½ hours, or until a tester comes out clean, then transfer to a rack to cool. Cool completely before flipping cake out of pan and onto a serving platter. Dust with confectioners' sugar and serve.

grapefruit olive oil pound cake

When it comes to baking, I keep waiting for the grapefruit to get the attention it deserves. Lemon layer cakes line bakery shelves, Key lime pies make even the president wax poetic, and you will never be unwelcome at brunch if you bring an orange-date bread. But grapefruit? Grapefruit seems to make people nervous.

It's particularly unfortunate if you, like me, are a grapefruit junkie. The grapefruit's peak season is, for me, the highlight of otherwise thanklessly cold Januaries, and its bracing flavor holds my interest longer than that of any other citrus fruit.

This recipe started as a rough adaptation of a pound cake made famous by Martha Stewart and Ina Garten. They both made it with lemon. Later, Ina made it with orange and chocolate. I waited and waited for one of them to use grapefruit, and neither of them did, so I took it upon myself, and we declared the results dreamy. But over the years I fiddled with it, because that's what I do. I discovered that, though the cake was good with butter, it was even better with olive oil, which complements the grapefruit's bitterness wonderfully. I started using some raw sugar as well, hoping to play up the natural flavors. But I kept intact the best parts of their lemon cake—the syrup that's brushed on it while the cake is still warm (though mine is less sweet, and I've found that poking holes in the cake helps to absorb it), and the glaze that should make it seem over the top but adds a great sweet contrast to grapefruit's intensity. This cake has become my favorite January treat—not too sweet, not too unhealthy, and bursting with ruby-red flavor.

* * *

make cake Heat the oven to 350 degrees. Butter and flour a 9-by-5-inch loaf pan.

In a large bowl, rub the grapefruit zest into the sugars with your fingertips. This will bruise it and help release as much grapefruit essence as possible. Whisk in the oil until smooth. Add the eggs one at a time, and whisk until combined. Scrape down the bowl.

yield: 1 loaf cake, serving 12

cake

Butter for pan

1½ cups (190 grams) all-purpose flour, plus more for pan

2 tablespoons freshly grated grapefruit zest (from 1 to 2 large grapefruits)

½ cup (100 grams) granulated sugar

½ cup (95 grams) raw or turbinado sugar (use granulated sugar if you can't find the raw variety)

½ cup (120 ml) olive oil

2 large eggs, at room temperature

1 teaspoon baking powder

¼ teaspoon baking soda

½ teaspoon table salt

2 tablespoons (30 ml) grapefruit juice

⅓ cup (80 ml) buttermilk or plain yogurt

syrup

2 tablespoons granulated sugar

⅓ cup (80 ml) grapefruit juice

glaze

1 cup (120 grams) confectioners' sugar

2 tablespoons (30 ml) grapefruit juice

Pinch of table salt

Combine the flour, baking powder, baking soda, and salt in a second bowl. In a liquid measuring cup, combine 2 tablespoons of grapefruit juice and buttermilk. Add the flour and the buttermilk mixtures, alternating between them, to the oil-and-sugar mixture, beginning and ending with flour.

Spread the batter in pan, smooth the top, and rap the pan on the counter a few times to ensure that there are no air bubbles trapped. Bake for 45 minutes to 1 hour, until a cake tester comes out clean.

make grapefruit syrup Combine 2 tablespoons of sugar with ⅓ cup grapefruit juice in a small saucepan, and cook over low heat until the sugar dissolves.

When cake is finished, let it cool for 10 minutes in the pan before inverting it onto a rack set over a tray. Poke holes in cake with a skewer or toothpick, then spoon or brush the grapefruit syrup over cake. Let the cake cool completely while it absorbs the syrup.

make glaze Combine the confectioners' sugar, grapefruit juice, and pinch of salt in a bowl, whisking until smooth. Pour the glaze over the top of cooled cake, and allow glaze to drizzle decoratively down the sides.

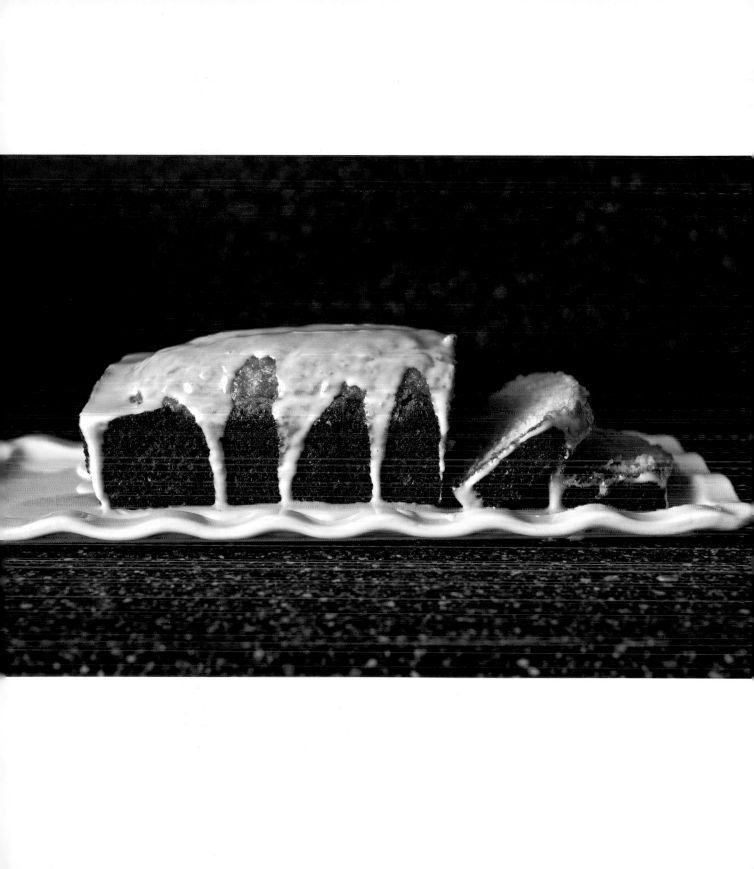

blueberry cornmeal butter cake

This recipe started with a whim: I imagined the place where a dense, buttery blueberry buckle would intersect with the kind of sweet, cakey cornbread that would make every Southerner I know shudder to hear it called "cornbread," and I wanted to go there. And what fun I had trying! There were versions with less lemon, some vanilla, buttermilk in place of milk, then sour cream for buttermilk, less liquid, more blueberries, more streusel, a crunchier streusel, a slip of cinnamon, a square cake instead of a round. Each time, I planned my next tweak, hit the market for more berries, and went at it again. Are we friends? You've probably had this cake twice.

A summer later, I was still playing with this cake, and it was time to accept the truth: We just loved it so much that I created excuses to make it some more. It's that kind of cake—dense and buttery, dotted with dreamy berries, portable, quick to make, and infinitely snacky—and I hope it won't be long until your version of this page is as spattered with berry, batter, and grit as mine.

*   *   *

Preheat your oven to 350 degrees. Line the bottom of an 8-inch square pan with parchment, then either butter and flour the bottom and sides, or coat them with a nonstick spray.

Whisk the flour, cornmeal, baking powder, and salt in medium bowl, and set aside. Using an electric mixer, beat the butter with sugar in large bowl until pale and fluffy, for at least 2 minutes. Beat in the eggs one at a time, scraping down the bowl between additions, then add the vanilla and zest. Add a third of flour mixture, all of sour cream, and another third of the flour, beating until just blended after each addition. Scrape down sides of bowl. Mix the remaining third of the flour mixture with the blueberries. Fold the blueberry-flour mixture gently into the cake batter.

Spread the cake batter in the prepared cake pan. Use your original dry-ingredients bowl (see how we look out for your dishpan hands?) to

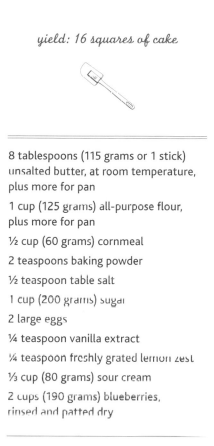

yield: 16 squares of cake

8 tablespoons (115 grams or 1 stick) unsalted butter, at room temperature, plus more for pan

1 cup (125 grams) all-purpose flour, plus more for pan

½ cup (60 grams) cornmeal

2 teaspoons baking powder

½ teaspoon table salt

1 cup (200 grams) sugar

2 large eggs

¼ teaspoon vanilla extract

¼ teaspoon freshly grated lemon zest

⅓ cup (80 grams) sour cream

2 cups (190 grams) blueberries, rinsed and patted dry

streusel

½ cup (100 grams) sugar

6 tablespoons (45 grams) all-purpose flour

2 tablespoons (15 grams) cornmeal

¼ teaspoon ground cinnamon

Pinch of table salt

2 tablespoons (55 grams) unsalted butter, cut into small pieces

blueberry cornmeal butter cake (continued)

combine the dry topping ingredients with a fork. Mash in the butter with your fork, fingertips, or a pastry blender. Scatter the topping over the batter.

Bake the cake until the top is golden brown and the tester inserted into center comes out clean, about 35 minutes. Cool the cake in the pan on a rack for 5 minutes. Run the spatula around the edges of the cake to loosen it, then flip out onto a cooling rack.

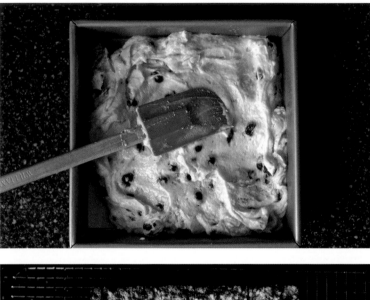

olive oil ricotta cake with concord grape coulis

*I*n a world of cakes named for special occasions—rolled Christmas *Bûches de Noël* (or should we say "Yule Logs"?), architecturally staggering Wedding Cakes, tufted and towering Birthday Cakes—I don't think every cake needs such a respectable reason to exist. In fact, I think that everyone should have in their repertoire a few cakes that are around only for lesser occasions, such as an Of Course We Can Come for Dinner Tonight, I'll Bring Cake, or a Just Because It's Tuesday Cake.

They needn't be fancy—in fact, they shouldn't be. They should be mildly sweet, as good with morning coffee as they are after dinner. They should keep at room temperature, preferably with a knife left on the cake plate on the counter, for when you walk by and the cake looks like it needs to be "evened." Ideally, they should be made in one bowl, and they should include things you already have around, like berries if they're in season or, in this case, a Concord grape sauce for September, when they're everywhere.

This is actually a riff on one of my favorite classic everyday cakes, the French yogurt cake. As things often do in my kitchen, this version came about one day when I realized I was out of yogurt but had a big tub of ricotta—no, not even the good stuff—languishing in my fridge. With the ricotta, olive oil seemed a better fit than a more neutral oil, and putting the Concord grapes in a sauce gave me a great way to make them toddler-friendly by removing those pesky seeds. The ricotta gives it an unmistakable richness, but the overall flavor is so mellow, the shot of grape sauce provides the perfect balance.

*　*　*

make the cake Preheat your oven to 350 degrees. Line the bottom of a 9-inch springform pan with parchment paper. Coat the paper and sides of the pan with butter, oil, or a nonstick cooking spray.

In a large mixing bowl, whisk together the ricotta, olive oil, granulated sugar, and lemon zest. Add the eggs one by one, whisking well after each

*yield: one 9-inch cake,
serving 8 to 12,
and 1⅓ cups sauce*

cake

Butter, oil, or nonstick spray, for pan

1 cup (250 grams) full-fat or fresh ricotta

⅓ cup (80 ml) olive oil

1 cup (200 grams) granulated sugar

½ teaspoon freshly grated lemon zest

2 large eggs

1½ cups (190 grams) all-purpose flour

1½ teaspoons baking powder

¼ teaspoon baking soda

¼ teaspoon table salt

Confectioners' sugar, for dusting
(see cooking note for other toppings)

grape coulis

⅔ cup (155 ml) water

3 tablespoons (40 grams) granulated sugar

1 tablespoon freshly squeezed lemon juice

Pinch of salt

2 cups (185 grams) Concord grapes

addition. Sift the flour, baking powder, baking soda, and salt together, right over the wet ingredients. Mix with a spoon until just combined.

Pour the batter into the prepared cake pan, and bake for 30 minutes, until the top is golden brown and a toothpick inserted in the center comes out clean. Transfer the pan to a cooling rack and let stand for 10 minutes. Run a knife around the pan to loosen the cake, unclasp the sides of the pan, and flip the cake out onto a cooling rack.

meanwhile, make the coulis Bring all coulis ingredients to a simmer. Cook for 3 minutes, crushing the grapes with spoon or potato masher to help them along, stirring occasionally. Pour the grape mixture through a fine-mesh strainer to remove seeds, and cool completely. Keep coulis covered in the fridge until needed; it keeps for up to a week and is delicious on pancakes and over yogurt too.

Serve cake in wedges, dusted with confectioners' sugar, if desired, and draped with grape coulis.

cooking note This is a flexible cake. Among my favorite things to include in it, in their limited season, are fresh currants (about 1½ cups) or tiny champagne grapes (same volume). When all the fresh berries and grapes are gone, I make a citrus glaze (1 cup confectioners' sugar with 2 tablespoons of lemon, lime, orange, or grapefruit juice). Don't have any fresh fruit around? Split the cake layer, slick the center with your favorite jam or marmalade, and put the lid back on, dusting the cake with confectioners' sugar. Preferably on a Tuesday, just because you can.

golden sheet cake with berry buttercream

Some people find out they're going to be parents and—you know, after the whole "Yay, babies!" cheer has simmered down a bit—freak out, because they haven't yet (a) traveled the world, (b) made their first million, paid off all of their debt, and saved up enough for the top tier preschool for which they put their kid on the waiting list as soon as they confirmed their due date, or (c) well, grown up yet. But, me, I actually had a moment of panic because I hadn't yet found the perfect yellow-layer-cake recipe. And apparently—and, yes, probably ridiculously—central to my image of the kind of mom I wanted to be was not to have to turn to a box of cake mix to get a reliably perfect *Ta-da!* of a birthday cake.

Now, I don't have anything against boxed cake mixes. In fact, I was always a bit jealous of how frighteningly often they made consistently perfect, moist, and plush yellow layer cakes. It's just that it had always been on my agenda to crack the code at home, using the kind of ingredients I was a little more proud to put my efforts behind. And so, with but ten weeks left before my due date, I came up with this cake, my two-to-four-layer 9-inch round yellow cake, and I made it whenever a great birthday cake was required—which is surprisingly often once word gets out that you make grand birthday cakes.

But a couple years later, once I actually had a kid and not just the idea of one, well, things shifted. I started looking enviously at cakes that didn't benefit from leveling and splitting layers and stacking. I realized people who made sheet cakes were on to something—one cake, one pan, lots of servings, and if you frosted them right inside the pan, you didn't even need to find a cake carrier, which was great, because it was currently being used as a life raft for a large stuffed Muppet family on the living-room carpet. The slices were usually smaller, which helps when you're trying to adjust portion size to people for whom reaching a doorknob requires the use of a step stool. And although I have never been the kind of mom who thought that a drop of food coloring here or there was going to harm her precious snowflake, it was hard not to be curious about ways to tint cakes more naturally. After all, nature provides us with such a pretty

yield: one 9-by-13-inch quarter sheet cake, serving 12 to 24. This same recipe can make 24 cupcakes, but you'll want to make 1½ recipes of the frosting if you like to frost them thickly.

12 tablespoons (170 grams or 1½ sticks) unsalted butter, at room temperature, plus more for pan

2¾ cups (345 grams) all-purpose flour

¼ cup (30 grams) cornstarch

1¼ teaspoons baking powder

½ teaspoon baking soda

¾ teaspoon table salt

1½ cups (300 grams) sugar

1½ teaspoons vanilla extract

3 large eggs, at room temperature

1½ cups (355 grams) buttermilk, well shaken

palette of berries—surely they can brighten any cake as well as Red No. 2, and add some flavor too?

*   *   *

Preheat your oven to 350 degrees. Butter a 9-by-13-inch cake pan, and line the bottom with parchment paper. Coat the parchment paper and the inner sides of the pan with butter or a nonstick cooking spray.

Whisk together the flour, cornstarch, baking powder, baking soda, and salt in a medium bowl. In a large mixing bowl, beat the butter and sugar with an electric mixer at medium speed until the mixture is pale and fluffy, then beat in the vanilla. Add the eggs one at a time, beating well and scraping down the bowl after each addition. At low speed, beat in the buttermilk until just combined (the mixture will look curdled). Add the flour mixture in three batches, blending until each addition is just incorporated into the batter.

Spread the batter evenly in the prepared cake pan. Bake until it is golden and a wooden pick inserted in center of cake comes out clean, 30 to 40 minutes. Cool the cake in the pan on a rack 10 minutes, then run a knife around edge of pan. Invert the cake onto rack and discard the parchment. Cool completely, for about 1 hour. Alternatively, you can leave the cake inside the pan and only frost the top, as is more traditional for sheet cakes (plus, the cake pan becomes your cake carrier).

cooking note

In my Berry Buttercream Experiments, I learned many things. One, raspberries and blackberries make nearly the same color tint, and that color is pink, with an almost indistinguishable purple edge to the blackberry one. Both of them together have a tartness and a surprisingly clear flavor that tempers the sweetness of the buttercream, just a bit. Together they're as pretty as a sundress. Two, blueberries were kind of a disaster, because their purée is not blue, but muddy, mucky purple. Also, if you leave the purée out at room temperature while you, say, bake a cake, it will gel, like Jell-O. Really! So—let's say you were trying to make blue, pink, and purple cupcakes for a baby shower, your blue will need a little something from a bottle—a single droplet of blue coloring added to the blueberry shade will make a very pretty hue.

berry buttercream

*   *   *

1 cup (140 grams) fresh raspberries, blackberries, or blueberries

16 tablespoons (225 grams or 2 sticks) butter, at room temperature

4 cups (approximately 480 grams or 1 pound) confectioners' sugar

Purée the berries in a food processor or blender until they are as smooth as possible. Press the purée through a fine-mesh strainer, discarding the skins and seeds. You'll have about ⅓ to a scant ½ cup of berry purée. Set aside.

In a large bowl, beat the butter until it is light and fluffy. Beat in the sugar, 1 cup at a time, beating well after each addition. Add ¼ cup purée and beat until the color is fully incorporated. If you're going for a bluer berry tint than the blueberries will provide, add a single drop of liquid blue food coloring to the blueberry-purée buttercream. Keep the frosting covered until it is needed.

To create the frosting design in the photos: I made four quarter-batches of this frosting, each one with 4 tablespoons (½ stick) butter, 1 cup confectioners' sugar, and 1 tablespoon berry purée. The first batch was blackberry, the second was raspberry, the third was blueberry, and the fourth was also blueberry, but blueberry with a drop of blue food dye. The frosting was piped with a small round pastry tip (about ¼-inch opening) in horizontal lines across the cake, alternating the frostings in stripes.* When the top of the cake is covered, drag a knife crosswise through the frosting (but not into the cake, or you'll pick up crumbs) in 1-inch intervals; the first drag should go in one direction, the second will go in the other. When you're done, your cake top will look like a Mossimo Zig Zag dress—you know, an affordable one.

*Realistically, you won't have four round pastry tips with the same size opening. I didn't! So—pipe your first line, and use the frosting tip to make three additional dot spacers at the end of your row with the same frosting; then pipe your next full line of the berry buttercream. Continue until the cake is covered, rinse the tip, and use the marker you made to pipe the lines for your next frosting until you are done. Yup, you'll have to wash the tip two more times.

chocolate hazelnut crepe cake

yield: serves 16

When my husband's family left Russia in the late 1970s, they spent a few months in Rome while waiting for their American paperwork to go through. They don't remember much from that time, although occasionally snippets leak out, like the extraordinarily dapper coat little Alex ended up with that winter, a secondary benefit of killing time in such a well-dressed country. They rented a furnished apartment, a place where many pantry items were stored in empty glass jars that bore the curious label "Nutella," which led them to buy a jar on a grocery run. Thus began a love affair with Nutella, the famed chocolate-hazelnut spread, that lasts through today.

Inspired by the famed mille-crepe cake at the Lady M bakery uptown, I made my first crepe cake in 2006 and declared it the very best kind of cake possible. Paper-thin crepes are stacked as tall, pretty, and dizzying as can be, and filled with anything from jam to curd to—my favorite—pastry cream. But my husband, a man who considers the Nutella-filled crepe to be the crepe's highest calling, had asked for such a riff on the cake for his birthday in the past. My first attempt was a simple stack of basic Nutella-filled crepes. I know this will be impossible to believe, but there is such thing as too much of a good thing—we had four stacked before the sweet heaviness of the spread became too much. It's almost like you're *supposed* to eat it in moderation?

So, for Alex's birthday last year, I took it upon myself to deconstruct Nutella spread into its hazelnut and chocolate parts, creating a Nutella crepe cake in summary, if not in its components. The end result incorporates a pastry cream that is louder with hazelnut flavor than I ever thought possible. It thinly fills a dozen and a half stacked crepes that are then draped with a thick chocolate ganache. I declared the combined flavor better than Nutella itself, because the chocolate and hazelnut flavors are even louder. My husband insisted the notion that anything could be better than Nutella was blasphemy, and I thought back to him in his little tweed coat in a foreign country and gave him a pass. Especially because he reached for a second slice.

* * *

crepes

9 tablespoons (127 grams) unsalted butter (will be used for both crepes and pastry cream)

2⅓ cups (550 ml) milk (I use whole milk but the fat level shouldn't matter if you prefer a different kind)

6 large eggs

1½ cups (190 grams) all-purpose flour

⅛ teaspoon salt

½ cup (100 grams) granulated sugar

1 tablespoon melted butter or neutral oil for brushing skillet

hazelnut pastry cream

1⅓ cups (190 grams) hazelnuts (will be used for both pastry cream and decorative hazelnuts)

1 cup (120 grams) confectioners' sugar

2 teaspoons hazelnut liqueur, such as Frangelico

¼ teaspoon table salt

3⅓ cups (785 ml) whole milk

7 tablespoons (90 grams) granulated sugar

5 large egg yolks

5 tablespoons (40 grams) cornstarch

Butter reserved from crepes (above)

make crepe batter In a small saucepan, melt the butter over medium heat. Once it's melted, reduce the heat to medium-low. The butter will melt, then foam, then turn clear golden, and finally start to turn brown and smell nutty. Stir the butter frequently, scraping up any bits from the bottom as you do. Don't take your eyes off the pot—you may be impatient for it to start browning, but the time between when the butter begins to take on color and the point where it burns is less than a minute. Once the butter is brown and nutty-smelling, remove it from the heat and transfer it to a bowl. Let it cool to a lukewarm temperature.

In a blender, combine the milk, eggs, flour, salt, granulated sugar, and 6 tablespoons of your cooled brown butter. (Alternatively, combine the ingredients in a bowl using an immersion blender, or whisk vigorously by hand.) Cover the finished mixture with plastic wrap, and refrigerate for an hour or up to 2 days.

toast and skin hazelnuts Preheat your oven to 350 degrees. Spread the hazelnuts out on a baking sheet, and toast them for 10 minutes, rolling them around once or twice so that they toast evenly—keep an eye on them so they don't burn, but let them get some color.

Let hazelnuts cool. Some people like to rub the nuts in a dish towel to loosen the skins, but I hate the mess this makes all over my kitchen when I inevitably forget that the towel is a mess of flakes and pick it up. Instead, with dry hands,

candied hazelnuts

⅔ cup (130 grams) granulated sugar

2 tablespoons water

Pinch of flaky or fine sea salt

Hazelnuts reserved from pastry cream (above)

chocolate draping

6 ounces (170 grams or about 1 cup) semisweet chocolate chips or finely chopped chocolate

¼ cup plus 2 tablespoons (90 ml) heavy cream

1 tablespoon hazelnut liqueur, such as Frangelico

I roll a few together between my palms until the skins come off—usually most, but not all do. This is fine—and the mess stays on the tray.

make hazelnut pastry cream In a food processor, grind 1 cup of the toasted hazelnuts (set the last ⅓ cup aside for decorating), confectioners' sugar, liqueur, and salt together. It will at first make a ruckus (warning: babies don't like this), then will grind to a coarse chop followed by a powder. Keep running the machine until the powder begins to come together in damp-looking crumbs that combine in small clumps, and then stop. If you keep running the machine, you'll end up with a more liquefied hazelnut butter as the oil from the nuts separates out; we don't want this.

In a saucepan, combine the hazelnut paste, milk, and sugar over medium-high heat, and bring to a simmer, stirring a bit so that it does not scorch. In a medium bowl, whisk together the yolks and cornstarch until smooth. Stream a small spoonful of the hot milk mixture into the egg-yolk bowl while whisking. Repeat this a few times with additional spoonfuls of hot milk, and by the time you've done five or six additions, you'll find that the egg-yolk bowl is hot; this is how you know you've added enough. Now go in reverse, slowly pouring the warm egg-yolk mixture back into the hot milk in the saucepan, whisking the whole time, until the two are combined. Return the saucepan to the stove and, continuing to whisk (sense a theme here?), bring the mixture to a boil and cook for 2 minutes; the mixture should thicken upon boiling, to a loose pudding consistency. Remove from the heat, and stir in the reserved 3 tablespoons of browned butter from the crepe-batter recipe above. Transfer it to a bowl (it will cool faster), press a piece of plastic wrap against the top of the custard (to prevent skin formation), and chill the pastry cream in the fridge until fully cold, which could take a couple hours. If you are more pressed for time, set the bowl of custard in a half-full bowl of ice water (i.e., not so full that it could spill into the custard bowl), and it will chill there faster, especially with some stirring to redistribute the temperatures.

make crepes Preheat a medium (9-inch) skillet or crepe pan over medium-high heat. Once it's heated, brush pan lightly with melted butter or oil. Pour ¼ cup batter into skillet, swirling it until it evenly coats the bottom, and cook, undisturbed, until the bottom is golden and the top is set, about 2 minutes. Carefully flip—I like to look for the driest-looking and darkest edge, lift it gently with a spatula so that it gets a second to cool, and use my fingers to hold on to it from that edge while flipping—and cook on other side for 5 to 10 seconds. In all likelihood, toss this one in the trash, and probably the next one too. The first two were never meant to be. I promise, you will eventually hit your stride and wonder why you ever feared the crepe. Transfer finished crepes to a paper-towel-covered plate to cool; it's safe to stack them as they cool, because you will miraculously still be able to separate them later. Continue with remaining batter. Your last

crepe—the one where you hoped you had enough batter for one more but indeed did not—will likely look like a cobweb. This is your snack; now take a break. The batter yields nineteen 9-inch crepes; pastry-cream volume is enough for the sixteen that will probably make it.

assemble cake Lay first crepe on your cake stand or plate. Spread with ¼ cup pastry cream. Repeat with all remaining crepes but the last one, which will act as your cake's lid. Chill the cake in fridge until you're ready to coat it in chocolate—the next step.

candy hazelnuts Spread out a piece of parchment paper on your counter, and have ready a small set of tongs or large tweezers. In a small, heavy saucepan, cook sugar and water together over high heat until the sugar melts and begins to turn a pale-beige color, about 3 to 5 minutes. Add a pinch of a flaky or fine sea salt and the hazelnuts, rolling the hazelnuts around to coat them. The caramel will cook a shade darker while you do this, to a light copper color. Once it has, remove the mixture from the heat. Remove the hazelnuts one by one with the tongs, spreading them out on the parchment paper so that they don't touch. Either cool the nuts on the counter, or slide the paper onto a plate and put the plate in the fridge for 5 minutes. Once firm, they'll fall right off the parchment paper. I like to leave some whole, and bash some up with the back of a heavy cup or pan, so they're in mixed-size pieces. I like them to look a little messy.

make chocolate draping Put chocolate in a heatproof bowl. Heat cream and liqueur to a simmer in a small saucepan and pour over chocolate. Let sit for a minute, then stir until smooth. If this wasn't enough heat to create a very thick but still (barely) pourable smooth mixture, put a little water in the saucepan that previously heated the cream, bring it to a simmer, place the bowl of chocolate and cream over it, and stir it until it thins and smooths out to the desired consistency.

to finish Remove the chilled crepe cake from fridge. Pour chocolate mixture over top, and spread with your spatula to cover the top crepe, gently nudging the chocolate over the edges in a few places. Decorate the top with the candied hazelnuts. Set the cake in fridge (allowing the chocolate to set) until needed.

s'more layer cake

Although I lack the planning-ahead trait in any other area of my life, it should be little surprise that I find myself plotting my son's birthday cakes months and months before they're needed. I knew I wanted his first birthday cake to be a two-layer banana and milk chocolate affair, shaped like a monkey, with a mini-monkey "smash" cake long before he even knew how to roll over, and I knew that his second birthday would have to involve graham crackers, which he delightfully called "tookies."

I hadn't planned for it to turn into a s'more cake, but as anyone who has ever camped before knows, with graham crackers around, chocolate and toasted marshmallows are inevitable. Getting the layers to taste exactly like graham crackers was surprisingly challenging; I only got it right in color and flavor when I actually used ground crackers as one of the "flours." Next, there was the milk chocolate filling. Though milk chocolate isn't terribly popular in baking—it's sweeter and less intense than darker varieties—I think a good pinch of salt is exactly what makes milk chocolate sing, and use it here.

The frosting, however, was easily the most fun part, mainly because it involved my ~~family cowering in the corner, pointing a fire extinguisher how in my direction a blowtorch!~~ And amazingly, it makes your kitchen smell like toasted marshmallows, too—hooray.

Needless to say, I've already got designs on Jacob's third birthday cake and am counting down the days until I can start testing it. I'll be putting away the blowtorch this year, sigh, but for the best of reasons: I hope it will be the first of many we can bake together.

*   *   *

make cake Preheat your oven to 350 degrees. Butter two 9-inch round cake pans, and line them with circles of parchment paper, then butter or coat with a nonstick cooking spray.

In a medium bowl, whisk together flour, graham-cracker crumbs, baking powder, baking soda, salt, and cinnamon. Set aside. In a large mixing bowl,

yield: one 2-layer 9-inch cake, serving 16

cake layers

16 tablespoons (225 grams or 2 sticks) unsalted butter, softened, plus more for pans

2 cups (250 grams) all-purpose flour

2 cups (170 grams) honey (not cinnamon-sugar-topped) graham-cracker crumbs, finely processed to a powder (from approximately fourteen 2½-by-4⅞-inch sheets)

2 teaspoons baking powder

¾ teaspoon baking soda

¾ teaspoon table salt

½ teaspoon ground cinnamon

⅔ cup (130 grams) granulated sugar

1 cup (190 grams) dark brown sugar

4 large eggs, at room temperature

2 cups (475 ml) buttermilk, well shaken (or 1⅓ cups milk and ⅔ cup sour cream)

filling

½ pound (225 grams) milk chocolate, chopped small

¾ cup (175 ml) heavy cream

2 pinches of salt

cream butter and sugars together until light and fluffy. Add eggs one at a time, scraping the bowl down after each addition. Add a third of the dry ingredients, then half the buttermilk, a third of the dry ingredients, the remaining buttermilk, and then the remaining dry ingredients, mixing between additions until combined. Scrape down bowl, and mix again briefly if needed.

Divide batter between prepared cake pans, smoothing tops. Bake until a toothpick inserted into the center comes out clean, about 30 to 35 minutes. Cool in pan on rack, then run a knife between the cake edges and pans before inverting each layer on a rack, discarding the parchment paper, and flipping back upright onto a rack. Let cool completely, a process you can speed up in the fridge (I always do).

make filling Place the chocolate in a heatproof bowl. Combine the heavy cream and salt in a small saucepan, and bring to a simmer. Pour over the chocolate, and let sit for 1 minute, then whisk until smooth. Set bowl over another bowl filled with ice water, and stir it until it firms up to a spreadable consistency. (If you have more time to kill, you can let it cool down in the fridge, but stir it from time to time so that it thickens evenly.)

prepare cake Arrange a single cake layer on a serving platter or cake stand. For a neat-looking cake, use a long serrated knife to level the top gently, taking off only the domed part (which shouldn't be much); place scraps in a bowl where husbands and other housemates can enjoy the pre-

view. Spread chocolate thickly over bottom layer. Place the top layer over bottom layer. Once again, for a neater appearance, you can level the top of the cake in the same manner, but I won't tell anyone if you don't share the scraps. Baking is exhausting work, after all.

make frosting Place the egg whites, granulated sugar, and cream of tartar in the heatproof bowl of an electric mixer. Set over a saucepan with simmering water. Whisk constantly until sugar is dissolved and whites are warm to the touch, about 3 minutes. Transfer the bowl to an electric mixer fitted with the whisk attachment, and beat, starting at low speed, gradually increasing to high, until stiff, glossy peaks form, 4 to 7 minutes. Add vanilla, and mix until combined. You'll want to use this immediately.

frost cake Spread a thin layer of the frosting over the top and sides, covering all of the crumbs (and binding them to the cake). Transfer the cake to the fridge for 5 or 10 minutes, to let it set a bit, then generously coat the top and sides with additional frosting. Put the remaining frosting in a piping bag, or disposable baggie with the corner nipped off, fitted with your largest round piping tip (I use an almost comically large one with a ½-inch opening). Create big marshmallowlike dollops decoratively over the top of the cake. Dipping your fingertip into a small dish of water between the dollops, use your fingertip to press down gently on the pointy top of each dollop, where you pulled the piping bag away. Remove any flammable objects and people from the immediate vicinity of the cake. With a kitchen torch on a low setting, lightly brown the dollops, creating a toasted-marshmallow effect (and—as you'll quickly discover—aroma).

red wine velvet cake with whipped mascarpone

*W*ho isn't charmed by red velvet cakes? They're cute: red-and-white striped, as adorable as a candy cane, as sweet as a valentine. They're typically towering and grand, and scream "party." Plus, just about anything covered in thick plumes of cream-cheese frosting is automatically delicious.

But behind the pretty façade, so much of it doesn't add up for me. The chocolate is barely perceptible and the "red velvet" is just red food dye, and a lot of it.

But one day, a reader left a comment on an everyday chocolate cake in my archives and told me she'd been out of the required buttermilk and used red wine instead. She'd turned a chocolate cake into a red wine–chocolate cake. And I'd never had one of these before, never even considered it, but I had to drop everything I was doing and try this substitution. It quickly became one of our favorite cakes. With its loud chocolate flavor and natural red tint—this was the *real* red velvet cake.

This is my favorite birthday cake for grown-ups, and, yes, I do mean grown-ups, because the wine does not fully bake out. (You're welcome.) The flavor trifecta is red wine, chocolate, and a slip of cinnamon, three things that you will quickly see have always been meant to be together. It's chocolate-flavored and naturally red, and the texture is so dense and moist that only a little frosting is required between the layers, and that frosting is whipped mascarpone cheese—or cream cheese for people who have taken a fancy to triple-creme cheeses.

* * *

make the cake Preheat your oven to 325 degrees. Line the bottom of three 9-inch round cake pans with parchment, and either butter and lightly flour the parchment and exposed sides of the pans, or spray the interior with a nonstick spray. In a large bowl, at the medium speed of an electric mixer, cream the butter until smooth. Add the sugars and beat until fluffy,

yield: 1 towering 3-layer 9-inch cake, serving 16 to 20

cake

16 tablespoons (225 grams or 2 sticks) unsalted butter, at room temperature, plus more for pans

2¾ cups (345 grams) all-purpose flour, plus more for pans

2 cups (380 grams) firmly packed dark brown sugar

⅔ cup (135 grams) granulated sugar

4 large eggs, at room temperature

2 cups (475 ml) red wine (any kind you like)

2 teaspoons vanilla extract

1⅓ cups (115 grams) Dutch cocoa powder

½ teaspoon baking soda

1 teaspoon baking powder

¾ teaspoon ground cinnamon

¾ teaspoon table salt

about 3 minutes. Add the eggs and beat well, then the red wine and vanilla. Don't worry if the batter looks a little uneven. Sift the flour, cocoa, baking soda, baking powder, cinnamon, and salt together, right over your wet ingredients. Mix until three-quarters combined, then fold the rest together with a rubber spatula. Divide batter between prepared pans (about 2½ cups batter per pan). Bake for 25 minutes, or until a cake tester inserted into the center of each layer comes out clean. The top of each cake should be shiny and smooth, like a puddle of chocolate. Cool in pan on a rack for about 10 minutes, then flip out of pan and cool the rest of the way on a cooling rack.

If your cakes have domed a bit and you want nice even layers in your stack, you can trim the tops. Use a long serrated knife, held horizontally, and use gentle back-and-forth motions with your hand on top of the cake to even it out. Share the cake scraps with whoever is around; no one will mind helping you remove "debris."

make the filling In a medium bowl, beat the mascarpone with the confectioners' sugar, pinch of salt, and vanilla extract at medium speed until the mixture is light and fluffy, about 1 to 2 minutes.

assemble cake Place the first cake layer on a cake stand or plate, and spread with one-third of the filling. Repeat with remaining two layers. Chill the cake in the fridge until you're ready to serve it.

filling

16 ounces (500 grams) mascarpone cheese

2⅓ cups (280 grams) confectionters' sugar

Pinch of salt

¼ teaspoon vanilla extract

cooking note

This recipe makes a three-layer cake with three layers of filling. You won't have enough to coat the sides—I liked the look of the cake stacked and open. You can double the frosting recipe to cover it, but I want to warn you that there is a bit of translucence to the whipped mascarpone, and the cake is likely to peep through anyway.

puddings and candy

strawberry cheesecake fools

white chocolate pudding with blackberry curd

tres leches rice pudding

apple cider caramels

coffee toffee

strawberry cheesecake fools

For the sake of honesty, I'm not going to pretend that I made my first strawberry fool in an exercise to better study classic British desserts. It wasn't because I often wish I could just sit there and eat a large bowl of whipped cream, though I won't say that hasn't crossed my mind. And it wasn't because I have any trouble using up pounds of strawberries, especially those as tiny and exquisite as the ones we get in June.

Nope, it was the name. I'm a sucker for fruit desserts with goofy names. I collect them the way some people might collect matches from Michelin-starred restaurants. I have to try each one at least once: the syllabub, the grunt, the buckle, the betty, and the pan-dowdy; the crisps, crumbles, cobblers, and clafoutis. But mostly, the fools. Because how can you not love a dessert called a fool?

Of course, I had to mess with it. I had to New York it up a little. First I made a classic fool—whipped cream, puréed fruit, served with a digestive biscuit for an extra British effect—but the combination of crumbs and fruit got me thinking about a great New York cheese-cake, the kind with fruit running off the top, and from that point, there was no going back. And so I made a cheesecake of a fool (perhaps a fool of a cheesecake?), and we proceeded to have to hide it in the back of the fridge to keep ourselves from eating more than one a day. Hey, I said I'd be honest here. But it's also that delicious, a pudding of a cheesecake as pretty as a ribbony striped candy cane.

* * *

prepare strawberries Hull and quarter the strawberries. Whisk together the granulated sugar and the cornstarch. Stir together the strawberries, sugar-and-cornstarch mixture, and lemon juice in a 2-to-3-quart saucepan, and let it stand, stirring occasionally, until juicy, about 15 minutes. Bring the strawberries to a simmer over medium heat, and cook for 2 minutes, stirring occasionally. Transfer the mixture to a bowl, cover, and chill completely in fridge, about 1 to 2 hours.

yield: 6 servings

---

fruit

4 cups (about 455 grams or 1 pound) strawberries

2 tablespoons (25 grams) granulated sugar

2 teaspoons cornstarch

1 tablespoon freshly squeezed lemon juice (from about ½ lemon)

---

brown sugar cookie crumb streusel

7 Carr's Whole Wheat Crackers, or 2 ounces (55 grams) of another digestive biscuit

¼ cup (25 grams) dark brown sugar

Pinch of ground cinnamon

---

whipped cream cheese

¾ cup (175 ml) heavy or whipping cream

6 ounces (170 grams) cream cheese, softened

¼ cup (25 grams) granulated sugar

Pinch of salt

¼ teaspoon vanilla extract

Once it's fully chilled, set a strainer over a bowl and pour the strawberry mixture into it. No need to strain the berries fully (i.e., over a long period of time)—you're just looking to remove a bit of the excess juiciness. Reserve ¼ cup of the strained juice, and set aside.

prepare crumbs Grind the crackers, brown sugar, and cinnamon together until powdery. Set aside.

make the creams In a small bowl, beat the whipping cream with a hand mixer until it holds stiff peaks; then set aside. In a large bowl, combine the cream cheese, sugar, salt, and vanilla. Beat until smooth, then fold in the whipped cream. Remove ½ cup of the cream-cheese–whipped-cream mixture and set it aside. Fold the ¼ cup of reserved strawberry juices into the larger volume of cream cheese and whipped cream.

assemble desserts Line up six champagne flutes or other tall, narrow 4-ounce glasses. In the bottom of each glass (using one of those long tea-spoons from your grandmother that you never use for anything else, or something along those lines), layer 1 tablespoon of the cooked straw-berry mixture, followed by 1 tablespoon of the crumb mixture, followed by 3 tablespoons of the strawberry-flavored cream cheese and whipped cream (you know, the pink stuff), followed by another tablespoon of crumbs and another tablespoon of strawberries. Add a dollop of the reserved, strawberry-free cream cheese and whipped cream to the top of each flute. Sprinkle some remaining brown sugar–cracker crumbs for garnish. Chill for 30 minutes or up to 3 days, and serve cold, with those very long spoons.

white chocolate pudding with blackberry curd

A small mix-up in the instruction department with my awesome unpaid assistant of a husband led to his purchasing not 2 to 3 *ounces* of white chocolate at the baking-supply store but, well, 2 to 3 pounds, or a whole kilo. That is a spectacular amount of white chocolate, at a spectacular price (it was, gulp, Valrhona Ivoire); there was way too much of it to ignore it until it went away. And so I decided to chip away at it until we made peace at last. And I learned a lot.

First, I learned a little empathy for this outcast of the chocolate world; white chocolate really has it tough. It shares a name with a confection that needs no improving upon, and it's so sweet that it requires (almost) no additional sugar, meaning that, if you use it in a recipe for which dark chocolate was intended, you'll find the dessert tooth-achingly inedible. Plus, it's barely white, more like a pale waxy shade of ivory. *Yum*, right?

Next, I realized that the easiest way to make peace with white chocolate was to think of it not as chocolate, but instead as a creamy, almost buttermilklike confection that flourishes when paired— in different proportions from the dark stuff—with a whole range of favorite ingredients. It's wonderful with salt, and salted nuts. It's fantastic with mint or peanut butter, rounding both flavors out delicately. And against berries, which I've never enjoyed when paired with dark chocolates, white chocolate simply *wins*. I can offer little better evidence than this pudding. White-chocolate pudding on its own is tasty—it's fine, sweet, even, pale. With a slick of sharp blackberry curd? It's delicious, balanced, and one of the prettiest things to come out of my kitchen in eons.

*　　*　　*

make the pudding Combine the cornstarch, sugar, and salt in a heavy saucepan. Before turning on the heat, slowly whisk in the milk, scraping the bottom and sides of the pan with a heatproof spatula to incorporate the dry ingredients. Place over gently simmering water, and stir occasionally, scraping the bottom and sides. Use a whisk as necessary, should lumps

white chocolate pudding

3 tablespoons (25 grams) cornstarch

1 tablespoon sugar

¼ teaspoon table salt

2¼ cups (530 ml) whole milk

4½ ounces (130 grams) white chocolate, chopped

¼ teaspoon vanilla extract

quick blackberry curd

½ cup (60 grams) fresh blackberries

1 tablespoon freshly squeezed lemon juice

¼ cup (25 grams) sugar

Pinch of salt

1 large egg

2 tablespoons (30 grams) unsalted butter, cut into small pieces

begin to form. After 15 to 20 minutes, when the mixture begins to thicken and coats the back of the spoon, add the chocolate. Continue stirring for about 2 to 4 minutes, or until the pudding is smooth and thickened. Remove from the heat and stir in the vanilla.

For perfectly silken texture, you can strain the pudding through a fine-mesh strainer (or skip this step if you're a slacker like me who can abide a lump or two in her puddin') into a bowl with a spout, and pour into individual serving dishes. Chill in fridge.

meanwhile, prepare the blackberry topping Puréee berries in a food processor or blender until as smooth as possible. Press through a fine-mesh strainer to remove seeds. You should have between 3 and 4 tablespoons of purée.

Whisk together the blackberry purée, lemon juice, sugar, salt, and egg in a heavy 1-quart saucepan. Stir in the butter, and cook over moderately low heat, whisking frequently, until the curd is thick enough to hold the marks of the whisk, and until the first bubble appears on surface, about 4 to 5 minutes. Pass through a strainer again if you want a perfect texture (though again, I don't usually bother). Divide curd among prepared cups, gently spreading it on pudding surfaces.

do ahead

Chill puddings in fridge for at least an hour and up to 3 days.

tres leches rice pudding

My list of rice pudding loves is long. There's the Danish *risala-mande*, with chopped almonds, whipped cream, and a sour cherry sauce, usually served at Christmas with a prize inside—one that I never win, not that I've been trying for thirteen years at my best friend's house or anything. There's *kheer*, with cardamom, cashews or pistachios, and saffron. There's rice pudding the way our grand-mothers made it, baked for what feels like an eternity, with milk, eggs, and sugar. And there's arroz con leche, which is kind of like your Kozy Shack went down to Costa Rica for a lazy weekend and came back enviously tan, sultry, and smelling of sandy shores. As you can tell, I really like arroz con leche.

But this—a riff on one of the best variants of arroz con leche I've made, which, in its original incarnation on my site, I adapted from Ingrid Hoffmann's wonderful recipe—is my favorite, for two reasons: First, it knows me. (That's the funny thing about the recipes I create!) It knows how preposterously bad I am at keeping stuff in stock in my kitchen, like milk, but that I seem always to have an unmoved collection of canned items and grains. Second, it's so creamy that it's like a pudding stirred into another pudding.

The rice is cooked first in water. I prefer to start my rice pudding recipes like this, because I'm convinced that cooking the rice first in milk takes twice as long and doesn't get the pudding half as creamy. Also, it gives me a use for those cartons of white rice left over from the Chinese take-out I only occasionally (*cough*) succumb to. Then you basically cook another pudding on top of it, with one egg and three milks—coconut, evaporated, and sweetened condensed—and the end result will be the richest and most luxurious rice pud-ding imaginable. But why stop there? For the times when the word "Enough!" has escaped your vocabulary, I recommend topping it with a dollop of cinnamon-dusted whipped cream, for the icing on the proverbial cake.

*   *   *

yield: serves 8

---

1 cup (180 grams) long-grain white rice

¾ teaspoon table salt

1 large egg

One 12-ounce can (1½ cups or 355 ml) evaporated milk

One 13.5-ounce can (1⅞ cups or 415 ml) unsweetened coconut milk

One 14-ounce can (1¼ cups or 390 grams) sweetened condensed milk

1 teaspoon vanilla extract

1 cup (240 ml) heavy or whipping cream, chilled

1 tablespoon confectioners' sugar

Ground cinnamon, to finish

---

tres leches rice pudding (continued)

cook the rice Put the rice, 2 cups of water, and the salt in a medium saucepan with a tight-fitting lid. Bring to a boil—you should hear the pot going all aflutter under the lid and puffing steam out the seam. Reduce to a low simmer, and let the rice cook for 15 minutes, until the water is absorbed. Remove the rice pot from the heat.

Once the rice is cooked, whisk the egg in a medium bowl, and then whisk in the evaporated milk. Stir the coconut and sweetened condensed milks into the rice, then add the egg mixture. Return the saucepan to heat and cook the mixture over medium-low heat until it looks mostly, or about 90 percent, absorbed (the pudding will thicken a lot as it cools), about 20 to 25 minutes. Stir in the vanilla extract, then divide the pudding among serving dishes. Keep the puddings in the fridge until fully chilled, about 1 to 2 hours.

to serve Whip the heavy cream with the confectioners' sugar until soft peaks form. Dollop a spoonful of whipped cream on top of each bowl of rice pudding, dust with ground cinnamon, then enjoy.

cooking note

If you have 2 cups of leftover white rice, you can skip the first step, and jump in with the egg and three milks.

apple cider caramels

$\mathcal{I}$f I could pack everything I love about New York City in October—the carpet of fiery leaves on the ground from the trees I didn't even know we had; the sky, impossibly blue; the air, drinkably crisp; the temperature finally delicious enough that it implores you to spend hours wandering around, sipping warm spiced apple cider from the greenmarkets—into one tiny square, this would be how I'd try to pull it off.

It would be impossible, of course. I mean, you can't smell the street vendors, with roasted nuts and pretzels that, well, at least *look* amazing. You can't feel the slightly irritating swish of strangers' scarves against your arm as they hurry past you. You can't hear the lull, the surprising hush that passes over the loudest city when the weather is unspeakably perfect.

I spent years making excuses for why I didn't make caramels. "Bleh, too sweet!" "I'm just not a candy person!" "It's too precise!"— but I was just avoiding it after one experience wherein I misread a recipe as 225, not 252 degrees and ended up with caramels that gummed permanently to your teeth. I had to toss the better part of a pound of chocolate into the trash. But my obsession with apple cider—and finding desserts that really taste like it, rather than invoking it in name only—finally got me over this. I'm so glad. This is my fall bliss. The apple cider is boiled and boiled and boiled until it's a slip of its original volume, leaving only a syrupy apple impact. The syrup is then expanded into a cinnamon-scented buttery caramel with hidden crunches of salt. They're the most intense caramels I've ever eaten, the kind that demand you close your eyes and consider how you've managed to shrink an entire weekend of leaf-peeping upstate into a paper-wrapped treat.

* * *

Boil the apple cider in a 3-to-4-quart saucepan over high heat until it is reduced to a dark, thick syrup, between ⅓ and ½ cup in volume. This takes about 35 to 40 minutes on my stove. Stir occasionally.

yield: about 64 caramels

4 cups (945 ml) apple cider

½ teaspoon ground cinnamon

2 teaspoons flaky sea salt

8 tablespoons (115 grams or 1 stick) unsalted butter, cut into chunks

1 cup (200 grams) granulated sugar

½ cup (110 grams) packed light brown sugar

⅓ cup (80 ml) heavy cream

Neutral oil for the knife

do ahead

Caramels keep, in an airtight container at room temperature, for two weeks, but really, good luck with that.

Meanwhile, get your other ingredients in order, because you won't have time to spare once the candy is cooking. Line the bottom and sides of an 8-inch straight-sided square metal baking pan with 2 long sheets of criss-crossed parchment. Set it aside. Stir the cinnamon and flaky salt together in a small dish.

Once you are finished reducing the apple cider, remove it from the heat and stir in the butter, sugars, and heavy cream. Return the pot to medium-high heat with a candy thermometer attached to the side, and let it boil until the thermometer reads 252 (not 225, okay?) degrees, only about 5 minutes. Keep a close eye on it.

(Don't have a candy or deep-fry thermometer? Have a bowl of very cold water ready, and cook the caramel until a tiny spoonful dropped into the water becomes firm, chewy, and able to be plied into a ball.)

Immediately remove caramel from heat, add the cinnamon-salt mixture, and give the caramel several stirs to distribute it evenly. Pour caramel into the prepared pan. Let it sit until cool and firm—about 2 hours, though it goes faster in the fridge. Once caramel is firm, use your parchment paper sling to transfer the block to a cutting board. Use a well-oiled knife, oiling it after each cut (trust me!), to cut the caramel into 1-by-1-inch squares. Wrap each one in a 4-inch square of waxed paper, twisting the sides to close. Caramels will be somewhat on the soft side at room temperature, and chewy/firm from the fridge.

cooking note

Apple cider (sometimes called sweet or "soft" cider), as I'm referring to it here, is different from both apple juice and the hard, or alcoholic, fermented apple cider. It's a fresh, unfiltered (it has sediment), raw apple juice—the juice literally pressed from fresh apples. It's unpasteurized, and must be refrigerated, because it's perishable. In the Northeast, I usually find it at farm stands and some grocery stores. I occasionally find vacuum-sealed bottles called apple cider in the juice aisle, but none of the bottled varieties that I've tried has the same delicate apple flavor as the more perishable stuff sold in the refrigerator section.

coffee toffee

When my kid was about two months old, I became obsessed with coffee. I'm sure it was just a coincidence that the coffee kick began just as the number of hours I slept each night decreased, which also coincided with my getting weepy with joy over the transcendent experience of wrapping my fingers around my first coffee each day, even if I was looked at like a weirdo at the coffee shop.

Still, I tried to limit my coffee intake; I always thought it was a slippery slope from enjoying a single small drip coffee each morning to becoming one of those people who need nothing short of a 31-ounce coffee tanker to make it in to work each day, and I was afraid to let my tidy coffee habit go. So, like any healthy adult, I sublimated my urges into baked goods, and soon coffee showed up everywhere. There was an espresso-soaked birthday cake, and mocha brownies, and chocolate-chip cookies made with chocolate-covered espresso beans. And, inspired by a pint of Ben & Jerry's Coffee Heath Bar Crunch ice cream, wherein toasted butter and brown sugar mingled dreamily with crunchy powdered espresso, there was this toffee.

This is grown-up toffee; it's almost as bitter as it is sweet, from both instant espresso powder and molasses, and it makes a great gift for coffee junkies (and new parents—eh, same thing). If a piece of candy could ever taste like a cup of coffee, this would be it.

*   *   *

yield: about 1½ pounds toffee

8 tablespoons (225 grams or 2 sticks) butter

½ cup (95 grams) light brown sugar

½ cup (100 grams) granulated sugar

1½ teaspoons molasses

¼ teaspoon table salt (or a heaping ¼ teaspoon flaky sea salt)

1½ teaspoons instant espresso powder

1 cup semisweet chocolate chips or 6 ounces (170 grams) semisweet chocolate, chopped

½ cup (70 grams) chopped hazelnuts (toasted, skinned, and cooled; see page 257), or another nut of your choice

Line a small baking sheet (mine is 9-by-13-inch, to fit in my puny oven) with parchment paper or a silicon mat, and set aside.

In a medium-sized heavy saucepan with a candy thermometer attached, melt butter, both sugars, molasses, salt, and espresso together over medium-high heat. Cook, stirring occasionally with a whisk, until the temperature approaches 250 degrees; then stir constantly until it reaches 300 degrees.

Pour immediately onto the prepared baking sheet—spread evenly with an offset spatula. Sprinkle the chocolate chips over the toffee, let them sit for a minute until soft, then spread the chocolate evenly over the candy base.

Sprinkle the chocolate with chopped hazelnuts, and then, if you're as impatient as we are, you can slide the sheet onto a cooling rack in the freezer until the toffee is set.

Break the toffee into pieces, and store in an airtight container. If your kitchen runs warm, you might prefer to keep it in the fridge so the chocolate doesn't get sticky.

party snacks
and drinks

how to throw a dinner party
(that you'll actually get to enjoy)

spicy brittled peanuts

pumpernickel grissini with horseradish
crème fraîche dip

smoky deviled eggs with crisped jamón
and crushed marconas

blue cheese and black pepper gougères

rosemary gruyère and sea salt crisps

baked potato crisps with the works

french onion toasts

broiled clams with chorizo breadcrumbs

spritzy ginger lemonade

muddle puddle battle

how to throw a dinner party

(that you'll actually get to enjoy)

*   *   *

As someone who recently prepared eight dishes for seven people in a tiny two-bedroom apartment, I can be trusted when I say that entertaining in small spaces is not impossible. Be ye not daunted by diminutive kitchens and minimal counter space, folding chairs, a full-time job that doesn't involve being a domestic diva, or the lack of proper serving utensils. All you really need is to make a few savvy decisions from the outset, and the rest will fall into place.

* *Call for take-out.* Fine, I'm kidding. But do consider what kind of things can be perfectly prepared elsewhere. There's no reason to bake a homemade baguette, for example—something I have been crazed enough to try in the past. A platter of cheeses, nuts, cured meats, and pickles makes an excellent first course, and requires minimal extra work on your part. Nobody is going to be disappointed you didn't cure your own meats.

* *You only need one pièce de résistance.* No matter how much you enjoy showing off your cooking prowess, you still only need one *Ta-da!* dish. Furthermore, it doesn't have to be the main

course. Maybe you did really want to try your hand at baking a homemade baguette; go for it. But then take it easy with the rest of your dishes. A fast track to pulling your hair out would be to make that baguette, plus pasta from scratch, plus homemade chicken stock, while soaking your own beans. They'll remember the baguette longer, anyhow.

* *Plan a savvy menu.* One you've picked your Big Ta-Da Dish, the rest of your items should be things that reheat easily or can be whipped together quickly; think tarts, quiches, soups, gratins, casseroles, and salads. Avoid anything that requires a last-minute pan-searing, especially if you have more items than fit in a single sauté pan.

* *Put time on your side.* I am a plan-ahead fiend. I hate rushing. What this translates to is my one above-all-else rule of party planning: If it can be done in advance, it should be. A week ahead of time, I make a list of the things I want to make and order them by date, from those items which can be made furthest in advance (tart dough, ice cream) to those which absolutely must be made at the last minute (tossed salad, things that cannot be reheated).

* *Buy some paper plates and cups.* Just in case! Most people own eight- or twelve-piece place settings and easily invite this many people for dinner. All goes well until it's time for the next course, and then—oops! Standing over the sink and frantically hand-washing dishes between courses, while all your friends are laughing and drinking in the next room, is no way to spend a party. You'll be glad you purchased a backup plan.

* *Liberate your inner domestic diva.* Here's the thing about too much perfectionism: It makes everyone a little uncomfortable. Perfectly matched table settings, and perfectly arranged everything while all dishes are presented just so, can be too much. People want to relax and have a good time; they don't want to feel that they are inside a china cabinet. So don't be afraid of mismatched table settings, and consider picking your battles.

* *Put your friends to work.* Your friends—yes, even those who have never turned on their ovens—want to help, so leave things for them to do. Easy ideas include whisking the vinegar, oil, and Dijon mustard into a salad dressing, plating food, slicing bread, stirring anything, and chopping garnishes. Figure out what the easily distributed tasks are, and start delegating.

* *Pick a quitting time.* About an hour before everyone is supposed to come over, I quit, take a shower, and put on some cute clothes. I cannot feel festive if I'm still wearing a filthy apron—and, yes, my aprons are filthy after I cook with them, never pressed and pristine like those you see in entertaining magazines. Whatever isn't done yet just isn't getting done. My time would be better used for other things, like testing the Prosecco to make sure it's good enough for guests, or sampling the snacks below, which are some of my favorites to make for a party.

spicy brittled peanuts

This recipe is for the people who know that the very best part of caramel popcorn is the peanuts, who root them out, ruining the bowl for others. It's for people who lamented the skimpy presence of peanuts in the Cracker Jack box (but kept buying them for the prize).

These spicy peanuts are addictive. They seem kind of harmless—candied nuts, nothing new here, right?—but they're loud with flavors, from a dark, almost over-toasted caramel, pops of crunchy salt, a little punch of spice, and the smallest amount of butter to make them even richer. I made them one day just to see what would happen if I completely forwent the popcorn part of the caramel popcorn. I left them out on their tray and came back to find the tray thinned of goodies. I moved them to a bowl, and then to a smaller bowl, until they were completely gone. I still don't know where they up and went to, but I know that, wherever they're hiding, the batch I made a few days later joined them. They have that kind of effect on people, and, should they ever last long enough to make it to a party, I believe they'd be a most welcome guest.

*   *   *

Line a baking sheet with parchment paper or a silicon mat. If you don't have either, coat your baking sheet with a thin slick of vegetable oil.

In a small bowl, whisk together the baking soda, sea salt, and cayenne, and set aside.

In a medium saucepan, the heaviest one you've got, heat the sugar, butter, and water over medium-high heat until it just begins to turn golden, about 7 to 10 minutes. Add the peanuts and start stirring, coating them with the sugar mixture. After a minute or two, the sugar will seize up a bit, making the peanuts look grainy and crusty, and it will be harder to stir them—you'll be convinced that it's gone irreversibly south, cursing me under your breath, but fear not, keep stirring, and in about 3 minutes it will melt back into a golden caramel. Keep stirring, breaking up any clumps with your spoon, until the nuts are evenly coated, then remove the pot

yield: 2 cups of candied nuts

½ teaspoon baking soda

½ teaspoon flaky sea salt

⅛ teaspoon cayenne pepper

1 cup (200 grams) sugar

1 tablespoon unsalted butter

¼ cup (60 ml) water

2 cups (280 grams) shelled raw or roasted unsalted peanuts, papery skins removed

from the heat. Stir in the baking-soda–spice mixture as fast and evenly as you can, then spill the caramelized nuts out onto your prepared sheet, spreading them in a single layer and breaking up any clumps that you can before they set. Cool completely.

Once they're cool, break the nut clusters into smaller pieces and put them in a serving dish. The nuts will keep in an airtight container for up to 2 weeks, but rarely do because they are habit-forming.

cooking note

Technically speaking, this recipe works best with raw peanuts, as they run the least risk of burning. However, I usually start with roasted ones, because I like the way their peanut flavor becomes toasty almost to the point of smokiness, which gives them an added depth

pumpernickel grissini with horseradish crème fraîche dip

My favorite recipe for pumpernickel bread has twenty ingredients, which start a little curious (apple cider, molasses), then get a little more worrisome (shallots, unsweetened chocolate), before finally getting so strange (espresso powder, ground fennel seeds) that it doesn't bother me in the least that the overwhelming majority of the visitors to that recipe's page click away a split second after reading the word "bran." This is because the ones who stay, the ones who shake off nagging concerns about caraway and make it, are like a special club—those of us who know that a slice of this with a pat of cultured butter, a cup of tea, and a good book has to be one of the greatest ways to spend a cold afternoon.

Needless to say, I don't make it very often, and when I do, we hoard it. Here, I whittle that ingredient list down to a Best Of, and then trim it further into a pencil-thin breadstick that can be cranked out easily, just because. I realize that most people don't get too excited about grissini; usually they arrive on tables at Italian restaurants and don't taste like terribly much. These—even without the fennel, espresso, and hours of labor—do. They make a surprisingly popular snack for my weirdo toddler and they're really fun to put out at a party with an unforgettable tangy, rich dip.

*   *   *

In a small dish, whisk together the water, yeast, molasses, and sugar. Set aside for 10 minutes, after which the mixture should be foamy. (If it's not, your yeast is probably past its prime, and should be replaced. Let's hope this hasn't happened.)

Combine the flours, cocoa, caraway seeds, and salt in a large bowl. Pour in the melted butter or olive oil and the yeast mixture, and stir until a craggy mass of dough comes together. Turn it out onto a lightly floured counter, and knead the dough for a few minutes, until it becomes smooth and somewhat elastic. Wipe out the mixing bowl, and coat it with olive oil.

yield: 4 dozen grissini and 1 cup dip

grissini

½ cup (120 ml) warm water

1 packet (2¼ teaspoons) active dry yeast

1 teaspoon molasses

1 teaspoon sugar

1 cup (125 grams) all-purpose flour, plus more for counter

¼ cup (30 grams) whole-wheat flour

½ cup (65 grams) rye flour

1 tablespoon cocoa powder

2 teaspoons caraway seeds

1½ teaspoons fine sea salt

2 tablespoons (30 grams or 30 ml) butter, melted and cooled, or olive oil, plus olive oil for bowl

dip

1 cup (225 grams) crème fraîche

4 teaspoons (20 grams) grated prepared horseradish, or more to taste

½ teaspoon table salt

1 teaspoon white wine vinegar

Return the dough to the bowl, cover the bowl with plastic wrap, and let it rise in a warm spot for an hour.

Meanwhile, oil two large baking sheets, or line them with parchment paper; set trays aside.

After an hour has passed, turn the dough back out onto your counter, and gently deflate it by pressing down on it with your palms. Divide the dough in half. Roll the first half into a rough rectangle, about 8 by 12 inches. Cut the dough lengthwise into ¼-inch strips, and transfer them to one of the prepared baking sheets, keeping them a breadstick width apart. Repeat with second half of dough on second tray. Cover the trays loosely with a towel, and let the grissini rise for another 30 minutes.

Meanwhile, preheat your oven to 400 degrees. Bake the breadsticks, one tray at a time, in the top third of the oven, until they're a shade darker and puffed, about 10 minutes. Rotate your tray halfway through if you fear your oven bakes unevenly. Bake remaining tray in the same manner. Cool trays completely on a rack.

When ready to serve, mix together the dip ingredients in a small bowl. Serve with grissini.

do ahead Grissini can be stored in an airtight container until needed. They keep for 1 week. The dip will keep for one week in the fridge.

smoky deviled eggs with crisped jamón and crushed marconas

I am pretty sure that if I didn't have a husband or a kid, and only had to feed myself for dinner each night, I would probably subsist solely on tomato bread—toasted bread with olive oil and salt that's been rubbed with a raw garlic clove and then a cut tomato—from July to October each year. I'd occasionally throw in some blistered Padrón peppers, and then, when the need for protein-rich food became overwhelming, I'd make an egg-and-potato tortilla. In short, I would either turn my apartment into a tapas bar or I'd move into one. Fine, I would definitely move into one.

Spain excels at bar snacks, and I excel at grazing—we make an excellent pair. This recipe wraps as many flavors as I can from that imaginary tapas bar into one deviled egg—a garlicky aioli, smoked paprika, crushed toasted marcona almonds, and crumbles of oven-crisped jamón serrano. Together, they make the kind of deviled egg I'd be overjoyed to eat at a party, or perhaps for dinner, if left to my own devices.

*　　*　　*

cook your eggs Follow procedure on p. 85. Fully chill eggs before proceeding. Rest your eggs in the fridge for a day or two (see cooking note) if time permits.

prepare garnishes Meanwhile, crisp your jamón. Preheat your oven to 350 degrees. Place the jamón slices in one layer on a foil-lined baking sheet. Crisp them in the oven for 5 to 10 minutes; keep an eye on them because the crisping time will vary according to the thickness of the ham. Once they're crisp, drain on paper towels and set aside to cool.

If your almonds are not toasted or not toasted enough, spread them on a different tray and toast them for 5 minutes. Cool them. Whether or not you've just toasted them, either crush them in a bag with a hammer (what? it's fun!) or chop them coarsely on a cutting board.

yield: 12 deviled eggs

6 large eggs

1 ounce (30 grams) thinly sliced jamón serrano (2 to 4 slices, depending on size and thickness)

2 tablespoons (20 grams) toasted, salted marcona almonds

3 tablespoons (40 grams) mayonnaise

½ teaspoon Dijon mustard, or more to taste

½ teaspoon finely minced garlic (from the tiniest of cloves)

1 teaspoon freshly squeezed lemon juice

1 teaspoon olive oil

¼ teaspoon hot or sweet smoked paprika, plus more for dusting

Salt

Freshly ground black pepper

fill eggs Peel your cold hard-boiled eggs. Split your eggs lengthwise, and pop out the yolks into a medium bowl. Arrange the whites on your serving platter. Mash the yolks with a fork or potato masher, then mix in the mayo, mustard, garlic, lemon juice, olive oil, and paprika. Season to taste with a couple pinches of salt and a few grinds of black pepper.

to serve Scoop filling into egg whites, and sprinkle with additional paprika. Just before serving (if they sit too long on the eggs, they'll soften), garnish with crumbled jamón and crushed almonds.

cooking notes

The mayo, garlic, olive oil, and lemon juice are mixed to approximate aioli—or fauxoli, as I call it because I think I'm really clever. If you have aioli left over from the chicken-egg salad (see p. 85), you can substitute 3 tablespoons of it here for those four ingredients.

If you can plan ahead on this recipe, older hard-boiled eggs peel far more easily than freshly cooked ones.

blue cheese and black pepper gougères

I can tell you from personal experience that when you're invited to a cocktail party and you bring a bottle of wine or bubbly, people are always happy to see you. But if you arrive with a bottle of wine and a tray of still-warm-from-the-oven gougères, well, they love you. And though I know that trying to make yourself more popular at a party is hardly the most earnest or brag-worthy goal, I—a person who just presented you with something like a hundred recipes and will now hold my breath until you tell me you love them and them only—am hardly in a place to pretend it's never been a motivator.

Gougères are the ingenious merger of something called choux paste (what, your husband didn't just say "Bless you!" too?) and saintly, glorious cheese.

They're traditionally made with Gruyère, but I like them even more with blue cheese and a hit of black pepper to accentuate the sharpness. I like the funkiness of them and respect anything that holds its own against a strong cocktail. I realize that suggesting the use of a saucepan, an electric mixer, and a piping bag to create a party snack that will be popped into mouths and disappear in one bite sounds a bit fussy, but I think you'll be surprised at how quickly they come together, how delightfully they reheat, and how fancy they'll seem for something you can probably throw together from ingredients you have around.

*   *   *

Preheat your oven to 375 degrees, and line two large baking sheets with parchment paper. In a large, heavy saucepan, bring the butter, water, and wine to a boil. Remove the saucepan from the heat. Add the flour, pepper, and salt, and stir to blend smoothly. Reheat pan over medium heat, and stir the mixture vigorously with a wooden spoon until it forms a ball, about 1 minute. A thin film should appear on the bottom and sides of the pan.

Transfer the mixture to the bowl of an electric mixer, then cool slightly. Add the crumbled cheese, then beat at a low speed to combine. Add the

yield: 30 to 36 gougères

4 tablespoons (55 grams or ½ stick) unsalted butter

½ cup (120 ml) water

½ cup (120 ml) white wine

1 cup (125 grams) all-purpose flour

¼ teaspoon freshly ground black pepper, plus more for sprinkling

½ teaspoon fine sea salt, plus more for sprinkling

1 cup (4 ounces or 115 grams) crumbled firm blue cheese

4 large eggs

do ahead

Gougères both freeze and reheat well.

first egg, beating until fully incorporated, then scrape down the sides of the bowl. Repeat the process with the remaining eggs.

To create your cheese puffs, you can use either a a tiny cookie scoop, a pastry bag with a ½-inch tip, or a plastic bag with a ½-inch opening cut across one corner. Create 1-inch rounds on prepared sheets, about 2 inches apart. If you've piped the mounds, dampen your finger with water and use your finger to tamp the points of dough down gently on top before baking the puffs. Sprinkle each gougère with a grind of black pepper and a tiny pinch of sea salt.

Bake the gougères in preheated oven until puffed, golden, and crisp-dry at the edges, about 20 to 25 minutes. Serve them warm or at room temperature.

cooking notes

You can replace the wine with additional water, if needed.

Instead of using an electric mixer, I've often used the food processor to mix in the cheese and eggs; just be sure to scrape down the sides between egg additions, as you would if using a mixer.

For extra color on top—a step I never bother with, mostly because I'm lazy—you can beat an additional egg with 1 teaspoon of water to create an egg wash that you can brush over unbaked gougères, then bake as described above.

rosemary gruyère and sea salt crisps

I never liked cheese crackers as a kid—you know, the *orange* kind. My husband thinks this means I am missing something essential, either in my taste buds or in my food/life experiences. But maybe if they'd tasted like this things would have gone differently: These are my Cheez-Its for grown-ups. Why grown-ups? Because they go better with wine than with milk. They belong on a cheese plate with olives and grapes, not in a plastic cup full of Cheerios with a vented lid so a small squishy hand can reach in and reload.

Or this was my theory. But what actually happened was, I went on my little stepladder to take a photo, because I'm short and stuff. And while I was on the top step, my toddler climbed onto the first step and scared the daylights out of me because he wanted a cracker. And then another one. Soon they were in the little plastic cup with the vented lid at the playground with him. But really, it should be no surprise that weird food tastes run in the family.

*   *   *

Preheat your oven to 350 degrees. Combine all ingredients in a food processor, pulsing until the mixture resembles coarse, craggy crumbs. Dump the mixture out onto a large piece of plastic wrap, gather it together into a ball, and flatten it into a loose, thick square. Wrap with plastic, and chill for 15 to 20 minutes, or until slightly firmed up.

On a floured counter, roll out your dough to about ⅛-inch thickness—you know, pretty thinly. The shape doesn't matter. Cut the dough into a large grid—I used a fluted pastry wheel and made 1-inch diamonds. Dock each cracker with a skewer or knife point, then dab lightly with water and sprinkle each with a tiny additional pinch of sea salt. Bake the crisps for 10 to 12 minutes, or until the ends are lightly browned. Set the baking sheet on a rack to cool.

yield: about 90 to 100 1-inch crackers

1½ cups (6 ounces or 170 grams) coarsely grated Gruyère cheese

4 tablespoons (55 grams or ½ stick) butter

¾ cup (95 grams) all-purpose flour, plus more for counter

1 teaspoon finely minced fresh rosemary

¼ teaspoon fine sea salt, plus more for sprinkling

do ahead

Dough can be made a day in advance. It will keep longer in the freezer: Baked crisps keep for up to 2 days at room temperature in an airtight container, and up to a month in the freezer. They will not last 5 minutes at a party.

baked potato crisps with the works

I am not sure when the baked potato fell from grace, but I am here, making it my cause to bring it back. Baked potatoes are one of those foods that were as ubiquitous during the dinner meal when I was growing up as Good Seasonings Italian dressing, in the hourglass bottle with the ingredient markings on the side. And then, sadly, the old-fashioned baked potato got pushed out by little reds cooked with freshly minced herbs—which are delicious but have nothing on a puff of carbs topped with cheese, sour cream, and bacon.

Here is your chance to have everything worth piling on a spud in something you can finish in a few bites, maybe even while holding a beer in your other hand. Skin-on discs of buttery, salted baked potato with baked-on cheddar cheese support a small dollop of sour cream, some crumbled bacon, and a shower of minced chives. You should serve them as soon as they come out of the oven and then go back into the kitchen to make more, because the first batch will be gone immediately. I'm sorry, they just have that effect on people.

*   *   *

Preheat your oven to 425 degrees. Line two large baking sheets with foil (I find this makes later potato removal easier) and generously butter each sheet with ½ tablespoon cold butter. Arrange the potato slices in one layer on the baking sheets. Melt the remaining 2 tablespoons of butter and brush the potato tops with it. Season the potatoes generously with salt and freshly ground black pepper. Roast them for 25 to 30 minutes, until golden brown underneath. Flip, and roast for an additional 10 minutes.

If you're using grated cheese, sprinkle each potato slice with a generous teaspoon of cheese, and bake for an additional 5 minutes, until the cheese is melted and bubbly.

Top each crisp with a small dollop of sour cream, bacon crumbles, and chives.

yield: about 42 crisps

3 tablespoons (40 grams) butter

3 russet potatoes, unpeeled, cut into ½-inch cross sections (should yield about 14 slices)

Salt

Freshly ground black pepper

½ cup grated cheddar (about 2 ounces or 55 grams) (optional)

1 cup (240 grams) sour cream

4 ounces (115 grams, or 4 or 5 slices) bacon, fried until crisp, and chopped or crumbled

3 tablespoons minced fresh chives

french onion toasts

I am convinced that, no matter what ails you, French onion soup is the answer. Never cooked before? Don't think you'll be able to pull off the kind of cooking you believe you can only experience in a restaurant? Start with onion soup. Have only $5 to spend on dinner? Refrigerator is almost bare? Onion soup is your friend. Want your home to have a transcendent aroma bouncing off every wall, the kind that's so distracting that you don't even know or care what's on the stove, only that you must have it now? Onion soup is waiting for you.

My love for onion soup is so profound that I wanted to take it to places with me too, but, really, there's nothing portable about soup. And so I made it handy, and now the most difficult thing is not taking it everywhere with me, because it's exactly what I want to eat at parties. The thing is, when I go to a party, I rarely want to bite into some really funky Brie that an enthusiastic cheese shop guy recommended, forgetting to mention that it would make guests smell mostly like a cave all night. I don't want greasy mini-quiche or foie gras–stuffed eggs. I want the very best foods I know how to make made portable and I want them to go well with wine. I want this. And I hope you like it too.

* * *

Melt the butter and olive oil together in a large skillet over medium heat. Add the onions to the pan, toss them gently with the butter and oil, reduce the heat to medium or medium-low, and cover the pan. Cook the onions for 15 minutes, then remove the lid, stir in the salt and sugar, and sauté without the lid for about 10 to 15 minutes, until the onions are fully caramelized and have taken on a deep-golden color. Pour in Cognac, if using it, and the stock, then turn the heat all the way up and scrape up any brown bits stuck to the pan. Simmer the mixture until the broth almost completely disappears (a small amount of slosh is okay; you don't want to cook it off so much that the onions seem dry), about 5 to 10 minutes. Adjust the salt, if needed, and season with freshly ground black pepper.

yield: approximately 32 toasts, about 2 cups cooked onion mixture

2 tablespoons (30 grams) butter

1 tablespoon olive oil

2 pounds (905 grams; about 4 medium-large) yellow onions, cut into dice of about ⅓ inch (about 4½ cups)

½ teaspoon table salt

Pinch of sugar

1 tablespoon Cognac, brandy, or vermouth (optional)

1 cup (235 ml) low-sodium beef, veal, or mushroom stock or broth

Freshly ground black pepper

Thirty-two ½-inch-thick slices from a long baguette

About 2 cups (8 ounces or 225 grams) finely grated Gruyère cheese (you might have a little extra)

Preheat your oven to 375 degrees. Line two baking sheets with foil. Dollop each round of bread with most of a tablespoon of the onion mixture (depending on the size of your baguette, 1 full tablespoon of onion may be too much to keep neatly on top). Add 1 tablespoon grated cheese to the top of each toast, mounding it a bit so it all stays in place. Bake the toasts for about 15 minutes, until bubbly and a bit browned. Serve immediately.

do ahead   The onion mixture can be made ahead of time and kept at room temperature for a couple hours in an airtight container. Longer, it should be kept in the fridge and gently rewarmed when needed.

broiled clams with chorizo breadcrumbs

This is the sort of dish that sounds exquisitely complicated but hinges on just five ingredients. Five *fantastic* ingredients, which I suppose helps.

As far as I'm concerned, clams are a perfect food, and they belong at your next party. They love everything that you do: garlic, butter, wine, lemons, and hot sauce. They're inexpensive, but most people don't bother preparing them at home, so it feels like an indulgence when you put them out. Clams go well on pasta or on pizza, and they're good fried—and if you haven't steamed them open in beer, set them on the half-shell, dotted them with butter, and broiled them with chorizo breadcrumbs, well, I want you to do so right now.

You can go large or small with these clams. Tiny are of course ideal for a cocktail party, but be sure to have that broiler blazing when you run them underneath, so they don't overcook. Larger clams work well as part of a plated appetizer, and remain briny, buttery puddles that made my husband so happy he cleaned out the fridge for me right after eating them. If that sounds like the kind of thing you need in your life right now, well, you know what to do next.

※　　※　　※

In a medium skillet, cook the chorizo over moderate heat until it is almost crisp, about 3 minutes. Add the panko, and cook, stirring frequently, until the crumbs are crisp as well, about 5 minutes. Transfer the chorizo breadcrumbs to a small bowl, and set aside until needed.

Soak your clams in cold water for 20 minutes, then check them. If any shells are open, tap on them. If they don't close, throw them away. Scrub your clams with a stiff brush, and rinse them well under cold water.

In a large pot, bring the beer to a boil. Add the clams to the pot, and cover it with a tight-fitting lid. Cook until the clams open, anywhere from 2 to 3 minutes for the tiny ones to 5 to 10 minutes for the larger ones. Don't overcook them! They're done as soon as they open, at which point, using

yield: 1 to 2 dozen, depending on clam size

4 ounces (115 grams) Spanish chorizo, casing removed and finely chopped

1 cup (55 grams) panko breadcrumbs (see cooking notes)

2 pounds hard-shelled cherrystone, littleneck, or steamer clams

One 12-ounce (355 ml) bottle or can of beer, whatever kind you have around but preferably on the pale side

2 tablespoons (30 grams) butter, chopped into small bits

¼ cup chopped fresh parsley leaves (optional)

tongs, you can remove them from the pot. Discard any clams that remain closed.

Preheat the broiler. Twist off and discard the top shell of each clam, being sure to keep the shell with the clam inside. Arrange the halved clams on a broiler-safe tray. Add a pea-sized bit of butter to each clam, and then sprinkle it with chorizo breadcrumbs.

Broil the clams until the breadcrumbs are golden, about 5 minutes. Garnish them with chopped parsley, if using, and serve immediately.

cooking notes

Just to confuse you, chorizo, a pork sausage, comes primarily in two different varieties: fresh and cured. The Mexican and Latin American variety is usually fresh and spiced; it must be used quickly. The kind you should look for here is the dry, aged, dark-red (from paprika, lots of it) Spanish-style variety. It is hard and keeps for some time.

Can't find panko breadcrumbs? See how I make my own on p. 170.

spritzy ginger lemonade

yield: serves 6

*n*ew York City is not a friend to people who brave the summer here. Not only does the city mostly empty out on the weekends, but then there are the ~~tumbleweeds~~ eh, empty plastic bags skittering around on broiling cement on the long weekends, reminding you that you're among the few who haven't yet reached the place in your life where you have a beach house, a boat, or a balcony overlooking Central Park. You might feel that the city is even rubbing it in, because the weather is mostly appalling and those window air-conditioning units never cut it. But it's best not to think about the unjustness of it all too long.

This is my liquid offering to the next heat wave. The lemonade is not terribly sweet, and you can control this level by adding more or less syrup. The ferocity of the ginger and spice are tamed deliciously in a lemon syrup, and leave you with a brighter and more cooling lemonade. And the club soda—or sparkling wine—breaks up the intensity of the drink and makes it twice as refreshing.

*   *   *

juice lemons Halve seven of the lemons, and roughly cut off the zest and part of white pith in large segments, leaving enough pith intact so that lemons retain their shape. Toss the peels into a small saucepan and reserve. Juice the lemons—you're looking for 1 cup (235 ml) of lemon juice. Set aside.

make syrup Add the ginger, cayenne, 1 cup water, and 1 cup sugar to the saucepan with the lemon peels. Bring the mixture to a boil, stirring until the sugar is dissolved. Cool completely, then strain the syrup. Discard ginger and peels.

assemble lemonade Mix the lemon juice, 2 cups cold water, and 1 cup spicy simple syrup in a large pitcher. Fill the glasses three-quarters of the way with ice cubes. Pour the lemonade two-thirds of the way up the glass, then top off with club soda or sparkling wine. Give it a quick stir, prop a lemon wedge from the remaining lemon on the rim, and cool off with a zing.

8 average-sized lemons

2 cups (475 ml) cold water

1 cup (235 ml) spicy simple syrup (below)

club soda or sparkling wine, for serving

spicy simple syrup

Lemon peels from lemons squeezed for juice above

2-inch segment fresh ginger, peeled, very thinly sliced

¼ teaspoon cayenne pepper, or to taste

1 cup (235 ml) water

1 cup (200 grams) sugar

muddle puddle battle

When our son was six months old, my husband and I, eager to unearth everything we loved about our own childhoods, starting reading our resident foot-chewer all the Dr. Seuss books we could get our hands on, but quickly focused in on *Fox in Socks*. Now, seriously, do you have any idea how hard it is to read this book out loud? We got kind of competitive about it, I admit, challenging each other to read the book quickly and without stuttering, and then, when friends would come over, we'd drag them into the game, and it wasn't long after that, on a night when the baby was at his grandparents', that it became a full-on drinking game, where stuttering over a word meant you had to drink.

Every drinking game needs a drink, and I found the perfect one for this game at a bar in my neighborhood, at which point I came home and re-created it myself. True to the muddle puddle battle described near the end of the book, the drink is a mess—carelessly muddled berries that spray red everywhere; salt and lime and sugar and black pepper and then some fizz. Together, however, the muddle puddle battle is one of my favorite summer cocktails, with just the right sweetness, freshness, and stutter-free bite.

*   *   *

In the bottom of a small pitcher, muddle the berries with lime juice, sugar, and several fresh grinds of black pepper until the berries are roughly puréed. Add the tequila and club soda and mix. Fill two glasses three-quarters of the way with ice, and divide the drink between them. Drink at once, then see if you can effortlessly recite a poem about Tweetle Beetles.

yield: 2 drinks

4 medium fresh strawberries, or handful of raspberries, or blackberries, or mixture

2 tablespoons (30 ml) freshly squeezed lime juice

4 teaspoons superfine sugar

Freshly ground black pepper

½ cup (4 ounces or 120 ml) white tequila

1 cup (8 ounces or 235 ml) club soda or sparkling water, plus more if needed

Lime wedges for garnish

measurements

metrics

$\mathcal{E}$ager to make this book as useful as possible to a wide range of readers, I have included metric weights in recipes. Because most digital scales these days switch easily between ounces and grams, I only listed most ingredients in grams. I did try to include ounces on items that most people in the United States buy by weight, such as meat and cheese, and items that are packaged by their weight. If your scale only reads in ounces, Google will happily do the math for you:

simply type, e.g., "15 grams in ounces" into the search bar, which will bring return the result ".52 ounces," or half an ounce. I have also included the spoon/cup-to-weight and volume equivalents below.

I also excluded very tiny weights, usually items that are a tablespoon, a teaspoon, or less, so small that including them bordered on quibbling.

Still new to scales? Please let me convert you.

how to use a kitchen scale
(and ditch your measuring cups forever)

Count me among those who rejoice whenever a recipe is presented in weights. Why? Because nothing is more accurate. A cup of flour, packed different ways, can clock in anywhere from 115 to 200 grams. You could end up with almost double the flour the recipe's writer intended in your cake! But a 125-gram cup will always be a 125-gram cup. Plus, I am all about using fewer dishes and nothing minimizes clutter in a kitchen like a scale. Measuring 2¾ cups flour into a bowl requires a 1-cup measure, a ½-cup measure, and a ¼-cup measure, plus a bowl—that's 4 dishes. On a scale, you *only* need that bowl and to fill it until

the number hits 345 grams. Then you can add your next ingredient, and the next, and voilà! You've nearly made a one-bowl recipe!

But enough of the sales pitch. So, you bought a kitchen scale. Now what?

Place your empty bowl on the scale and "tare" or "zero out" its weight. (On scales without "tare" button, the "on/clear" button usually does the same job.) Add your first ingredient, slowly, until the scale reaches the weight you need. Zero it out again. Add the next ingredient. Zero it out again. If the recipe calls for you to whisk, whip, or blow gentle kisses across the surface of your ingredients, go do that too, but when it calls for the next ingredient, re–zero out the weight of the bowl so that you can continue.

You'll have this method down in no time. You'll wonder why you didn't try it sooner. And now, you can use all the extra space in your drawer that was once devoted to a tangle of measuring cups and spoons to stash more chocolate.

useful conversions

Fahrenheit/Celsius/Gas Mark Equivalents
275°F = 140°C = gas mark 1
300°F = 150°C = gas mark 2
325°F = 165°C = gas mark 3
350°F = 180°C = gas mark 4
375°F = 190°C = gas mark 5
400°F = 200°C = gas mark 6
425°F = 220°C = gas mark 7
450°F = 230°C = gas mark 8
475°F = 240°C = gas mark 9

Length Equivalents
¼ inch = .5 cm
½ inch = 1 cm
1 inch = 2.5 cm
6 inches = 15 cm
1 foot (12 inches) = 30 cm

Volume Equivalents
½ teaspoon = ⅛ fluid ounce
1 teaspoon = ¼ fluid ounce
2 teaspoons = ½ fluid ounce
1 tablespoon = 3 teaspoons = ¾ fluid ounce
2 tablespoons = 1 fluid ounce

3 tablespoons = 1½ fluid ounces
¼ cup = 4 tablespoons = 2 fluid ounces
⅓ cup = 2⅔ fluid ounces
½ cup = 4 fluid ounces
⅔ cup = 5⅓ fluid ounces
¾ cup = 6 fluid ounces
1 cup = 8 fluid ounces
1 pint = 2 cups = 16 fluid ounces
1 quart = 4 cups = 32 fluid ounces
2 quarts = 8 cups = 64 fluid ounces
1 gallon = 4 quarts = 128 fluid ounces

Weight Equivalents
½ ounce = 15 grams (rounded/approximate/
    practical equivalent; exact is 14)
1 ounce = 30 grams (exact = 28)
2 ounces = 55 grams (exact = 56)
4 ounces = ¼ pound = 115 grams (exact = 113)
5⅓ ounces = ⅓ pound = 150 grams (exact = 151)
8 ounces = ½ pound = 225 grams (exact = 227)
12 ounces = ¾ pound = 340 grams (exact)
16 ounces = 1 pound = 455 grams (exact = 454)
24 ounces = 1½ pounds = 680 grams (exact)
32 ounces = 2 pounds = 905 grams (exact = 907)

build your own smitten kitchen
(deb's kitchen essentials)

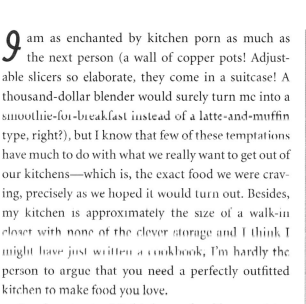

$\mathcal{I}$ am as enchanted by kitchen porn as much as the next person (a wall of copper pots! Adjustable slicers so elaborate, they come in a suitcase! A thousand-dollar blender would surely turn me into a smoothie-for-breakfast instead of a latte-and-muffin type, right?), but I know that few of these temptations have much to do with what we really want to get out of our kitchens—which is, the exact food we were craving, precisely as we hoped it would turn out. Besides, my kitchen is approximately the size of a walk-in closet with none of the clever storage and I think I might have just written a cookbook, I'm hardly the person to argue that you need a perfectly outfitted kitchen to make food you love.

So where to start? I think you should get cooking with whatever junk you have around, no matter how inefficient or pathetic. Old spoons still stir, stained pots still hold food. I have never let the absence of a pizza stone (I have a terrible track record with them) keep me from making pizza for dinner, and neither should you. From there, you keep a list—a list of things you are lost without or dying to replace because they are the bane of your cooking existence. You can't figure this out in a store; it's gotta happen in the kitchen.

And while my list may be different from yours—for example, I don't deep-fry a whole lot, but I have friends who do and right near the top of their list of essentials is a deep-fryer—I think you can get far with just a handful of things. Below are some of my earliest kitchen purchases that are still in heavy rotation today.

1. *a great big sharp knife* You don't need a knife block with twelve knives with mythical special ties—you just need one that works and to keep it really sharp. In a single-hour knife skills class, you will likely learn how to sharpen yours on an inexpensive stone and be self-sufficient forever. Have time and loose change for a second knife

purchase? Get a great bread knife (which doubles as a tomato knife/cake leveler/my favorite way to cut bars and brownies as that sawing motion goes easy on their crumb) and you'll have it forever.

2. *a digital scale* These days, kitchen scales are inexpensive, take up very little space (and a heck of a lot less than a set of cups and spoons), and open up a world of recipes to you (seeing as only the U.S. is cups-and-spoons-centric). For more on getting started with your scale, see p. 305.

3. *measuring cups and spoons too* Of course, you'll still need these. I know it's tempting, but I recommend buying ones designed for accuracy over cuteness. I figure I'm perfectly capable of messing up a good recipe in my own kitchen; I don't need my cute measuring cups to do it for me.

4. *a wooden spoon* Get one with a handle long enough that you're not scalding yourself on blurps and splatters from the pot.

5. *rubber and silicone spatulas* Remember how I said I was a minimalist in the kitchen? These tell a different story: I have eight, and there are days that all are dirty. I use them to mix, to fold, to sauté in nonstick pans, and to clean out bowls.

6. *a flexible fish spatula* "But Deb, you don't like fish!" Nevertheless, these thin spatulas are fantastic for pancake flipping, cookie transfers, and tossing vegetables midroasting. I have not once used a regular spatula since I bought mine.

7. *two whisks* A big sturdy one for eggs, whipping cream, and wet ingredients and a tiny one for salad dressing. Most of the time, I'm making a tiny batch of salad dressing, and using a full-size whisk to make a couple tablespoons of dressing is like trying to touch up paint trim with a 1-foot roller.

8. *bench scraper* I use this almost as much as I use my fish spatula, not only to divide and lift doughs. Nothing does a faster job of cleaning up a post-rugelach (p. 212) floured, sticky, and sugar-crustedc ounter.

9. *tongs* I use tongs for everything, from tossing salads to moving around large pieces of food in a pan or oven and, you know, getting items down from the cabinet that I can't reach. They're like my hand extensions.

10. *bowls* I love glass bowls because they look great on the table too. Who wants to transfer food to make it look prettier? If you're getting them just for the kitchen, however, I'd go with large glass measuring cups (1 quart, 2 quart, and so on) with a spout. The markings on the side and the spout come in handy regularly.

11. *mandoline* For paper-thin slices and the easiest matchstick cuts, the mandoline makes everything that comes out of your kitchen look totally "profesh." Here, too, buy the cheap one. I paid well under $20 for mine, it's the exact one I always see on cooking and restaurant shows, and in five years, the blade has barely dulled.

12. *four-sided box grater* I have so many flat graters and zesters that work wonderfully, but none has succeeded in replacing my box grater for efficiently grating and containing the mess of a block of cheese.

13. *mesh strainers in a few sizes* I use mine for everything from sifting (you don't need a sifter!) to dusting cakes with powdered sugar to straining foods (i.e., pressing out seeds from fruit and draining pasta). My favorite ones are all metal (i.e., no easily melted parts)—they can be suspended over a pot of water for use as a steamer—and have long long handles, which feel more natural for sifting and dusting, and hang easily from pot racks.

14. *pots and pans* Pots and pans top my list of things you should buy as you need, or as the absence of them has become a frequent nuisance in your kitchen. I prefer to buy open stock so I don't end up with pieces I don't need, and I gravitate toward basics that work for any kind of cooking, oven or stovetop. Here are the ones I get the most use out of:

a. *two cast-iron skillets* A 9-inch and a 12-inch. I use these for everything, from pancakes to upside-down cakes to roasting small birds. I roast potatoes in the big one in the oven and I swear it makes the most perfect latkes. I bet you can get them for less than $30 together, and even pass them on to your grandkids.

b. *a dutch oven* This is my favorite thing to buy people as a wedding or other big occasion gift. I recommend buying a larger size first (7 to 8 quarts), which should be big enough to roast a bird and will cover you for all soups and stews, even for a crowd. If you find you need it down the road, a moderate-sized one (5 quarts) is ideal for most 4- to 6-portion recipes. You can make a lifetime of great meals in a single pot.

c. *two heavy rimmed baking sheets* You can use these for everything from cookies to pizza to roasting vegetables.

d. *the cake pan size that will allow you to make your favorite cake* Nobody should be denied their favorite cake, even if it uses an unusual

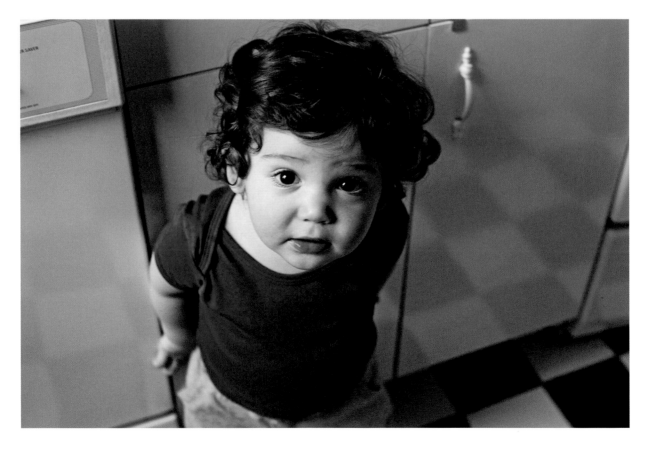

pan. Don't have a favorite cake yet? Get a 9-inch springform (for layer or cheesecakes), a 9 by 13 (which can also be used for casseroles and gratins), and a loaf.

15. *food processor* I would be lost without mine, as it, in one second flat, reduces a potato to shreds or perfectly chops nuts. People, you can make Nutella in one. Need I say more?

16. *electric mixer* If you bake a lot, a KitchenAid is a fantastic investment. If you're an occasional baker and short on storage space, an electric hand mixer will cover 90 percent of what you need to do. *Psst:* I spent $16 on my first one in 1999 and $60 on my second one in 2010. Guess which one I dislike so much I want to throw it out the window? Next time, I won't assume I have to pay up for a good one.

17. *immersion blender* I know people who use their immersion blender daily to purée soups, smoothies, and even baby food. I don't, but every single time I use it, I want to give it a hug (but don't, you know, because that would be dangerous) for being so awesome. It makes quick work of any blending, takes up almost no room, and is a cinch to clean.

18. *gadgetry* The five tools other people could probably live without, but I wouldn't want to:

a. *garlic press* A great one will leave no garlic behind, and will make 5-second work out of mincing a clove to paste.

b. *melon baller* It doesn't just make for a cute fruit salad; I use it to remove cores from halved apples and pears for baking.

c. *ruler* This probably is more about me being a little obsessive over details than it is about something your kitchen needs, but isn't it nice to know that if I say something makes a 2-inch biscuit, it actually does? I use mine more than you could possibly imagine.

d. *fancy grapefruit knife* Mine is double-ended; one side piths (piths!) and the other loosens segments, and it's a must for grapefruit fans.

e. *pastry blender* I really like making pie dough by hand, but I find my fingertips warm the butter too much. The blender makes quick work and single-bowl efforts out of pie, which leads to more pie for everyone (All Butter, Really Flaky Pie Dough, p. 226).

19. *something pretty on which to display your hard work* Pick a platter, the prettiest platter you have ever seen, the one you want to serve main dishes on forever, and ask loved ones for it for your birthday. The next year, do the same with a cake or dessert stand. I find that the sturdiest platters and cake stands tend to be the least expensive; sturdy is a good quality in heavily used items.

acknowledgments

To smittenkitchen.com readers, commenters, and emailers, who nudged, cheered, and inspired me to become a better cook by asking hundreds of great questions a day. Without you, this would be no fun at all.

To my husband, a very good reason to be smitten. Even if you didn't run out to the store without grumbling every time I ran out of an ingredient, even if you didn't say something positive about every dish, no matter how awful, and even if you did not pour us Bailey's when it is cold and grumpy out, you'd still be a total keeper.

To our families, for their endless support and countless babysitting hours that have enabled me to complete this project at a lightning pace (cough) of three or so years. Without you, I'd still be plugging away at the breakfast section.

To "Zana," whose loving care of our son (and many sinkfuls of dishes, even when I insisted you let me clean my own messes) enabled me to work away at this book without a shred of doubt that he was in the very best hands that weren't mine.

To Alison Fargis, my agent, and her Stonesong team, whose office I waddled into at thirty-two weeks pregnant for the sole purpose of telling her all the reasons I considered writing a book a terrible idea and whose office I left two hours later, telling my husband over the phone, "I am going to write a book and Alison says it's going to be the best book ever!" ("At last!" he said.)

To Lexy Bloom, my editor, whom I should thank for a lot of things: perseverance, patience, good cheer, asking good questions, promising and delivering a gorgeous book, etc. but whom we both know I'm mostly going to thank for the bottle of bourbon she included in a manuscript delivery to make the editing go down easier.

To everyone at Knopf: Although I have no idea what you're doing with the likes of a food blogger with no professional training who routinely burns pots of rice, I couldn't be more honored that you've invited me to be part of your great cookbook tradition.

To Olga Massov and Rachel Holtzman, recipe testers extraordinaire, for having the patience of saints and a level of attention to detail that helped whip this book into shape.

To Anna Painter, for your recipe testing, for the granola, and for the constant kitchen inspiration.

To David Lebovitz, for the endless rounds of help translating this book from cups-and-spoons to something everyone could use. Also, for that time you lugged a kilo of cocoa across the ocean for me.

To Angela Moore, for making this cookbook one halibut dish tastier, and for making the right choice when I sat in your backyard in the summer of 2006, asking, "Should the blog be called Deb's Kitchen? Kitchen Smitten? . . ."

Index

Page references in *italics* refer to illustrations.

Aioli, Lemon, 85–86
Alex's Chocolate Raspberry Rugelach, 212–14, *214–15*
Alfredo, Sweet Peas and Shells, *120*, 121–22
All Butter, Really Flaky Pie Dough, 226–28
almond(s):
    Broccoli Slaw, 72–73, *73*
    Date Breakfast Bars, *20*, 21–22
    Marconas, Crushed, Smoky Deviled Eggs with Crisped Jamón and, 290–91, *291*
    Pesto, Zucchini Ribbons with, *56*, 57–58
    Rhubarb Hamantaschen, *198*, 199–200
    and Sweet Cherry Galette, 229–30, *230*
apple:
    Cake, Mom's, 239–40, *240*
    Pie, Deepest Dish, 231–32, *233*
apple cider:
    Caramels, 277–79, *279*
    Pork Chops with Horseradish, Dill and, 177–78, *178*
Apricot Breakfast Crisp, 23–24, *24–25*
Artichoke Heart–Stuffed Shells in Lemon Ricotta Béchamel, 125–26, *127*
Arugula Fennel Salad, 169–70, *170–71*
Asparagus, Shaved, Pizza, *108*, 109–10
Avocado Tartine with Cucumber and Sesame Seeds, 82, *83*

bacon:
    Baked Potato Crisps with the Works, 296, *296*
    Maple Biscuits, 28–29, *29*
bagels, in New York Breakfast Casserole, *42*, 43–44
baking powders, xiii
baking sheets, rimmed, 310
Balsamic and Beer–Braised Short Ribs with Parsnip Purée, 179–81, *181*
Banana Butterscotch Tarte Tatin, 220–21, *221*
bars:
    Almond Date Breakfast, *20*, 21–22
    Cranberry Crumb, with Mulling Spices, 206, *206*
    Gooey Cinnamon Squares, 207–8, *209*
    Salted Brown Butter Crispy Treats, 201–2, *202*
    Whole Lemon, 217–18, *218–19*
basil, in Everyday Margarita Pizza, 106–7, *107*
bean(s):
    Black, and Spaghetti Squash Tacos with Queso Fresco, 143–44, *144–45*
    Black, Ragout, Slow-Cooker, 137–38, *139*
    Chickpeas, Cumin-Crisped, Roasted Eggplant with Yogurt-Tahini Sauce and, 146–47, *147*
    Cranberry, Salad with Walnuts and Feta, 74–75, *75*
    White, Pancetta, and Swiss Chard Pot Pies, *162*, 163–65

White, Roasted Tomatoes and Cipollini Onions with, *140*, 141–42
Béchamel, Lemon Ricotta, 125–26
beef:
    Brisket, Maya's Sweet and Sour Holiday, and Roasted Fingerling and Carrot Coins, *182*, 183–85
    Meatloaves, Tomato-Glazed, with Brown Butter Mashed Potatoes, *186*, 187–88
    Short Ribs, Balsamic and Beer–Braised, with Parsnip Purée, 179–81, *181*
bench scrapers, 308
Berry Buttercream, *252*, 255
Big Cluster Maple Granola, 26–27, *27*
Biscuits, Maple Bacon, 28–29, *29*
black bean:
    Ragout, Slow-Cooker, 137–38, *139*
    and Spaghetti Squash Tacos with Queso Fresco, 143–44, *144–45*
blackberry(ies):
    Berry Buttercream, *252*, 255
    Curd, White Chocolate Pudding with, *272*, 273–74
    Muddle Puddle Battle, 302, *303*
Black Pepper and Blue Cheese Gougères, 292–93, *293*
blenders, immersion, 311
Blintzes, Jacob's, or Sweet Potato Blintzes with Farmer's Cheese, 131–33, *133*
blueberry(ies):
    Berry Buttercream, *252*, 255
    Cornmeal Butter Cake, *244*, 245–46

blue cheese:
  and Black Pepper Gougères, 292–93, *293*
  Iceberg Stack with Radishes and, 61–62, *62–63*
Bourbon Hard Sauce, Peach Dumplings with, *234*, 235–37
Bourguignon, Mushroom, 151 52, *152–53*
bowls, 309
box graters, 309
bread:
  Cinnamon Toast French Toast, 7–8, *9*
  Fig, Olive Oil, and Sea Salt Challah, 45–48, *47*
  see also toasts
breadcrumbs, panko, 170
breakfast, 3–50
  Almond Date Breakfast Bars, *20*, 21–22
  Buns, Cheddar Swirl, 49–50, *51*
  Casserole, New York, *42*, 43–44
  Chocolate Chip Brioche Pretzels, 17 18, *19*
  Cinnamon Toast French Toast, 7–8, *9*
  Crisp, Apricot, 23–24, *24–25*
  Fig, Olive Oil, and Sea Salt Challah, 45–48, *47*
  Gingerbread Spice Dutch Baby, *10*, 11
  Greens, Eggs, and Hollandaise, 33–34, *35*
  Latkes, Big, *30*, 31 32
  Maple Bacon Biscuits, 28–29, *29*
  Maple Granola, Big Cluster, 26–27, *27*
  Peach and Sour Cream Pancakes, *4*, 5–6
  Plum Poppy Seed Muffins, 12–13, *13*
  Potato Frittata with Feta and Scallions, 39–40, *41*
  Ranchero Eggs, Baked, with Blistered Jack Cheese and Lime Crema, *36*, 37–38
  Whole-Wheat Raspberry Ricotta Scones, *14*, 15–16
Brioche Pretzels, Chocolate Chip, 17–18, *19*
Brisket, Maya's Sweet and Sour Holiday, and Roasted Fingerling and Carrot Coins, *182*, 183–85
Brittled Peanuts, Spicy, 286–87, *287*

Broccoli Rabe Panini with Mozzarella, 93–94, *94*
Broccoli Slaw, 72–73, *73*
brown butter:
  Mashed Potatoes, *186*, 188
  Salted Crispy Treats, 201–2, *202*
Brownie Roll-Out Cookies, 210–11, *211*
Buns, Cheddar Swirl Breakfast, 49–50, *51*
butter(ed):
  All, Really Flaky Pie Dough, 226–28
  Blueberry Cornmeal Cake, *244*, 245–46
  Popcorn Cookies, 195–96, *197*
  see also brown butter
Buttercream, Berry, *252*, 255
buttermilk, xiii
Butternut Squash and Caramelized Onion Galette, 99–100, *101*
Butterscotch Banana Tarte Tatin, 220–21, *221*

cabbage:
  Napa, in Sugar Snap Salad with Miso Dressing, 69–70, *71*
  Vinegar Slaw with Cucumbers and Dill, 54, *55*
cake pans, 310–11
cakes, 238–68
  Apple, Mom's, 239–40, *240*
  Blueberry Cornmeal Butter, *244*, 245–46
  Chocolate, Tiny but Intense, 250 51, *251*
  Chocolate Hazelnut Crepe, 256–60, *260–61*
  Golden Sheet, with Berry Buttercream, *252*, 253–55
  Grapefruit Olive Oil Pound, 241–42, *243*
  Olive Oil Ricotta, with Concord Grape Coulis, 247–48, *248–49*
  Red Wine Velvet, with Whipped Mascarpone, *266*, 267–68
  S'more Layer, *262*, 263–65
cake stands, 311
Calzone, Eggplant and Three Cheese, 111–12, *113*
candy, 277–81
  Apple Cider Caramels, 277–79, *279*
  Coffee Toffee, 280–81, *281*

Caramels, Apple Cider, 277–79, *279*
carrot(s):
  and Fingerling Coins, Roasted, 185, *185*
  Honey and Harissa Farro Salad, 78–79, *79*
cast-iron skillets, 310
Cauliflower Pesto, Linguine with, 123–24, *124*
Celery, Pickled, 59
Challah, Fig, Olive Oil, and Sea Salt, 45–48, *47*
cheddar:
  Baked Potato Crisps with the Works, 296, *296*
  Swirl Breakfast Buns, 49–50, *51*
cheese:
  Blue, and Black Pepper Gougères, 292–93, *293*
  Blue Cheese, Iceberg Stack with Radishes and, 61–62, *62–63*
  cheddar, in Baked Potato Crisps with the Works, 296, *296*
  Cheddar Swirl Breakfast Buns, 49 50, *51*
  Emmentaler on Rye with Sweet and Sour Red Onions, 87–88, *89*
  Farmer's, Jacob's Blintzes, or Sweet Potato Blintzes with, 131–33, *133*
  Feta, Cranberry Bean Salad with Walnuts and, 74–75, *75*
  Feta, Potato Frittata with Scallions and, 39 40, *41*
  fontina, in Butternut Squash and Caramelized Onion Galette, 99–100, *101*
  Goat, Whipped, Tomato Scallion Shortcakes with, *64*, 65–66
  Gruyère, in French Onion Toasts, 297–98, *298*
  Gruyère, Rosemary, and Sea Salt Crisps, 294, *295*
  Jack, Blistered, Baked Ranchero Eggs with Lime Crema and, *36*, 37–38
  Queso Fresco, Spaghetti Squash and Black Bean Tacos with, 143–44, *144–45*
  Swiss, Baby, Wild Rice Gratin with Kale, Caramelized Onions and, 148, 149–50
  Three, and Eggplant Calzone, 111–12, *113*
  see also mozzarella

cheesecake:
  Marbled Pumpkin Gingersnap Tart,
    224–25, *225*
  Strawberry, Fools, *269*, 270–71
cherry(ies):
  Kale Salad with Pecans and,
    67–68, *68*
  to pit or not to pit, 230
  Sweet, and Almond Galette, 229–30,
    230
Chiarello, Michael, 156
chicken:
  and Egg Salad Toasts with Lemon
    Aioli and Fennel, *84*, 85–86
  Flat Roasted, with Tiny Potatoes,
    172, 173–74
  Harvest Roast, with Grapes, Olives,
    and Rosemary, 175–76, *176*
  Mustard Milanese with Arugula
    Fennel Salad, 169–70, *170–71*
chickpea(s):
  Cumin-Crisped, Roasted Eggplant
    with Yogurt-Tahini Sauce and,
    146–47, *147*
  Smashed, Salad with Lemon and
    Sumac, *166*, 168
chocolate:
  Brownie Roll-Out Cookies, 210–11,
    211
  Cake, Tiny but Intense, 250–51, *251*
  Chip Brioche Pretzels, 17–18, *19*
  Hazelnut Crepe Cake, 256–60,
    260–61
  Peanut Butter Cookies, 203–4, *205*
  Raspberry Rugelach, Alex's, 212–14,
    214–15
  Red Wine Velvet Cake with
    Whipped Mascarpone, *266*,
    267–68
  Silk Pie, 222–23, *223*
  S'more Layer Cake, *262*, 263–65
  White, Pudding with Blackberry
    Curd, *272*, 273–74
Chorizo Breadcrumbs, Broiled Clams
  with, 299–300, *300*
cider, *see* apple cider
cinnamon:
  Squares, Gooey, 207–8, *209*
  Toast French Toast, 7–8, *9*
Cipollini Onions, Roasted Tomatoes
  and, with White Beans, *140*,
  141–42
Clams with Chorizo Breadcrumbs,
  Broiled, 299–300, *300*

coconut, in Big Cluster Maple Granola,
  26–27, *27*
Coffee Toffee, 280–81, *281*
Colwin, Laurie, 85
Concord Grape Coulis, 247–48,
  248–49
conversions, 306
cookies, 194–214
  Brownie Roll-Out, 210–11, *211*
  Buttered Popcorn, 195–96, *197*
  Chocolate Peanut Butter, 203–4,
    205
  Chocolate Raspberry Rugelach,
    Alex's, 212–14, *214–15*
  Cranberry Crumb Bars with
    Mulling Spices, 206, *206*
  Gooey Cinnamon Squares, 207–8,
    209
  Rhubarb Hamantaschen, *198*,
    199–200
  Salted Brown Butter Crispy Treats,
    201–2, *202*
Cornmeal Blueberry Butter Cake, *244*,
  245–46
Corn Risotto–Stuffed Poblanos,
  134–36, *136*
cornstarch, xiii
Coulis, Concord Grape, 247–48,
  248–49
cranberry(ies):
  Broccoli Slaw, 72–73, *73*
  Crumb Bars with Mulling Spices,
    206, *206*
  Syrup, 131, 133, *133*
Cranberry Bean Salad with Walnuts
  and Feta, 74–75, *75*
cream:
  Cumin Crema, 137–38
  Garlic Lemon, *128*, 129–30
  whipping and heavy, xiii
crema:
  Cumin, 137–38
  Lime Mexican, 38
crème fraîche, xiv
  Horseradish, Dip, 288–89, *289*
Crepe Cake, Chocolate Hazelnut,
  256–60, *260–61*
Crisp, Apricot Breakfast, 23–24,
  24–25
Crumb Bars, Cranberry, with Mulling
  Spices, 206, *206*
cucumber(s):
  Avocado Tartine with Sesame Seeds
    and, 82, *83*

Gazpacho Salsa, 159–60, *160–61*
Mint Raita, 189–90
Vinegar Slaw with Dill and, 54, *55*
cumin:
  Crema, 137–38
  -Crisped Chickpeas, Roasted
    Eggplant with Yogurt-Tahini
    Sauce and, 146–47, *147*

Date Almond Breakfast Bars, *20*, 21–22
Deepest Dish Apple Pie, 231–32, *233*
desserts, 193–281
  see also cakes; candy; cookies; pies
    and tarts (sweets); puddings
Deviled Eggs, Smoky, with Crisped
  Jamón and Crushed Marconas,
  290–91, *291*
Dijon-Shallot Vinaigrette, 59–60
dinner parties, how to throw, 284–85
Dip, Horseradish Crème Fraîche,
  288–89, *289*
dressings:
  Blue-Cheese, 62
  Buttermilk, 61–62
  Dijon-Shallot Vinaigrette, 59–60
  Honey-Dijon, 67–68
  Honey-Harissa, 78–79
  Lemon Aioli, 85–86
  Sesame-Miso, 69–70
  Sherry-Shallot Vinaigrette,
    76–77, *77*
  Tomato Vinaigrette, 159
drinks:
  Muddle Puddle Battle, 302, *303*
  Spritzy Ginger Lemonade, 301, *301*
Dumplings, Peach, with Bourbon
  Hard Sauce, *234*, 235–37, *237*
Dutch Baby, Gingerbread Spice, *10*, 11
dutch ovens, 310

egg(s), xiv
  Baked Ranchero, with Blistered
    Jack Cheese and Lime Crema, *36*,
    37–38
  and Chicken Salad Toasts with
    Lemon Aioli and Fennel, *84*,
    85–86
  Cinnamon Toast French Toast,
    7–8, *9*
  Greens, and Hollandaise, 33–34, *35*
  New York Breakfast Casserole, *42*,
    43–44
  Potato Frittata with Feta and
    Scallions, 39–40, *41*

Sieved, Fingerlings Vinaigrette with
Pickled Celery and, 59–60, *60*
Smoky Deviled, with Crisped Jamón
and Crushed Marconas, 290–91,
291
whites, in Frosting, *262*, 264–65
eggplant:
Ratatouille Sub, *90*, 91–92
Roasted, with Yogurt-Tahini Sauce
and Cumin-Crisped Chickpeas,
146–47, *147*
and Three Cheese Calzone, 111–12,
113
Emmentaler on Rye with Sweet and
Sour Red Onions, 87–88, *89*
equipment, essential, 307–11

Farmer's Cheese, Jacob's Blintzes,
or Sweet Potato Blintzes with,
131–33, *133*
Farro Salad, Honey and Harissa,
78–79, *79*
fennel:
Arugula Salad, 169–70, *170–71*
Chicken and Egg Salad Toasts with
Lemon Aioli and, *84*, 85–86
feta:
Cranberry Bean Salad with Walnuts
and, 74–75, *75*
Potato Frittata with Scallions and,
39–40, *41*
Fig, Olive Oil, and Sea Salt Challah,
45–48, *47*
fingerling(s):
and Carrot Coins, Roasted, *185*, 185
Vinaigrette with Sieved Eggs and
Pickled Celery, 59–60, *60*
flour, measuring, xiv
fontina cheese, in Butternut Squash
and Caramelized Onion Galette,
99–100, *101*
food processors, 311
Fools, Strawberry Cheesecake, *269*,
270–71
French flavors:
Mushroom Bourguignon, 151–52,
152–53
Ratatouille Sub, *90*, 91–92
French Onion Toasts, 297–98, *298*
French Toast, Cinnamon Toast,
7–8, *9*
Fries, Tarragon Oven, 156–58, *157*
Frittata, Potato, with Feta and
Scallions, 39–40, *41*

Fritters, Leek, with Garlic and Lemon,
128, 129–30
frostings:
Chocolate Draping, 257, 260, *260–61*
marshmallowlike, for S'more Layer
Cake, *262*, 264–65

gadgetry, 311
Galette, Butternut Squash and
Caramelized Onion, 99–100, *101*
garlic(ky):
Lemon Cream, *128*, 129–30
Toasts, 137–38
garlic presses, 311
Garten, Ina, 163, 241
Gazpacho Salsa, 159–60, *160–61*
Gingerbread Spice Dutch Baby, *10*, 11
Ginger Lemonade, Spritzy, 301, *301*
Gingersnap Marbled Pumpkin Tart,
224–25, *225*
glazes:
Cider and Horseradish, 177
Grapefruit, 241–42
Tomato, 187
Gnocchi in Tomato Broth, *116*,
117–19
Goat Cheese, Whipped, Tomato
Scallion Shortcakes with, *64*,
65–66
Golden Sheet Cake with Berry
Buttercream, *252*, 253–55
Gooey Cinnamon Squares, 207–8,
209
Gougères, Blue Cheese and Black
Pepper, 292–93, *293*
graham cracker crumbs, in S'more
Layer Cake, *262*, 263–65
Granola, Big Cluster Maple, 26–27, *27*
grape(s):
Concord, Coulis, 247–48, *248–49*
Harvest Roast Chicken with Olives,
Rosemary and, 175–76, *176*
grapefruit knives, 311
Grapefruit Olive Oil Pound Cake,
241–42, *243*
graters, box, 309
Gratin, Wild Rice, with Kale,
Caramelized Onions, and Baby
Swiss, *148*, 149–50
Greens, Eggs, and Hollandaise,
33–34, *35*
Grissini, Pumpernickel, with
Horseradish Crème Fraîche Dip,
288–89, *289*

Gruyère cheese:
French Onion Toasts, 297–98,
298
Rosemary, and Sea Salt Crisps, 294,
295

Halibut, Seared, and Gazpacho Salsa
with Tomato Vinaigrette, 159–60,
160–61
Hamantaschen, Rhubarb, *198*,
199–200
Hard Sauce, Bourbon, 235–36
Harissa and Honey Farro Salad,
78–79, *79*
Harvest Roast Chicken with Grapes,
Olives, and Rosemary, 175–76,
176
hazelnut(s):
Candied, 257, 260
Chocolate Crepe Cake, 256–60,
260–61
Heart-Stuffed Shells in Lemon Ricotta
Béchamel, 125–26, *127*
herbs, xiv
Hoffmann, Ingrid, 275
Hollandaise, Greens, Eggs and,
33–34, *35*
Home Cooking (Colwin), 85
Honey and Harissa Farro Salad,
78–79, *79*
Horseradish Crème Fraîche Dip,
288–89, *289*

Iceberg Stack with Blue Cheese and
Radishes, 61–62, *62–63*
immersion blenders, 311
Indian flavors, in Pistachio Masala
Lamb Chops with Cucumber
Mint Raita, 189–90, *190–91*
ingredients, basic vs. expensive, xiv
Italian flavors:
Broccoli Rabe Panini with
Mozzarella, 93–94, *94*
Eggplant and Three Cheese Calzone,
111–12, *113*
Mustard Milanese with Arugula
Fennel Salad, 169–70, *170–71*
Potato Frittata with Feta and
Scallions, 39–40, *41*
see also pasta; pizza

Jack Cheese, Blistered, Baked
Ranchero Eggs with Lime Crema
and, *36*, 37–38

Jacob's Blintzes, or Sweet Potato
    Blintzes with Farmer's Cheese,
    131–33, *133*
Jamón, Crisped, Smoky Deviled Eggs
    with Crushed Marconas and,
    290–91, *291*
Jewish cooking:
    Big Breakfast Latkes, *30*, 31–32
    Chocolate Raspberry Rugelach,
        Alex's, 212–14, *214–15*
    Fig, Olive Oil, and Sea Salt Challah,
        45–48, *47*
    Jacob's Blintzes, or Sweet Potato
        Blintzes with Farmer's Cheese,
        131–33, *133*
    Rhubarb Hamantaschen, *198*,
        199–200

kale:
    Salad with Cherries and Pecans,
        67–68, *68*
    Wild Rice Gratin with Caramelized
        Onions, Baby Swiss and, *148*,
        149–50
knives, 307–8
    grapefruit, 311

Lamb Chops, Pistachio Masala, with
    Cucumber Mint Raita, 189–90,
    190–91
Latkes, Big Breakfast, *30*, 31–32
Leek Fritters with Garlic and Lemon,
    128, 129–30
lemon:
    Aioli, 85–86
    Garlic Cream, *128*, 129–30
    Ricotta Béchamel, 125–26
    Whole, Bars, 217–18, *218–19*
Lemonade, Spritzy Ginger, 301,
    301
lime:
    Crema, 38
    -Pickled Red Onions, 138
Linguine with Cauliflower Pesto,
    123–24, *124*

mandolines, 309
maple:
    Bacon Biscuits, 28–29, *29*
    Granola, Big Cluster, 26–27, *27*
    Marbled Pumpkin Gingersnap Tart,
        224–25, *225*
    Margarita Pizza, Everyday, 106–7,
        107

marshmallow(s):
    flavor, in S'more Layer Cake, *262*,
        263–65
    Salted Brown Butter Crispy Treats,
        201–2, *202*
Masala Pistachio Lamb Chops with
    Cucumber Mint Raita, 189–90,
    190–91
Mascarpone, Whipped, Red Wine
    Velvet Cake with, *266*, 267–68
Maya's Sweet and Sour Holiday Brisket
    and Roasted Fingerling and
    Carrot Coins, *182*, 183–85
measurements, 305–6
measuring cups and spoons, 308
measuring dry ingredients, xiv
Meatballs, Sesame-Spiced Turkey, and
    Smashed Chickpea Salad, *166*,
    167–68
Meatloaves, Tomato-Glazed, with
    Brown Butter Mashed Potatoes,
    186, 187–88
melon ballers, 311
mesh strainers, 309
Mexican flavors:
    Baked Ranchero Eggs with Blistered
        Jack Cheese and Lime Crema, *36*,
        37–38
    Black Bean Ragout, Slow-Cooker,
        137–38, *139*
    Corn Risotto–Stuffed Poblanos,
        134–36, *136*
    Spaghetti Squash and Black Bean
        Tacos with Queso Fresco, 143–44,
        144–45
Mint Cucumber Raita, 189–90
Miso-Sesame Dressing, 69–70
mixers, electric, 311
Mom's Apple Cake, 239–40, *240*
mozzarella:
    Broccoli Rabe Panini with, 93–94, *94*
    Eggplant and Three Cheese Calzone,
        111–12, *113*
    Everyday Margarita Pizza, 106–7, *107*
    Shaved Asparagus Pizza, *108*, 109–10
Muddle Puddle Battle, 302, *303*
Muffins, Plum Poppy Seed, 12–13, *13*
Mulling Spices, Cranberry Crumb
    Bars with, 206, *206*
mushroom:
    Bourguignon, 151–52, *152–53*
    Wild, Tart, 95–98, *97*
Mussels, Vermouth, with Tarragon
    Oven Fries, 156–58, *157*

Mustard Milanese with Arugula
    Fennel Salad, 169–70, *170–71*

New York Breakfast Casserole, *42*,
    43–44

oats:
    Apricot Breakfast Crisp, 23–24,
        24–25
    Big Cluster Maple Granola, 26–27, *27*
olive oil:
    Fig, and Sea Salt Challah, 45–48, *47*
    Grapefruit Pound Cake, 241–42, *243*
    Ricotta Cake with Concord Grape
        Coulis, 247–48, *248–49*
Olives, Harvest Roast Chicken with
    Grapes, Rosemary and, 175–76,
    176
onion(s):
    Caramelized, and Butternut Squash
        Galette, 99–100, *101*
    Caramelized, Wild Rice Gratin with
        Kale, Baby Swiss and, *148*, 149–50
    French, Toasts, 297–98, *298*
    Red, Lime-Pickled, 138
    Red, Sweet and Sour, Emmentaler
        on Rye with, 87–88, *89*

pancakes:
    Gingerbread Spice Dutch Baby, *10*, 11
    Peach and Sour Cream, *4*, 5–6
Pancetta, White Bean, and Swiss
    Chard Pot Pies, *162*, 163–65
Panini, Broccoli Rabe, with
    Mozzarella, 93–94, *94*
panko breadcrumbs, 170
Parmesan:
    Eggplant and Three Cheese Calzone,
        111–12, *113*
    Sweet Peas and Shells Alfredo, *120*,
        121–22
parsnip(s):
    Honey and Harissa Farro Salad,
        78–79, *79*
    Purée, 181, *181*
party snacks and drinks, 283–302
    Blue Cheese and Black Pepper
        Gougères, 292–93, *293*
    Clams with Chorizo Breadcrumbs,
        Broiled, 299–300, *300*
    Deviled Eggs, Smoky, with Crisped
        Jamón and Crushed Marconas,
        290–91, *291*
    French Onion Toasts, 297–98, *298*

Muddle Puddle Battle, 302, *303*
Peanuts, Spicy Brittled, 286–87, *287*
Potato Crisps, Baked, with the
    Works, 296, *296*
Pumpernickel Grissini with
    Horseradish Crème Fraîche Dip,
    288–89, *289*
Rosemary Gruyère and Sea Salt
    Crisps, 294, *295*
Spritzy Ginger Lemonade, 301, *301*
pasta:
    Gnocchi in Tomato Broth, *116,*
    117–19
    Heart-Stuffed Shells in Lemon
    Ricotta Béchamel, 125–26, *127*
    Linguine with Cauliflower Pesto,
    123–24, *124*
    Sweet Peas and Shells Alfredo, *120,*
    121–22
pastry blenders, 311
Pastry Cream, Hazelnut, 256–57
peach:
    Dumplings with Bourbon Hard
    Sauce, *234,* 235–37, *237*
    and Sour Cream Pancakes, *4,* 5–6
Peanut Butter Cookies, Chocolate,
    203–4, *205*
Peanuts, Spicy Brittled, 286–87, *287*
Peas, Sweet, and Shells Alfredo, *120,*
    121–22
Pecans, Kale Salad with Cherries and,
    67–68, *68*
peppers:
    Gazpacho Salsa, 159–60, *160–61*
    Ratatouille Sub, *90,* 91–92
pesto:
    Almond, Zucchini Ribbons with,
    56, 57–58
    Cauliflower, Linguine with, 123–24,
    124
pickled:
    Celery, 59
    Lime-, Red Onions, 138
pies and tarts (sweets), 216–37
    All Butter, Really Flaky Pie Dough,
    226–28
    Almond and Sweet Cherry Galette,
    229–30, *230*
    Apple Pie, Deepest Dish, 231–32, *233*
    Butterscotch Banana Tarte Tatin,
    220–21, *221*
    Chocolate Silk Pie, 222–23, *223*
    Marbled Pumpkin Gingersnap Tart,
    224–25, *225*

Peach Dumplings with Bourbon
    Hard Sauce, *234,* 235–37, *237*
    Whole Lemon Bars, 217–18, *218–19*
Pistachio Masala Lamb Chops with
    Cucumber Mint Raita, 189–90,
    190–91
pizza, 102–10
    equipment for, 102–3
    Margarita, Everyday, 106–7, *107*
    Shaved Asparagus, *108,* 109–10
pizza dough, 102–5
    Leisurely, 105
    Rushed, 104
platters, 311
Plum Poppy Seed Muffins, 12–13, *13*
Poblanos, Corn Risotto–Stuffed,
    134–36, *136*
Popcorn, Buttered, Cookies, 195–96,
    197
Poppy Seed Plum Muffins, 12–13, *13*
Pork Chops with Cider, Horseradish,
    and Dill, 177–78, *178*
potato(es):
    Brown Butter Mashed, *186,* 188
    Crisps, Baked, with the Works, 296,
    296
    Fingerling and Carrot Coins,
    Roasted, 185, *185*
    Fingerlings Vinaigrette with
    Sieved Eggs and Pickled Celery,
    59–60, *60*
    Flat Roasted Chicken with Tiny, *172,*
    173–74
    Frittata with Feta and Scallions,
    39–40, *41*
    Gnocchi in Tomato Broth, *116,*
    117–19
    Latkes, Big Breakfast, 30, 31–32
    Tarragon Oven Fries, 156–58, *157*
Pot Pies, Pancetta, White Bean, and
    Swiss Chard, *162,* 163–65
pots and pans, 310
Pound Cake, Grapefruit Olive Oil,
    241–42, *243*
Pretzels, Chocolate Chip Brioche,
    17–18, *19*
puddings, 269–76
    Strawberry Cheesecake Fools, *269,*
    270–71
    Tres Leches Rice, 275–76, *276*
    White Chocolate, with Blackberry
    Curd, *272,* 273–74
puffed-rice cereal, in Salted Brown
    Butter Crispy Treats, 201–2, *202*

Pumpernickel Grissini with
    Horseradish Crème Fraîche Dip,
    288–89, *289*
Pumpkin Gingersnap Tart, Marbled,
    224–25, *225*

Queso Fresco, Spaghetti Squash and
    Black Bean Tacos with, 143–44,
    144–45
quinoa, in Roasted Baby Roots with
    Sherry-Shallot Vinaigrette, 76–77,
    77

radishes:
    Iceberg Stack with Blue Cheese and,
    61–62, *62–63*
    Sugar Snap Salad with Miso
    Dressing, 69–70, *71*
Ragout, Slow-Cooker Black Bean,
    137–38, *139*
Raita, Cucumber Mint, 189–90
Ranchero Eggs, Baked, with Blistered
    Jack Cheese and Lime Crema, *36,*
    37–38
raspberry(ies):
    Berry Buttercream, 252, *255*
    Chocolate Rugelach, Alex's, 212–14,
    214–15
    Muddle Puddle Battle, 302, *303*
    Whole-Wheat Ricotta Scones, *14,*
    15–16
Ratatouille Sub, *90,* 91–92
red wine:
    Mushroom Bourguignon, 151–52,
    153–53
    Velvet Cake with Whipped
    Mascarpone, *266,* 267–68
Rhubarb Hamantaschen, *198,* 199–200
rice:
    Corn Risotto–Stuffed Poblanos,
    134–36, *136*
    Pudding, Tres Leches, 275–76, *276*
    puffed-, cereal, in Salted Brown
    Butter Crispy Treats, 201–2, *202*
ricotta:
    Eggplant and Three Cheese Calzone,
    111–12, *113*
    Lemon Béchamel, 125–26
    Olive Oil Cake with Concord Grape
    Coulis, 247–48, *248–49*
    Whole-Wheat Raspberry Scones,
    14, 15–16
Risotto, Corn, –Stuffed Poblanos,
    134–36, *136*

Roots, Roasted Baby, with Sherry-
    Shallot Vinaigrette, 76–77, *77*
Rosemary Gruyère and Sea Salt Crisps,
    294, *295*
Rugelach, Chocolate Raspberry, Alex's,
    212–14, *214–15*
rulers, 311
Rye, Emmentaler on, with Sweet and
    Sour Red Onions, 87–88, *89*

salad(s), 53–79
    Arugula Fennel, 169–70, *170–71*
    Broccoli Slaw, 72–73, *73*
    Chicken and Egg, Toasts with
        Lemon Aioli and Fennel, *84*,
        85–86
    Chickpea, Smashed, with Lemon
        and Sumac, *166*, 168
    Cranberry Bean, with Walnuts and
        Feta, 74–75, *75*
    Farro, Honey and Harissa, 78–79, *79*
    Fingerlings Vinaigrette with
        Sieved Eggs and Pickled Celery,
        59–60, *60*
    Iceberg Stack with Blue Cheese and
        Radishes, 61–62, *62–63*
    Kale, with Cherries and Pecans,
        67–68, *68*
    Roots, Roasted Baby, with Sherry-
        Shallot Vinaigrette, 76–77, *77*
    Sugar Snap, with Miso Dressing,
        69–70, *71*
    Tomato Scallion Shortcakes with
        Whipped Goat Cheese, *64*,
        65–66
    Vinegar Slaw with Cucumbers and
        Dill, 54, *55*
    Zucchini Ribbons with Almond
        Pesto, *56*, 57–58
Salsa, Gazpacho, 159–60, *160–61*
Salted Brown Butter Crispy Treats,
    201–2, *202*
salts, xiii
sandwiches, 82–94
    Avocado Tartine with Cucumber
        and Sesame Seeds, 82, *83*
    Broccoli Rabe Panini with
        Mozzarella, 93–94, *94*
    Chicken and Egg Salad Toasts with
        Lemon Aioli and Fennel, *84*,
        85–86
    Emmentaler on Rye with Sweet and
        Sour Red Onions, 87–88, *89*
    Ratatouille Sub, *90*, 91–92

sauces:
    Almond Pesto, 57
    Cauliflower Pesto, 123–24
    Concord Grape Coulis, 247–48,
        248–49
    Cranberry Syrup, 131, 133, *133*
    Hollandaise, 33–34, *35*
    Lemon Ricotta Béchamel, 125–26
    Ranchero, 37–38
    Tomato, Quick, 111–12
    Yogurt-Tahini, 146–47, *147*
scales, kitchen, 308
    how to use, 305–6
scallion:
    Biscuits, 65–66, *66*
    Tomato Shortcakes with Whipped
        Goat Cheese, *64*, 65–66
Scones, Whole-Wheat Raspberry
    Ricotta, *14*, 15–16
seafood:
    Clams with Chorizo Breadcrumbs,
        Broiled, 299–300, *300*
    Halibut, Seared, and Gazpacho Salsa
        with Tomato Vinaigrette, 159–60,
        160–61
    Mussels, Vermouth, with Tarragon
        Oven Fries, 156–58, *157*
sesame (seeds):
    Avocado Tartine with Cucumber
        and, 82, *83*
    Miso Dressing, 69–70
    -Spiced Turkey Meatballs and
        Smashed Chickpea Salad, *166*,
        167–68
shallot:
    Dijon Vinaigrette, 59–60
    Sherry Vinaigrette, 76–77, *77*
shells (pasta):
    Heart-Stuffed, in Lemon Ricotta
        Béchamel, 125–26, *127*
    and Sweet Peas Alfredo, *120*,
        121–22
Sherry-Shallot Vinaigrette, 76–77, *77*
Shortcakes, Tomato Scallion, with
    Whipped Goat Cheese, *64*, 65–66
Short Ribs, Balsamic and Beer–
    Braised, with Parsnip Purée,
    179–81, *181*
sides:
    Cucumber Mint Raita, 189–90
    Fingerling and Carrot Coins,
        Roasted, 185, *185*
    Fries, Tarragon Oven, 156–58, *157*
    Parsnip Purée, 181, *181*

Potatoes, Brown Butter Mashed,
    186, 188
    see also salad(s)
Simple Syrup, Spicy, 301
skillets, cast-iron, 310
slaws:
    Broccoli, 72–73, *73*
    Vinegar, with Cucumbers and Dill,
        54, *55*
slow-cooker:
    Black Bean Ragout, 137–38, *139*
    Sweet and Sour Holiday Brisket,
        Maya's, *182*, 183–84
Smoky Deviled Eggs with Crisped
    Jamón and Crushed Marconas,
    290–91, *291*
S'more Layer Cake, *262*, 263–65
snacks, *see* party snacks and drinks
Sour Cream and Peach Pancakes, *4*,
    5–6
spaghetti squash:
    and Black Bean Tacos with Queso
        Fresco, 143–44, *144–45*
    seeds, roasting, 144
Spanish flavors:
    Seared Halibut and Gazpacho Salsa
        with Tomato Vinaigrette, 159–60,
        160–61
    Smoky Deviled Eggs with Crisped
        Jamón and Crushed Marconas,
        290–91, *291*
spatulas:
    fish, flexible, 308
    rubber, 308
Spicy Brittled Peanuts, 286–87, *287*
spoons, wooden, 308
Spritzy Ginger Lemonade, 301, *301*
squash (winter):
    Butternut, and Caramelized Onion
        Galette, 99–100, *101*
    Pumpkin Gingersnap Tart, Marbled,
        224–25, *225*
    Spaghetti, and Black Bean Tacos
        with Queso Fresco, 143–44,
        144–45
    spaghetti, roasting seeds of, 144
Stewart, Martha, 241
strainers, mesh, 309
strawberry(ies):
    Cheesecake Fools, *269*, 270–71
    Muddle Puddle Battle, 302, *303*
streusel:
    Brown Sugar Cookie Crumb, 270–71
    Topping, 231–32, 245–46

Sub, Ratatouille, *90*, 91–92
sugar:
   brown, xiv
   confectioners' or powdered, xiii
Sugar Snap Salad with Miso Dressing, 69–70, *71*
Sweet and Sour Holiday Brisket, Maya's, and Roasted Fingerling and Carrot Coins, *182*, 183–85
Sweet Potato Blintzes with Farmer's Cheese, or Jacob's Blintzes, 131–33, *133*
sweets, 193–281
   see also cakes; candy; cookies; pies and tarts (sweets); puddings
Swiss, Baby, Wild Rice Gratin with Kale, Caramelized Onions and, *148*, 149–50
Swiss Chard, Pancetta, and White Bean Pot Pies, *162*, 163–65
syrups:
   Cranberry, 131, 133, *133*
   Grapefruit, 241–42
   Simple, Spicy, 301

Tacos, Spaghetti Squash and Black Bean, with Queso Fresco, 143–44, *144–45*
Tahini-Yogurt Sauce, 146–47, *147*
Tarragon Oven Fries, 156–58, *157*
Tarte Tatin, Butterscotch Banana, 220–21, *221*
Tartine, Avocado, with Cucumber and Sesame Seeds, 82, *83*
tarts (savories), 95–100
   Butternut Squash and Caramelized Onion Galette, 99–100, *101*
   Wild Mushroom, 95–98, *97*
tarts (sweets), *see* pies and tarts (sweets)
tequila, in Muddle Puddle Battle, 302, *303*
toasts:
   Chicken and Egg Salad, with Lemon Aioli and Fennel, 84, 85–86
   French Onion, 297–98, *298*
   Garlicky, 137–38
Toffee, Coffee, 280–81, *281*
tomato(es):
   Broth, Gnocchi in, *116*, 117–19
   Everyday Margarita Pizza, 106–7, *107*

Gazpacho Salsa, 159–60, *160–61*
-Glazed Meatloaves with Brown Butter Mashed Potatoes, *186*, 187–88
Ranchero Sauce, 37–38
Roasted Cipollini Onions and, with White Beans, *140*, 141–42
Sauce, Quick, 111–12
Scallion Shortcakes with Whipped Goat Cheese, *64*, 65–66
Vinaigrette, 159
tongs, 308
Tortilla Strips, Crisp, 37–38
Tres Leches Rice Pudding, 275–76, *276*
Turkey Meatballs, Sesame-Spiced, and Smashed Chickpea Salad, *166*, 167–68

vegetarian main dishes, 115–52
   Black Bean Ragout, Slow-Cooker, 137–38, *139*
   Blintzes, Jacob's, or Sweet Potato Blintzes with Farmer's Cheese, 131–33, *133*
   Corn Risotto–Stuffed Poblanos, 134–36, *136*
   Eggplant, Roasted, with Yogurt-Tahini Sauce and Cumin-Crisped Chickpeas, 146–47, *147*
   Gnocchi in Tomato Broth, *116*, 117–19
   Heart-Stuffed Shells in Lemon Ricotta Béchamel, 125–26, *127*
   Leek Fritters with Garlic and Lemon, *128*, 129–30
   Linguine with Cauliflower Pesto, 123–24, *124*
   Mushroom Bourguignon, 151–52, *152–53*
   Peas, Sweet, and Shells Alfredo, *120*, 121–22
   Spaghetti Squash and Black Bean Tacos with Queso Fresco, 143–44, *144–45*
   Tomatoes and Cipollini Onions, Roasted, with White Beans, *140*, 141–42
   Wild Rice Gratin with Kale, Caramelized Onions, and Baby Swiss, *148*, 149–50
Vermouth Mussels with Tarragon Oven Fries, 156–58, *157*

vinaigrettes:
   Dijon-Shallot, 59–60
   Sherry-Shallot, 76–77, *77*
   Tomato, 159
Vinegar Slaw with Cucumbers and Dill, 54, *55*

walnuts:
   Big Cluster Maple Granola, 26–27, *27*
   Cranberry Bean Salad with Feta and, 74–75, *75*
washing greens and other gritty vegetables, xiv
Waters, Alice, 93
wheat germ, in Big Cluster Maple Granola, 26–27, *27*
whisks, 308
white bean(s):
   Pancetta, and Swiss Chard Pot Pies, *162*, 163–65
   Roasted Tomatoes and Cipollini Onions with, *140*, 141–42
White Chocolate Pudding with Blackberry Curd, *272*, 273–74
Whole Lemon Bars, 217–18, *218–19*
Whole-Wheat Raspberry Ricotta Scones, *14*, 15–16
Wild Rice Gratin with Kale, Caramelized Onions, and Baby Swiss, *148*, 149–50
wine:
   Mushroom Bourguignon, 151–52, *152–53*
   Red, Velvet Cake with Whipped Mascarpone, *266*, 267–68
   sparkling, in Spritzy Ginger Lemonade, 301, *301*
wooden spoons, 308

yellow squash, in Ratatouille Sub, *90*, 91–92
yogurt:
   Cucumber Mint Raita, 189–90
   Tahini Sauce, 146–47, *147*

zucchini:
   Ratatouille Sub, *90*, 91–92
   Ribbons with Almond Pesto, 56, 57–58
Zuni Café Cookbook, The (Rodgers), 173

A NOTE ABOUT THE AUTHOR

DEB PERELMAN is a self-taught home cook and photographer, and the creator of SmittenKitchen.com, an award-winning blog with a focus on stepped-up home cooking through unfussy ingredients. In previous iterations of her so-called career, she's been a record store shift supervisor, a scrawler of "happy birthday" on bakery cakes, an art therapist, and a technology reporter. She likes her current gig—the one where she wakes up and cooks whatever she feels like that day—the best. *The Smitten Kitchen Cookbook* is her first book. Deb lives in New York City with her husband and delicious baby son.

A NOTE ON THE TYPE

This book was set in Minion, a typeface produced by the Adobe Corporation specifically for the Macintosh personal computer, and released in 1990. Designed by Robert Slimbach, Minion combines the classic characteristics of old-style faces with the full complement of weights required for modern typesetting.

Typeset by North Market Street Graphics,
Lancaster, Pennsylvania

Printed and bound by Toppan Printing Co.,
(Shenzhen) LTD., China

Designed by Cassandra J. Pappas